HOLDING
THE
LINE

FLAVEL CLINGAN BARBER

Courtesy of Margaret Hill Pruitt

HOLDING THE LINE

The Third Tennessee Infantry, 1861–1864

by

Flavel C. Barber

edited by

Robert H. Ferrell

The Kent State University Press

KENT, OHIO, & LONDON, ENGLAND

©1994 by The Kent State University Press,
Kent, Ohio 44242
Library of Congress Catalog Card Number 94-8653
ISBN 0-87338-504-7
Manufactured in the United States of America

Library of Congress Cataloging-in-Publication Data

Barber, Flavel C., 1830–1864.
    Holding the line : the Third Tennessee Infantry, 1861–1864 /
    by Flavel C. Barber ; edited by Robert H. Ferrell.
        p.   cm.
    Includes bibliographical references and index.
    ISBN 0-87338-504-7 (cloth : alk. paper) ∞
    1. Confederate States of America. Army. Tennessee Infantry
Regiment, 3rd.   2. Barber, Flavel C., 1830–1864.   3. Tennessee—
History—Civil War, 1861–1865—Regimental histories.   4. United
States—History—Civil War, 1861–1865—Regimental histories.   5.
Tennessee—History—Civil War, 1861–1865—Personal narratives.
6. United States—History—Civil War, 1861–1865—Personal
narratives, Confederate.   7. Soldiers—Tennessee—Biography.   I.
Ferrell, Robert H.   II. Title.
E579.5 3rd .B37   1994   94–8653
973.7'468—dc20   CIP

British Library Cataloging-in-Publication data are available.

Contents

E
579.5
3rd
.B37
1994

Illustrations & Maps

Acknowledgments

MY THANKS to the many individuals who have helped with this book. First of all, thanks to the daughters of Nat U. Hill II of Bloomington, Indiana—Margaret Hill Pruitt, Elizabeth Hill Dinsmore, and Anna Jane Hill Andrews—who together with Mrs. Nat U. Hill III deposited the Barber Papers in the Lilly Library of Indiana University, Bloomington. William Cagle, head of the library, enthusiastic collector that he is, and knowing that I like to hear of his accessions, one day pointed out his new treasure and recommended a look at it. Historian friends thereafter gave much assistance: Frank L. Byrne and Lawrence S. Kaplan of Kent State University; John T. Hubbell, editor of *Civil War History* and director of the Kent State University Press; Richard J. Sommers of the U.S. Army Military History Institute at Carlisle Barracks; Charles P. Roland of the University of Kentucky; and Nathaniel Cheairs Hughes, Jr., descendant of Maj. Nathaniel F. Cheairs of the Third Tennessee Regiment. Margaret Butler of Pulaski, Tennessee, and historian of Giles County, offered every assistance, including a reconnaissance of nearby Bryson. Chris Barber of Toney, Alabama, journeyed to Pulaski in search of a diary book missing from the Barber Papers in Bloomington, and Richard Fanning of Mississippi State University searched the Jackson archives for the book. Sue Edgerton helped make an exact transcription of the four books in the Lilly Library. C. Patricia Riesenman, reference librarian of the Indiana University Library, was also extraordinarily helpful.

Joanna Hildebrand, editorial assistant at The Kent State University Press, went over the manuscript with technical skill and imagination, preventing many errors. I am grateful for her dedication. My thanks also to Julia Morton and Linda Cuckovich at the Press.

Lynne McCaffry of Monroe, Wisconsin, a skilled scholar-librarian, is responsible for the combined alphabetical and keyed roster of members of the Third Tennessee. John M. Hollingsworth drew the maps.

Again, thanks to Lila and Carolyn, who make every task easier.

HOLDING
THE
LINE

Introduction

FLAVEL CLINGAN BARBER, born on January 30, 1830, in Union County, Pennsylvania, was an unlikely individual to join the Army of the Confederate States of America. While the family line did include a group of Virginians (who spelled the name "Barbour"), most of the Barbers were from New Jersey, Rhode Island, and Pennsylvania, the latter descended from Robert Barber, who came to America from Yorkshire, England, in about 1699 as an apprentice shoemaker. He joined his uncle, Robert, in Chester, Pennsylvania, and upon the elder's death inherited a considerable part of the family estate. Flavel Clingan, of the fifth generation of Barbers, was the eighth child of Thomas Barber (1785–1856) and Elizabeth Clingan (1787–1872), a niece of Flavel Roan.[1]

What moved Flavel Clingan to go to Tennessee is impossible to say. Nor do we know much about his activities there. We do know that he was attracted to and attended Giles College, an institution of higher learning in Pulaski, the seat of Giles County; but, unfortunately, the date of Barber's graduation is unknown, for college records have long since disappeared. Upon graduation, however, the young Pennsylvanian must have turned to farming or business, or both, and done reasonably well, for the 1860 census lists him as possessing one thousand dollars' worth of real estate and two thousand dollars in personal property—not the means of a schoolteacher.[2]

By 1860, though, he was established as a teacher in Bryson, a little community near Elkton, fifteen or so miles southeast of Pulaski. In 1858 the leaders of Bethany Presbyterian Church had decided to build an "up-to-date" private academy and, with community support, gave liberally of time and money. With these generous resources, and even a sizable endowment for "poor but worthy" students, Bryson built a handsome two-story school-house and was granted a state charter, with its course of study primarily classical and musical.[3]

Barber taught at the Bryson school until the war began, and it was here that he met his future wife, Mary Paine Abernathy, of one of the most prominent Giles County families. Upon the declaration of war, Barber helped raise a company of what became the Third Tennessee Infantry, and on May 15, 1861, the evening before the company left Elkton for Pulaski, she and Barber were married.

Thereafter everything moved rapidly. At about midday on May 16, Barber's company, together with one raised by Capt. Calvin J. Clack, left "on the cars" from Pulaski. Near Lynnville he and his men joined other companies to form a regiment, and, in the democratic way of the time, the assembled men and officers voted in their field officers: colonel, John C. Brown; lieutenant colonel, Thomas M. Gordon; and major, Nathaniel F. Cheairs.

Colonel Brown, who became prominent in the Confederate cause, had graduated from Jackson College in Columbia, Tennessee. After a stint of teaching, he read law and passed the bar, returning to his native Giles County in 1848 to practice law in Pulaski. After capture at Fort Donelson and imprisonment at Fort Warren in Boston Harbor, he was exchanged and promoted to brigadier and, later, major general. Prominent in postwar Tennessee politics, Brown was twice elected governor. He was also involved in the construction of the Texas and Pacific Railway, becoming its president in 1888, a year before his death.[4] Lieutenant Colonel Gordon, born in 1827, had served as a lieutenant in the Mexican War in a Tennessee brigade. After the Civil War, he became a physician and practiced in Lynnville. He died in 1901.

Major Cheairs was born in 1818 near Spring Hill, Tennessee. He married in 1841 and in 1855 moved to Rippavilla, his magnificent house near Spring Hill. Though antisecessionist, Cheairs went with his state, even raising a company of 110 men in just forty-eight hours. After capture at Donelson, where he carried the surrender request to General Grant, he was imprisoned at Fort Warren. There he lived in style, arranging for the importation of six thousand dollars' worth of food, wine, and cigars, for which

Mary Paine Abernathy Barber.
Courtesy of Margaret Hill Pruitt.

officer friends paid him back in Confederate money. Upon exchange, he was present at the reorganization of the regiment in
Jackson, Mississippi, in September 1862. Not reelected major, he
returned to Tennessee, tried unsuccessfully to organize a cavalry

command, and then served with Generals Nathan B. Forrest and Joseph E. Johnston. Again captured, Cheairs spent nearly a year at Camp Chase in Columbus, Ohio. Rejoining Forrest, he shortly thereafter surrendered with the end of the war. After the war, President Johnson gave Cheairs a full pardon for his "Confederate sins." He died in 1914 at the age of ninety-five. "I am perhaps unfortunately constituted," he wrote his sister on June 25, 1862. "I am high tempered. I can be overpowered but not conquered (so long as I am satisfied I am right), and when trampled upon I am like the Texas scorpion, I'll sting if I can. Such is, as you know, my nature, and I can't help it."[5]

Having chosen officers, the men of the Third Tennessee entrained for Nashville, where they arrived late on the night of May 16 and marched from the railroad station to the fairground to set up camp. The next day they were formally inducted into state service, and at about noon the mustering officer, Col. James L. Scudder, made his appearance. Troops lined up in single file, and Colonel Scudder and an inspector, Dr. Snyder, passed along examining each man and swearing in whoever passed inspection. The inspector rejected one of Barber's men for faulty eyes, and the captain remembered that the man sat down and wept bitterly.

After a march though the streets to the capitol building to receive percussion-lock muskets, the Third Tennessee was on its way. The companies again took railcars to a locality four miles beyond Springfield, Camp Cheatham. In following days and weeks, routine took over: roll call, squad drills, and company drills; officers received instruction in tactics.

During the summer of 1861, many of the men—a July report showed 885 present at Camp Cheatham—became ill. There was much typhoid fever, measles, and what was known generally as "camp fever," which included chills, indigestion, and dysentery—all doubtless tinged with, and in some cases indelibly marked by, pneumonia. It was not long before camp fever was carrying off the weak and sometimes even the strong. But the men tended to take it philosophically—that is, those who did not come down with it—by reasoning that in war the weak could have little place and that it was an act of Providence to dislodge them before weakness in battle endangered other men. Barber caught camp fever, and, after lying ill for two weeks and finding himself growing weaker every day, he went home in late July to "recruit" his health. He returned to duty on September 1.

While Barber was home in Giles County, during the latter part of July the regiment transferred to Sumner County and Camp Trousdale, a much larger and more attractive facility than Cheatham. And it was here that on August 7 the Third Tennessee was inducted into Confederate service. And it was also at Trousdale that three other regiments, a battalion of cavalry, a cavalry company under Capt. Thomas G. Woodward, and a battery of six pieces under Capt. Thomas K. Porter joined the Third in forming a brigade under Colonel Brown.

In the third week of September the units were moved yet again, this time taking the railroad through Franklin, Kentucky, to Bowling Green. For their first night in Bowling Green, the troops bivouacked on the banks of the Barren River above the bridge; the next day the officers marked out the location of a camp. Troops kept arriving, and a detachment went up the railroad and formed another camp on the south bank of the Green River near Woodsonville. Troops also settled at Russellville. It began to appear as an effort to occupy all of southern Kentucky, with Brig. Gen. Simon Bolivar Buckner in command.[6]

The first real taste of war came for the Third while at Bowling Green. On the second day after arrival, September 23, Barber and company were ordered to move along the Green River and break up Federal camps. Half the units in the five-hundred-man provisional force under Lt. Col. Benjamin H. Helm were from Kentucky regiments, and in support was Woodward's cavalry company.[7] As Barber described the beginning of this adventure, the men set off along "a hot, dusty, country road" through Warren County and upon striking hills went right on among them until midnight, when the force reached a small tributary, the Gasper River. During the latter part of the march, and indeed throughout the night, rain came down in torrents. Footsore and nearly exhausted, Barber and his company found their way into an old church; there, without putting out sentinels, they slept until morning. Setting off again, they crossed the Gaspar and once more marched all day, halting for the night in a creek bottom, but

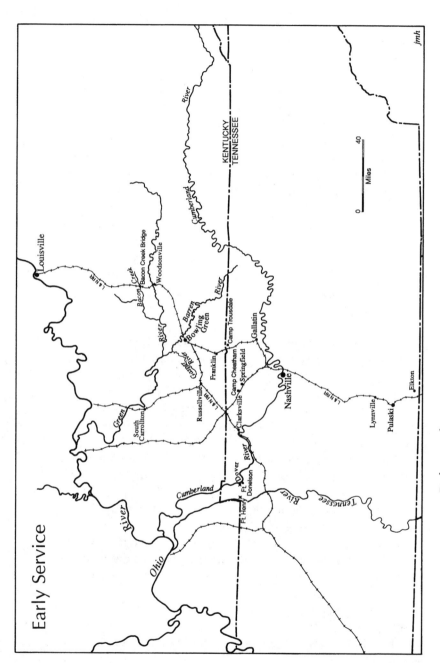

Early Service

Barber's early service in Tennessee and Kentucky, 1861–62

this time putting out guards and a picket. They sensed that the enemy was close. Indeed, Federal soldiers were hovering around their camp. One of Barber's men, going out in search of water, stumbled into unfriendly hands but managed to escape. The next day the expedition waited to see how strong the enemy was and sent out scouts to ascertain whether, as rumored, the Federals were one thousand strong: "We were in Butler County, one of the most notorious Lincolnite counties in the state, and the inhabitants were nearly all unfriendly." Hostilities in the following days were slight; the privations of service in the field, however, continued.

It was an exhausting and fruitless chase of the Federals. Colonel Helm's force, the rear guard of Buckner's force, became separated from the main force and marched on wearily, lost, until finally, by chance, hooking up with them again. On one occasion during the march, Captain Barber and a friend, beginning to have their fill of Kentuckyland, played a joke on their hosts, the Kentucky companies under Helm.

> One day while we were encamped in Butler County, Dr. Bowers and myself, taking a stroll, found a dilapidated old squirrel rifle sitting outside the door of a deserted log house.[8] We brought it to camp with us and gave it to Dr. Grant who at the time was going with us as an independent volunteer. Grant took out his knife and engraved on the breech the following inscription, "Dan Boon, 1777," and rubbed powder into the cut so as to make it appear of great antiquity. We then hung it on a sapling, muzzle downward, placed two men with fixed bayonets to guard it, and circulated through the camp a report that Daniel Boone's rifle had been captured by our scouts and was to be seen at my quarters. Soon a crowd collected, principally of Kentuckians, who looked at the gun with great curiosity and reverence. Some of their officers came down and wished to examine it closely but our faithful sentinels would allow no person to put his hands upon it. One man became so eager that he got down on his knees before it and tried to look into the muzzle. It was more than an hour before the

deception was discovered, and the Kentuckians, badly sold, returned to their quarters.

Autumn in Bowling Green passed in hard labor on the drill field and on fortifications. Lt. Gen. Albert Sidney Johnston arrived and took command of the army, and Maj. Gen. William J. Hardee came with his Arkansas troops. Buckner drilled the Tennesseans incessantly in "movements in masses," and on Sundays either he or Johnston held reviews. The town was fortified everywhere and became a perfect Gibraltar. On the Federal side, Maj. Gen. Don Carlos Buell took command and sent out skirmishers in the vicinity of Green River, to which the Confederates responded by sending Capt. John H. Morgan, whose first exploit was the burning of the Bacon Creek bridge. At length, Brig. Gen. Thomas L. Crittenden of the Federal forces advanced to South Carrollton on the lower part of Green River and threatened Russellville, to which Barber's brigade was sent. And after the fall of Fort Henry, the Third was moved on to Fort Donelson.[9]

Arrival at Fort Donelson seemed to be just one more in a series of moves. But unbeknownst to Barber and his regiment, it was a fateful move indeed. And when they found themselves in the company of Brig. Gen. Gideon J. Pillow, they might have realized what the future had in store. The commander at Donelson, this Tennessee politician was an ill-starred officer. Wherever Pillow went during his short-lived military career, he was apt to scatter confusion. A native of Tennessee, he graduated from the University of Nashville and became friendly with James K. Polk—perhaps the most important thing he did to advance himself militarily. When the Mexican War began, the president appointed Pillow brigadier and then major general of volunteers. During the campaigning, he got into a public contention with Gen. Winfield Scott but was defended by the president, who declared that Pillow had been "greatly persecuted." This was hardly the case, since at Cerro Gordo Pillow had managed to expose his troops to enemy fire and then disappear during the subsequent action. Similarly, appointed a brigadier general in the Confederate army in 1861 and finding himself in command at Donelson, he chose to escape, leaving General Buckner to surrender. During the remainder of the war he received no important command. Major Cheairs, who hated Pillow, wrote to his daughter from Fort Warren on April 22, 1862, "I understand that Gid Pillow has gone to his plantation, a miserable man, wishing himself dead, and if wishing would do any good, he could have any amount of help. He is the man that made a speech in Clarksville to the soldiers on their way to Donelson and then again at Donelson just before the fight commenced, in both of which he boasted of what he intended to do, stating in his closing remarks that the words *retreat* and *surrender* was not in his vocabulary." Cheairs said of Pillow that if he had been at home, tied to his wife's apron strings, the gallant little army at Donelson would still have been in Dixieland.[10]

Indeed, affairs were very bad when Barber and his men reached Donelson. The garrison was manned by mostly raw regiments and fugitives from the rout at Fort Henry. Barber wrote of his fear that a thousand resolute men might take the fort almost without a blow. On Sunday, February 9, the Third, with a strength of 743 men, took its position in the line occupying the top ridge running at right angles to a hollow, and General Pillow rode up and spoke a few words of encouragement. At dark, the men bivouacked on the crest and western slope of the hill. The next day a detail cut down trees at the regimental position; so by early the next morning, February 11, all the timber for three or four hundred yards in front had been leveled, forming an almost impenetrable abatis. Meanwhile, reinforcements arrived at Dover, and camps were set up, with rifle pits dug in front and built up with logs and earth.

About midday on Wednesday, February 12, rapid firing began to the southwest, and the Federals, reportedly in great force, drove in the Confederate pickets, and by evening they had advanced to within sight of Rebel lines. Four companies of the Third were in ditches, with the remaining six in reserve, but there were not enough troops to man the ditches. Barber's first platoon stood on the extreme left of the regiment, with Capt. William Peaton's company on its right and Col. Edmond C. Cook's regiment on the left.[11] Barber's second platoon remained in reserve.

Everything was ready for the battle.

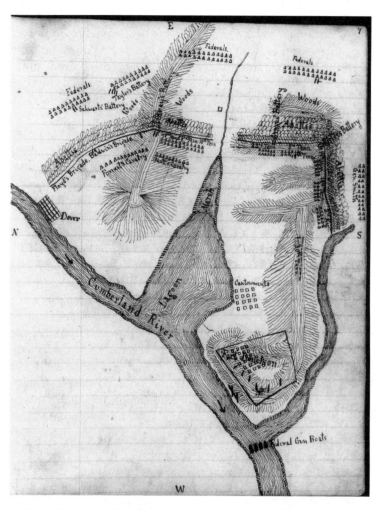

Map of Fort Donelson drawn by Barber in 1862 while a prisoner on Johnson's Island in Lake Erie. Courtesy of the Lilly Library, Indiana University, Bloomington.

As Barber remembered Donelson and the disposition of Confederate troops there just before the battle: "Fort Donelson is situated on a bluff on the south side of Cumberland River and consists of strong earthworks almost entirely surrounding it. Colonel Sugg's and Bailey's regiments were stationed inside the fort. On the side next the river several pieces of cannon (one 128-pounder) were mounted, and two pieces under the bluff at the water's edge. Just above the fort a lagoon set back from the river about half a mile, and from the shores of this lagoon steep and lofty hills rose on either side. From the head run high ridges, parallel with each other, and deep ravines or gorges set up from the valley toward the crests of the opposite ridges. The valley was mostly clear of timber but the hills were thickly covered with trees and in many places with undergrowth. Beyond the ridges on the north side of the valley is the town of Dover, on the banks of the Cumberland. Our lines extended across the little valley nearly north and south, facing eastward, from the summit of one ridge to that of the other. When they reached the top of the southern ridge they turned to the right, passed along the crest several hundred yards, and then ran down a spur of the ridge to a bayou setting back from the river below the fort. When the lines reached the top of the northern ridge they passed down the northern declivity, which was much more gentle than the southern, and turned to the left toward Dover.

"Colonel Cook's regiment, the Thirty-Second Tennessee, with Captain Graves' battery, occupied the lines from the valley extending up the hill toward the right. Our regiment, the Third Tennessee, was posted on the brow of the hill, facing eastward toward a low ridge which ran parallel to our works at a distance of about three hundred yards. The ravine and slopes of the hill in front of us were covered and rendered almost impassable by fallen trees. On our right was Captain Porter's battery, and beyond this the Fourteenth Mississippi (Major Doss) and the Eighteenth Tennessee (Colonel Palmer). The Second Kentucky (Colonel Hanson) occupied our extreme right. On the north side of the valley were the Tenth Tennessee (Colonel Heiman), the Fifty-Third Tennessee (Colonel Abernathy), and the Forty-Eighth Tennessee (Colonel Voorhies), extending from the valley to the top of the ridge, where Captain Maney's battery was placed. Beyond this hill I know nothing of the disposition of our troops, except that General Floyd's brigade occupied the extreme left and a brigade commanded by Colonel Baldwin of Mississippi was posted on the right of Floyd.

"General Floyd was the ranking officer but as he only arrived the day before the battle he did not assume the chief command but left that position to General Pillow. General Buckner commanded the division on the right and General Floyd and General Bushrod Johnson were on the left."

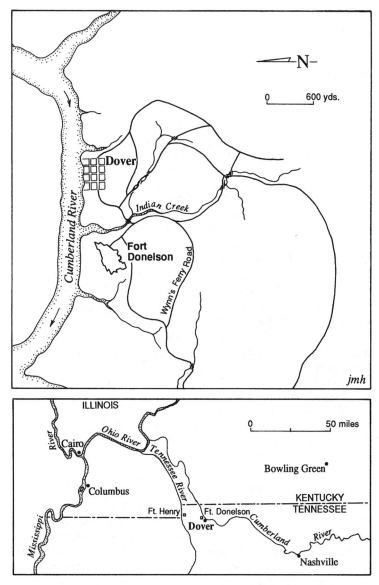

Modern map of Fort Donelson site

The pages that follow pick up here with the account of the battle at Fort Donelson. Barber's narrative of the enlistment and organization of the Third Tennessee in the early summer of 1861 and his other activities throughout that year are not included here, since, for the most part, this period of his military service was humdrum.

Barber wrote partly in the form of a straight narrative—accounts written somewhat after the event—and partly in the form of a diary. With the best of intentions he sought to keep up with events, and when he fell behind he resorted to detailed updating. At one juncture, beside himself with boredom while a prisoner on Johnson's Island, he recalled events of several months, the fall of Fort Donelson and his reception into captivity. "To while away the tedious hours of imprisonment," he wrote, "I commence an unpretending narrative of some events that have fallen under my notice within the past few months. This narrative will not take the form of a consecutive history, nor that of a diary, but will be merely a series of sketches of life in camp, on the battlefield, and in a military prison, written not for the public eye, and therefore under the influence of feelings fearless of public criticism."[12] Similarly, after a home leave, he recounted vicissitudes in rejoining the regiment. After both the above narratives he began daily entries.

Whether in retrospect of weeks or months or hot upon events, Barber's accounting is remarkably literate and does not succumb to the sentimentalism so typical of the Civil War era. Not merely is it straightforward in the way readers now admire, but it describes piquant incidents and scenes and often turns to soliloquy. Perhaps the author sensed what fate had in store. A thoughtful man, Barber put down everything that crossed his mind—not just the course of the march or the weather. His writing moves toward tragedy. The reader senses the war's grand drama, but also its futility, so far as concerned the prospects of Flavel Clingan Barber.

So while the narrative indeed shows marked literary quality, is there any historical novelty? There is. The analysis of the battle at Fort Donelson offers an acute sense of not only what that fight meant for a participant but also a very real description of the chaos of surrender. The author's detailing of his experience in captivity, first at Camp Chase and then on Johnson's Island, is vivid, as is the memorable, stark description of the attempt of Rear Adm. David G. Farragut to pass his squadron up the Mississippi past Port Royal.

But the centerpiece of *Holding the Line* is Barber's account of the Battle of Chickasaw Bayou in December 1862, in which a small Confederate force roundly defeated a much larger force under Maj. Gen. William T. Sherman—an object lesson on how not to send troops against an impregnable position. The Third Tennessee occupied a crucial position in the Confederate line and held off Sherman's attack virtually by itself, a fact that has long remained shrouded in the postwar efforts of certain Confederate commanders, notably Brig. Gen. Stephen D. Lee, to distribute the laurels. But in Barber's telling, the course of the battle finally becomes clear.

An essential comment about this manuscript must be its provenance. After Barber's death his widow remarried and then died not long afterward. The diaries were passed to his sister Sarah and, through marriage, came two generations later to the Hill family of Bloomington, Indiana. Years ago, Margaret Hill Pruitt and her sister, Elizabeth Hill Dinsmore, made a typescript of Barber's books, for they rightly sensed their historical value. Mrs. Pruitt and Mrs. Dinsmore, together with Anna Jane Hill Andrews and Mrs. Nat U. Hill III, kindly deposited the four diary books in the Lilly Library of Indiana University in 1987.

All of the diary books except one survived, that for August 25 through December 2, 1863. Barber was on leave for part of this period, but for the rest of it he undoubtedly kept a diary, as evidenced when, while at Dalton, Georgia, he wrote, "I again commence another volume of my diary. The last one was commenced at Enterprise, Mississippi, last August." Unfortunately the book has disappeared without a trace. Richard Fanning searched the Mississippi Department of Archives and History in Jackson without result, as I did the holdings of the Tennessee State Library and Archives in Nashville. And inquiries to several Georgia manuscript depositories likewise failed.

The books are in excellent condition, considering their peregrinations after Barber's death. The first diary was written in a fine eight-by-ten-inch notebook with boarded covers and lined pages; Barber had secured the book from his captors while on Johnson's Island. He wrote in a bold hand, testimony to the schoolteacher he was, and the ink on this book's pages is as clear and legible as the day he wrote it. So for this first book the task of transcription was easy; I merely had to copy the Hill sisters' transcription and check it against the manuscript. The subsequent books, however, posed more of a challenge. In these three smaller books the ink had run through the pages, making reading very difficult. Moreover, the Hill sisters had not transcribed the final book on the Atlanta campaign.

Editorially, I have maintained the integrity of Barber's prose. Departing from Barber, but for the benefit of the reader, I have divided the published material into chapters, each of which commences with a list of topics or events. Likewise, for clarity's sake, I have amended some of his original paragraphing. The punctuation, however, as quirky the comma usage sometimes is, stands as he wrote it, reflecting his pauses and emphases and, perhaps, distractions. As Barber was extraordinarily literate, only in a few instances was it necessary to resort to bracketed explanations or clarifications or to correct spelling errors, spell out any abbreviations, or lower-case his occasional Victorian capitalization.

1 Fort Donelson

February 12–16, 1862

FEDERAL CANNONADE. SHARPSHOOTERS MAKE LIFE MISERABLE. GUNBOATS OPEN ON THE FORT. ENEMY INFANTRY ATTACK. THE WOODS CATCH FIRE. A NIGHT OF DRIZZLING RAIN. ANOTHER CANNONADE. SURROUNDED. WE DRIVE THE SHARPSHOOTERS. FEROCIOUS ACTION. GENERAL PILLOW SAYS "TAKE THAT BATTERY." CONFUSION CAUSED BY LIEUTENANT COLONEL GORDON. STUPIDITY OF PILLOW PREVENTS ESCAPE. LAST RESERVES THROWN IN. TERRIBLE NIGHT. THE TERRIBLE TRUTH.

The sun set clear and beautiful. The air was cool and bracing, and so clear that the outlines of distant objects could be distinctly seen. On each side as far as we could see extended our breastworks with the long line of men behind them. Everyone was waiting and watching with every sense strained to discover the approach of the enemy, whose glittering bayonets were seen through the trees in the distance.

Suddenly the silence was broken by the boom of a cannon, a light puff of smoke appeared high in the air in front of our line, then the bursting of the shell was heard, and the smoke ascended in the form of a delicate ring up into the heavens out of sight. Many a time have I seen it ascend from the bowl of a pipe in a quiet room in exactly the same manner.

Then came another shell and then another in quick succession, and the air was full of missiles exploding in front, above, and behind us.[1]

The enemy were trying to provoke a return of our fire, so as to ascertain the position of our batteries, but all along our line everything was silent as death. Not a gun responded. At dark the fire ceased, and we lay down to sleep on the eve of our first battle in silence. On the breastworks could be seen the dark and silent forms of our sentinels, each wrapped in his blanket, standing motionless on the berm. No sound reached our ears save the distant and confused murmur from the Federal camp, the sound of axes busily plied, and now and then the distant echo of a voice. We could see the faint reflection of the Federal watch fire against the sky. I lay down on my blankets by the side of the trench, with sword and pistol belt buckled round me, and my Maynard rifle by my side.[2] Leaving directions to be roused, should anything uncommon occur, I was soon sound asleep.

Thus passed the night before our first battle. I have read that great commanders before their first battle have not been able to sleep, but I suppose that subordinates do not partake of the same anxiety—at least I never slept more soundly in a featherbed at home. During the night I was awakened by a sentinel who fancied that he heard someone approaching, but I could hear nothing and soon went to sleep again. . . .[3]

On Thursday morning, the thirteenth, the sun rose bright and clear. As soon as it was fairly light our batteries for the first time opened upon the enemy. They soon returned the fire with shot and shell, mostly overshooting us, many of their shells exploding in the ravine back of our tents. As they learned our range they fired lower, some of their shot almost grazing our breastworks and passing in close proximity to our heads. As we were raw troops and had not yet acquired the coolness and steadiness of veterans there was considerable dodging as they whizzed by us and each shot received our respectful obeisance as it passed. But the novelty of this danger soon wore off, and it became almost impossible to keep our men from exposing themselves unnecessarily on the works.

But a new species of danger soon arose. The enemy's sharpshooters concealed themselves in the fallen timber at the head of the ravine and in the woods on top of the hill in front of us, and commenced firing at every head that was raised above the breastworks, and swept the crest of the hill behind our trenches, so that it became quite hazardous to pass and repass from the rifle pits to the camp. Every tent within their range was riddled with bullets, and nearly every tree and bush on the crest was well marked. But the whistling of the Enfield rifle balls and the peculiar hornet-like singing of the Belgian balls soon grew familiar to our ears, and our men moved about among them almost as coolly as on parade. The sharpshooters would sometimes become visible and our men would return their fire with musketry, but they were out of the range of our guns and we had to endure a provoking fire all day without being able to return it with much effect.

About nine o'clock the attack commenced in earnest. The Federal gunboats coming up the river opened upon the fort and the fort replied with heavy ordnance. At the same time the enemy advancing under cover of the woods attacked our lines to the right of Porter's battery where the Fourteenth Mississippi were stationed. They rushed out of the woods and advanced among the fallen timber. The Fourteenth and the Eighteenth Tennessee received them with a tremendous volley of musketry which for fifteen or twenty minutes was kept up continuously. Porter opened upon them with murderous effect. Some of them, it is said, advanced to within fifty yards of our works, when they recoiled and fled in wild confusion. As they fled past Porter's battery he ploughed their routed ranks with grape and canister. Just at this moment I could see them passing the head of the ravine like a flock of sheep, leaving their track in mangled corpses. They were beyond the reach of the guns of our regiment, and except a few on our right we did not fire. A wild yell arose all around our lines at our first success.

Meanwhile the bombardment of the fort continued. Some of the shells from the gunboats passed over the fort and exploded on the hills to the rear of our camp. Above the rattle of musketry, the boom of cannon, and the bursting of shells, could be heard the deep roar of our 128-pounder. At length a loud cheer from the fort, repeated along the lines, announced that the gunboats had retired, disabled from the conflict, and floated down the river out of sight.

Thus disastrously ended the first attack of the Federals. The spirits of the men rose high. They thought the battle already won, and demanded to be led forth that they might drive back the enemy to the Tennessee River.

Between twelve and one o'clock the attack recommenced on our left. The enemy could be seen advancing through the woods on the left of the valley, crawling along the ground and covering themselves with logs and trees, directly in front of Colonel Abernathy's lines. As soon as they arrived within range Graves and Maney opened upon them with shell and grape, and the lines in front of them kept up a continuous fire of musketry and rifles. They recoiled several times but were again urged on to the charge by their officers. At the height of the battle I walked up to the crest of the hill where I could see distinctly, and while gazing upon the exciting scene, forgetting everything else, I was brought to my senses by the whiz of several rifle balls close to my head, and became conscious that I was the fair mark of the sharpshooters at the head of the ravine. I stepped behind a tree and continued to gaze upon the fight. Our batteries continued to plough their ranks, while the incessant fire of small arms in front cut them down as fast as they advanced. They at length fled in wild confusion, followed by the cheers of our men and by Graves' canister, until they disappeared in the woods, leaving the ground covered with wounded and dead.

And now occurred the most heart-rending scene of the whole battle. The woods had caught fire during the engagement and when the enemy had retreated the ground on which their dead and wounded were lying was burnt over. The groans and screams of the poor helpless men suffering this double torture were agonizing, but no help was sent and death finally put an end to their misery. One poor fellow was heard late at night by our advanced picket, calling most piteously for help. Our sentinel called to the enemy's picket, informing him of the condition of his comrade and offering to go to his assistance if they would refrain from firing, but the picket refused, neither would they go to his relief on the assurance of our sentinel that he would offer no violence, and the poor wretch was left to linger till morning.

In the course of the evening heavy firing was heard on the left, where General Floyd attacked the enemy, and after a severe battle and heavy loss on both sides succeeded in driving them back.[4] It was said by those who visited that part of the field that in many places the ground was literally covered with the bodies of the slain. Over three hundred prisoners were captured. The enemy now drew off, completely beaten at every point on land and water. The sharpshooters, however, continued to annoy us, and picked off many of the cannoneers from our batteries. There were a few long-range rifles among our men and occasionally one of them was made to bite the dust. My own rifle was in use throughout the day, either in my own hands or in those of some good marksmen of my company.

Toward night a cold, drizzling rain set in, which soon turned to snow. Our poor fellows who had been in the rifle pits for thirty hours were now relieved by the Forty-First Tennessee Regiment (Colonel Farquharson), which had just arrived from Cumberland City. The night which followed was one of the coldest of the season, and the ditches were in some places half full of snow and freezing water. Some of the men, worn out with cold, fatigue, and want of sleep, sat with their feet in the trenches until the water rose round them and froze them fast, utterly unconscious. Many a poor soldier who escaped the dangers of the battlefield carried with him from these trenches the seeds of incurable disease. Worn out with fatigue and cold, I crept into a tent without fire and was soon buried in slumber. About midnight I was awakened by the sound of the drum, the trampling of many feet in the snow, and the low hum of voices. There was evidently an alarm, but I never felt so much unwillingness to do my duty in my life as I did just then, to go out of my warm bed and face the cold and snow and perhaps the bullets of the enemy. I went out and found Colonel Cook's regiment forming on the hill to our left. I met Lieutenant Colonel Moore and asked him the cause of the alarm. He told me that the enemy were said to be advancing, but as I could neither hear nor see them, and turning round I could not see a single one of the Third Tennessee stirring, I went back to my tent and was soon asleep, satisfied that the sentinels in the trenches would give the alarm in time to rouse us to meet the enemy.

Friday morning, the fourteenth, dawned cold and cheerless, the coldest day of the season. The ground was covered with a few inches of snow and everything was frozen hard and stiff. As soon as it became light the Federal sharpshooters were at their posts and bullets were again whizzing about our ears. After sunrise our regiment was drawn up in the ravine occupied by our reserve yesterday, in rear of Porter's battery. The arms were then stacked and the men were allowed to remain around their fires, ready at a moment's warning to seize their muskets. They retained this position throughout the day as a reserve. I had my tent moved down to the bottom of the ravine where it was less exposed to bullets than it had been the day before, and remained nearly all day at the fires, vainly striving to keep warm.

At an early hour the batteries on both sides opened on each other, and continued to fire at intervals all day. Several of their pieces were silenced, but our gunners one by one were picked off by the enemy's riflemen until there were scarcely enough left to work the guns. About one o'clock the gunboats again opened upon the fort, and after a tremendous cannonade on both sides they again withdrew, repulsed and disabled, and thenceforth gave us no further trouble. Only one man was killed in the fort during the entire battle.[5]

We passed a very disagreeable day. Our men were constantly suffering from cold; many of them were sick, lying in tents without fire. The balls of the sharpshooters were striking the trees all around us and above our heads, shells were occasionally flying over us and exploding in disagreeable proximity, in fact we had all the annoyances and many of the dangers of battle without any of its excitement.

For the first time we began to realize that we were surrounded and actually besieged by the enemy. We had heretofore thought of nothing less than driving them back to Fort Henry and into the Tennessee River. But they had been largely reinforced and were receiving fresh troops daily and almost hourly, and during the whole of Friday whilst they amused us with their cannonade and their sharpshooters they were drawing tightly around us, from river to river, a double line of troops nearly five miles in length. Repulsed at every point where they had attacked our breastworks, they seemed to have almost ceased active operations and were waiting till famine, weariness, and want of ammunition should place us at their mercy. Hereafter our contest was to be not an effort for victory but a desperate struggle to escape and break through the toils that our enemy had placed around us.[6]

But we knew nothing of this and it even seemed to escape the knowledge of our commander-in-chief, General Pillow. Buckner, the only man who seemed really to appreciate our condition, saw clearly on Friday that we were fighting for escape and not for victory, and he finally brought Pillow, for a time at least, over to his own opinion.

On Friday evening Lieutenant Colonel Gordon ordered me to select thirty good marksmen and report to Major Doss of the Fourteenth Mississippi for the purpose of driving back the enemy's sharpshooters who were making such havoc with Captain Porter's gunners. I received the impression from the order that we were to make a night attack, and selecting the men from my own company, accompanied by Lieutenants Jones and McCoy, we moved in high spirits to the top of the hill. When we arrived at Major Doss' quarters I found that we were to be put on a much less desirable service. All he wanted with us was to relieve the Mississippians, a few of whom had been kept in the brushwood in front of the works to annoy the enemy's skirmishers. He refused to give me permission to attack them at close quarters, as they were strongly supported, and stated that as it was then growing dusk we could be of no use till morning. I sent six men over to the Mississippi rifle pits and directed the rest to return to camp. We had to pass immediately through the battery, then silent and deserted and swept by the balls of the sharpshooters in every direction. The men passed over at a run, one at a time, to avoid attracting the notice and drawing the fire of the enemy, this being the most exposed position on our whole line. After learning all I could from Major Doss about the ground in front of the works I went over to the rifle pits and found that two of my men had already gone over the breastwork. Just as we arrived the Mississippi skirmishers came in and the fire of the sharpshooters ceased, with the exception of a stray bullet or two. It was nearly dark and they had returned to their camp for the night. I called in our men, and making an arrangement to return in the morning before daylight and take up our position as skirmishers for the day, we went back to our tents down the ravine.

Dr. Beaty stayed with me this night. We partook of a hearty supper, talked of our strong hopes of victory on the morrow, around a blazing log fire, and lay down to that dreamless sleep of exhaustion which the soldier only knows. Little did we know of our real condition—twelve thousand men surrounded by nearly sixty thousand, our ammunition running short, our provisions becoming scarce, so many of our gunners disabled that the guns could scarcely be worked, and no hope of succor from abroad. We went to sleep that night hoping that on the morrow we would be led forth to certain victory and the invaders would be driven from the soil of the state.

But while we poor soldiers were feeding ourselves upon the illusive hopes that we should soon follow our fleeing enemies to the banks of the Ohio, a council of war was held and it was resolved that on tomorrow the army should cut its way through the lines of the enemy and make its way to Nashville.

Saturday morning, February 15, before daylight, Lieutenant Colonel Gordon waked us up and ordered us to prepare rations, pack knapsacks, and get ready to march. The men were eager, expecting these preparations were made to follow the enemy after the victory they felt sure of obtaining. Our regiment was soon in line and together with several other regiments was in motion before daylight. We proceeded down that hateful ravine where we had been cooped up so long, crossed the little valley, and mounted the opposite ridge by the time day dawned. We were then thrown into the rifle pits on the left of our lines. On our left was the Seventh Texas Infantry and two guns of Graves' battery occupied a post on the left wing of our regiment.

We had been there but a short time when sharp firing was heard on our left and in front. General Floyd was attacking the enemy on the extreme left and driving him back. At the same time Graves opened vigorously upon the batteries in front of us. The enemy's guns commenced a heavy cannonade upon our line and they threw out sharpshooters in the woods to annoy us. The shells, shot, and minié balls again flew familiarly over us, but much thicker and faster than we had ever seen them before.

The firing on our left grew still hotter and nearer, though both Floyd and the enemy were concealed from view by thick woods, which lay not much more than a hundred yards in front of our lines. Floyd on their right flank was evidently driving them back, as we could hear the loud shouts of his men. Our regiment was strung along the rifle pits more than a quarter of a mile, two or three companies on the left and the rest on the right of Graves' guns. The field officers were on our center and right, far remote, out of sight and out of hearing of those to the left of the battery.

Just then Adjutant Tucker came to the left and told the officers that when the command should be given to take that battery we should leap over our breastworks and rush upon it.[7] None of us knew where the battery was which it was intended to charge— the adjutant did not know and the field officers were too remote to inquire of. We supposed, however, it would be all right, that our officers knew where it was and would direct our course when we made the charge.

Soon the adjutant returned and ordered us to close in along the trenches to the right of Graves' guns and then charge the battery, neither he nor we knowing where it was. We closed up rapidly toward the right (my company being on the extreme left) until we passed Graves. When we arrived there the right wing of the regiment was not anywhere in sight, neither was any field officer there to direct our movements, but Company I was passing over directly in front of us.

My company at the word immediately leaped the breastworks and rushed down the cleared glacis in the midst of a storm of shells and bullets. We reached the woods in safety—no one was hurt, though several had their clothes riddled by balls. When we arrived at the little ravine in the woods I found three companies, H, I, and K, and no one else in sight. I was requested by the other captains to take command. The woods and undergrowth were very thick, firing was heard all around us, bullets struck the trees above our heads and all around us, and the enemy having no doubt seen us entering the woods commenced throwing shells and grape at our little detachment. We knew not what to do nor in what direction to find the enemy of our own troops.

I formed the detachment in a line, and making them sit down for shelter sent back a sergeant to report our position and ask for orders. He returned with the reiterated orders from General Pillow to "take that battery," but with no explanation where "that battery" was. Of course we could do nothing but stand still and send out scouts in different directions through the woods to ascertain the whereabouts of the enemy.

While doing this we received intelligence from the trenches that the rest of our regiment had retreated thither. We then immediately rejoined them. The Third Tennessee and Fourteenth Mississippi had both retired to the breastworks, after severe loss and after killing great numbers of the enemy. General Floyd continued to advance on the left, and on the approach of Forrest's cavalry the enemy, already thrown into confusion, abandoned their cannon and fell back toward the right.

It is said that at the very moment when our men were pouring a destructive fire into the enemy's ranks and they were falling back from their cannon, our lieutenant colonel gave the order to retreat. The inefficiency of our field officers was perfectly manifest to the men by this time and they lost all confidence in them. The failure to give any intelligible orders to the left wing, the failure to halt the right wing in the hollow until the left came up, and then to advance on the battery, and finally the unlucky command to retreat at the wrong time, all satisfied our regiment that it had no field officer worthy of his position. Colonel Brown, in whom we all had the utmost confidence, was in command of the brigade and of course separated from us. Captain Wade was severely wounded in the retreat and carried back to the trenches. Schwartz' battery was taken, but our men were in a bad humor because they were not at the taking of it.

As soon as our men were in the trenches the enemy again opened fire upon us from a battery farther to the right. Our regiment assisted by several others was ordered to attack this battery consisting of six rifled guns and styled Taylor's Chicago Battery. As we afterwards learned, it was supported by General Wallace's entire division of Illinois troops.[8] The shot and shells were poured hot and heavy upon our trenches and upon the crest of the hill behind them. Our regiment retired from the trenches, which were too much crowded, and formed in a line behind the hill farther to the right and close to a six-pounder. Generals Pillow and Buckner and Colonel Brown came up and we were ordered to attack

Taylor's battery. Forward we went in double column, over the breastworks, down the hill, through thick bushes and fallen tree-tops. We emerged from the woods, crossed an open field, and entered a road where we were halted and deployed into line. We marched along this road by the flank toward the right and passed by Schwartz' battery which had been taken. Nothing was to be seen there but a few guns, one of them dismounted, and a half-finished breastwork made of wickerwork and earth. Farther along were dead bodies scattered through the woods, all in the Federal uniform. In the rear of the battery under a little shelter of brush lay the corpse of an officer wrapped in a cloak, the top of his head carried away by a cannon ball, the most ghastly spectacle I ever saw. The enemy in their retreat had carried away their wounded and covered the bodies of the dead with blankets. All around were strewn blankets, knapsacks, guns thrown away by the Federals. One of our men found a coffee pot with its contents still hot.

Our regiment was now thrown into divisions, right in front, and advanced through the woods, throwing the fifth division of which I had command in the rear. Onward we went through the woods, the bushes in many places being so thick that the men could not keep their ranks, believing that before us lay an easy task and that the enemy were in full retreat, not knowing that before us lay the main force of the Federal army.

General Pillow was exulting in his supposed victory and had entirely forgotten that his day's work was completed, that the enemy's lines were broken through, and that now was the time to save ourselves. By the capture of Schwartz' battery the road to Nashville lay open and there was nothing to prevent our army from making good its retreat. But the temporary success of the morning had turned Pillow's brain, and with a few exhausted regiments he talked boldly of driving back the enemy to their boats. Buckner ominously shook his head and opposed our farther advance but yielded to the orders of his superior.

But of all this we knew nothing. Down the hill, across the ravine, and up the opposite declivity, on the top of which was supposed to be the enemy's battery, we kept steadily on. On the left was the Second Kentucky, on the right were the Eighteenth and Thirty-Second Tennessee, and immediately in our rear was the Fourteenth Mississippi. The Federals were ominously silent. No one was yet in sight. Not a gun nor a voice was heard from the enemy. Our regiment which was in advance was halted on the side of a hill, less than one hundred yards from the battery.

Just then a Federal soldier, who had been out in the bushes, rose from his hiding place and ran toward his friends. A few muskets were leveled at him and at the word of command he halted and suffered himself to be taken. He was brought to Colonel Brown who was on the left of our column on horseback, and after a few questions were asked him he was sent to the rear. Colonel Brown ordered the first division, Companies A and B (Captains Clack and Gordon), to deploy as skirmishers. These companies instantly advanced.

Just then a tremendous fire opened up on us by the battery and the regiments supporting it. We were ordered to lie down while our skirmishers who had arrived in sight of the battery sheltered behind logs and trees attempted to pick off their gunners. Grape and canister, shot and shell and rifle balls, fell like hail upon us. Scarcely three seconds seemed to intervene between the discharge of the cannons, while the balls fell like a driving rainstorm into our crowded ranks. The balls generally struck the trees about four feet from the ground and frequently lower. If we had been standing upright the Third Tennessee would have been swept away from the earth by that terrible storm. Not a tree, not a bush, but what was literally riddled by bullets and grape.

Colonel Brown, who was on our left, a little out of the range of the battery, dismounted and stood behind his horse. He now gave the command, "Forward! Storm the battery!" The men commenced rising to their feet. Just at this moment the man next to me was grazed on the shoulder by a shot and, believing himself desperately wounded, rolled over on top of me. Before I could shake him off and rise to my feet we were run over by the men in advance falling back in disorder. At the same time that Colonel Brown gave the order, "Forward!" Lieutenant Colonel Gordon, who was on our right, was struck by a ball through the arm, and apparently, it is said, losing his presence of mind, gave the command, "Retreat!" The front division, being at a distance from

Brown, and not hearing his command in the midst of the rattle of rifles and the thunder of cannon, obeyed Gordon's command.

Our column was in very close order in a bushy place, the front divisions fell back in disorder on those in rear of them, and the whole column was soon a confused mass. Colonel Brown assisted by several of the officers strove in vain to arrest the retreat. I called upon my company to rally or at least to retreat in order, and they tried to halt, but were borne down by the retreating masses. They fell back across the ravine and to the top of the next hill, still in the midst of the hail from the enemy's battery. Here where balls were falling thick and fast Buckner succeeded in rallying them and forming them in line. Here we found the other regiments who had also fallen back. General Pillow now came up and ordered us to renew the charge. Buckner replied that it would be little better than murder to attack such an overwhelming force with exhausted troops, but if General Pillow ordered it he would lead the charge. Pillow gave way sullenly and ordered the troops back to the breastworks.

Now was the time to take up our march for Nashville; we had found the enemy too strong in numbers for us, but his lines were broken and there was no hindrance to our retreat. But the golden opportunity passed away, never to return: we were doomed.[9]

As we slowly and gloomily wended our way back to the trenches we passed by what I supposed to be a dead body lying in the snow, covered with a blanket. As we came close to it I saw a tremulous motion of the eyelids and a wistful look from the eyes, the only sign of life, and discovered an acquaintance, one of Captain Clack's company. The poor fellow had a leg shattered by a grapeshot and had been lying more than an hour on the snow. While we were resting ourselves behind the trenches an ambulance came up laden with wounded soldiers. As it passed through the gap in the breastwork where the ground was very rough the careless driver urged his horses forward. The vehicle passed over with a severe jolt and the cries and groans of the poor, mangled sufferers were heart-rending.

The evening was already far spent when our regiment was formed behind the trenches. Slowly and sadly we wended our way back to our camp. Without being allowed for a moment to halt at our tents the right wing was ordered to their former place in the rifle pits and the left wing was again placed on the side of the hill in the ravine. The exhausted men lay down in the snow, their stiffened fingers still holding tightly to their muskets.

But even such rest as this was denied them. When our men had been withdrawn in the morning from the right of our lines to the left, a few had been left in the trenches to keep up appearances. By good luck the enemy had refrained from an attack on our right all day. But just at the moment of our return to our old camp, before the Second Kentucky had reached their trenches, General Smith's Federal division rushed suddenly upon their breastworks defended by only sixty men.[10] This little band was swept away like chaff before overwhelming numbers. While we were lying on the snow the roar of artillery and the rattle of musketry announced that the battle had again commenced. Shells and rifle balls flew over us in every direction, but Porter's battery nobly responded and the ceaseless volleys of musketry from our men in the trenches showed that the day was not yet lost. The rattle of firearms resounded thicker and faster. Porter was disabled by a wound, his gunners were falling fast around him, the bullets whistled still more thickly over our heads. Just then one of Buckner's aides ran down the hill in an excited manner and ordered the Forty-First Tennessee to the trenches to support the Second Kentucky. That regiment moved up over the brow of the hill and disappeared.

The battle raged fiercer than ever. Our excitement became intense, almost uncontrollable. In our position we could hear everything and see nothing. At length a cry came over the hill, that the enemy were entering our works, and a crowd of skulkers came dashing down the ravine to our right. Almost a continuous stream of wounded men was carried to the rear.

Just then came an order for the five companies of the Third Tennessee to advance to the support of our wavering line. We were the last of the reserve. I glanced along our ranks, already frightfully thinned by the two desperate charges of the morning, and saw there no longer the buoyancy of hope but, depicted on every countenance amid traces of physical exhaustion, the calm resolution of despair.

We advanced in column by company over the hill, through the storm of balls which swept the crest, and into the trenches. After firing a few rounds we were ordered farther to the right. We leaped out of the trenches and rushed to the spot where the battle raged most fiercely. The enemy had driven back the Second Kentucky and entered their works, captured their camp, and were following them up the hill so as to gain a position between us and the fort. Everything was in wild confusion. The Kentuckians were huddled in a mass behind the crest of the hill. Four of our companies formed on their right. I threw mine into a vacant space on their left. General Buckner stepped out in front and formed our line. The enemy kept advancing up the hill and we met them at the crest with bayonets fixed ready for a charge.

A perfect tornado of balls swept our ranks. Buckner called to us not to cross the hill and expose ourselves to certain destruction. I saw here more individual instances of heroism than during the whole previous three days of battle. One poor fellow was taking deliberate aim at the enemy when his left arm fell powerless to his side by a ball. He coolly grasped his musket in the right and walked to the rear. Our standard bearer fell mortally wounded, but as he fell handed it to his comrade with the exclamation, "Never give it up!" A private of my company who stood next to me in the ranks fell dead with a ball in his throat. I bent over him—he was quite dead when he reached the ground, but a smile was on his face.

But the Federals though vastly outnumbering us did not dare to charge upon our serried ranks. One of Porter's guns was now brought up and opened upon them. They fell back behind the breastworks and the firing ceased. Our imminent danger was over for the present.

About the dusk of the evening when everything had become quiet, Floyd and Pillow rode up and held a short interview with Buckner. In that interview it was determined to send out scouts to ascertain the exact strength and position of the enemy on the left and if it were possible make another desperate attempt to cut our way out early next morning. To Buckner's division was to be assigned the perilous task of covering the retreat.

The night set in, bitter cold and gloomy. The men lay down on their arms without supper, too tired to cut fuel for their fires. A few chips scraped together, a little brush piled up, and a blanket apiece, alone kept them from freezing on their beds of snow. Major Cheairs, worn out, retired to his tent. Colonel Brown sent for me and gave me command for the night of our five companies on that cheerless hill. We were ordered to keep a strict watch, as the enemy lay on the other side only a short distance from us. I could scarcely rouse the men to stand guard. In spite of the cold and danger they slept the deep sleep of exhaustion. I could not sleep myself. I knew that the morning would bring with it a renewal of the terrible strife and that if we should escape it would only be by cutting our way through with fearful loss, leaving behind our sick and wounded and the unburied bodies of the dead. The word "surrender" had not been mentioned nor even thought of. The determination of all was to cut our way out, even if half our number should be left dead on the ground. Slowly that terrible night wore away, truly "la noche triste" of this war. Money could not buy me to pass through such another.

Late at night a council of war was held and the results of that council are well-known to the public. In General Buckner's opinion it was impossible for the army to cut its way out without a loss greater than he was willing to encounter, and he therefore decided upon a surrender. General Floyd determined to make his way out with as many of his troops as possible, carrying with him the only means of escape for the rest of the army. General Pillow, the actual commander-in-chief, announced his intention of escaping in person, leaving the army to its fate. Of course it does not become an humble and obscure subaltern to criticize the conduct of officers so superior in rank and reputation, nor even to offer an opinion as to whether, by the code of military honor, a commander is always bound to share the fate of his brave and faithful soldiers.[11]

About three o'clock on Sunday morning Major Cheairs came to me and in a hurried whisper told me to bring my men down to the ravine where the regiment was to assemble, and that we were to fight our way out. Slowly and silently we assembled. It was almost impossible to rouse the men. Exhaustion and suffering had made them reckless and regardless of orders, and many of them would have slept under the fire of a battery. Some who were sick and weary could only be aroused by telling them if left behind they would certainly fall into the hands of the enemy. Our whole line of breastworks were silently deserted, the enemy lying but a few yards beyond.

Our whole force was halted in the ravine and kept standing in the intense cold for nearly an hour. While standing here in the darkness and the cold, one of General Buckner's aides rode by us from Dover with a white flag. Then the terrible truth began to dawn upon us. We were about to be surrendered.

We were thunderstruck. We had expected a desperate fight at break of day, but no one had dreamed of a surrender. We thought even yet there must be some mistake about it, that the white flag was but a pretext to gain time and to give us a chance for escape. We knew not what Buckner knew, that we were surrounded by an army of nearly five times our number, that nearly all our batteries were silenced for want of gunners, that our ammunition and provisions were running short, and that in fact we were at the mercy of the enemy.[12]

The regiments were ordered back into the trenches and Colonel Brown directed me to take a hundred men and go to Dover and report to General Buckner. I took my own company and Company I, went to Buckner's headquarters in town, and there received orders to prevent the town from being plundered and burnt during the confusion consequent upon the surrender— a most disagreeable and thankless task.

Day soon dawned and revealed to us General Floyd on the riverbank passing his brigade over as fast as two steamboats could transport them. He had a strong guard posted between the river and the town to keep back the mass of disorganized soldiers who were trying to get on board the boats. Leaving a few men as a guard at headquarters I took the rest down to the river, mingled with Floyd's guard, and watched an opportunity of getting them on board the boat. It was now quite light. Floyd had passed three regiments over and only one remained to cross. The boat returning suddenly rounded in the middle of the river, turned her head upstream, and soon disappeared. The last hope of escape was cut off.

I returned with my company to the town, despairing. Soldiers from all the regiments were now crowding into Dover and everything was in confusion and disorder. Major Cassidy, Buckner's aide, asked me to place a guard over the army stores to prevent their being plundered by our own men. I refused to do so, telling him that many of our men were destitute of clothing and that I hoped they would seize the last rag of clothing in the quartermaster's stores and destroy what they could not use. I went back to my company, told them that we were unconditionally surrendered, and advised them to make their escape if possible and to seize all the provisions and clothing they might need. They were not slow in obeying. Pants, coats, hats, shoes, bacon, hams, loaves of bread, army crackers, sugar, coffee, and whiskey by the bucketful were soon scattered over the streets. Many broke their muskets or threw them into the river. Cartridge boxes were broken open and their contents destroyed. Men wild with rage and liquor mounted upon stray horses and rode through the town cursing the Yankees and their own generals.[13]

In the meantime many had made their escape. Colonel Forrest with the greater part of his regiment of cavalry dashed through the enemy's pickets on their extreme right and made his way out by crossing a slough which set back from the river. Many stragglers followed him on horseback or on foot. Some swam the river on logs and planks, although the water was icy cold. Some escaped through the lines in various disguises, and all the roads to Clarksville were full of fugitives hastening from the disastrous field of Donelson.

Our regiments abandoning their works came pouring into Dover. The Federals soon made their appearance upon the heights and marched into town. Regiment after regiment of our army formed on the riverbank, stacked their arms, and dispersed. The Federals placed a strong guard against us, making it almost impossible to escape. I took up my abode in a small house in which were several sick and wounded soldiers and remained there throughout the day without interruption. Occasionally an officer or soldier would look in at the door and, seeing the wounded men, would apologize for the intrusion and retire.

The Federals generally behaved well. But few insults were offered to our soldiers. They seemed anxious to converse with us and tried to persuade us that they were our friends, but they met with but little success. Candor compels me to say that their officers acted toward us as gentlemen and in their conversation with us carefully avoided saying anything which might irritate our feelings already so sore from defeat and surrender.

Thus passed away Sunday, February 16, the longest, dreariest day I ever experienced. We who had been accustomed to tread the earth in the proud consciousness of freedom were learning our first lesson in slavery.

But nothing that we suffered ourselves was to be compared with the agony we felt when we thought of the bitter tears and the breaking hearts at home. We did not despond of our cause but it seemed hard to be carried away to a foreign prison while our country and our families were left at the mercy of a foreign soldiery. We had strong hopes, however, of a speedy release either by exchange or parole. Assurances to that effect were given by our captors. I wrote a hasty note to my wife, gave it to a citizen who hoped to be allowed to return home, and resigned myself to my fate.

2 | Captivity

February 16–September 16, 1862

ABOARD THE *TECUMSEH*. UP THE MISSISSIPPI TO ST. LOUIS. THE CARS TO COLUMBUS, OHIO. CAMP CHASE. THE CAMP BECOMES MORE CONGENIAL. VISIT BY PARSON BROWNLOW. EN ROUTE TO LAKE ERIE. JOHNSON'S ISLAND. SPIRITS SLOWLY IMPROVE. NEWS OF GENERAL EXCHANGE. A COLD-BLOODED MURDER. JOY. THROUGH YANKEE-LAND TO FREEDOM.

After dark on Sunday night we were ordered on board a steamboat. Slowly and sadly our regiment moved down to the river through the cold and mire. We were there divided and put on different boats to sleep.[1] Passing along the lower deck with my company I was accosted by a Federal sergeant who demanded my arms with the assurance that they would be restored in the morning. I gave up my sword and pistol, my rifle having been taken to pieces and safely stowed away in the knapsack of one of the men. I laid down on the floor in the midst of my company, and the first night of captivity I slept soundly till morning.

All day Monday, the seventeenth, we lay at anchor at Dover, and in the course of the day our regiment was put on board the *Tecumseh* and preparations were made for departure. I had neither blanket nor clothing except what was on my person, but was kindly furnished by Sergeant Beaty. I never was more kindly treated in my life than by the men of my company during captivity, and the slightest request was as punctually obeyed as the most positive order during my days of authority.

Unless otherwise indicated, ellipsis points in this chapter and subsequent chapters show omission of what Barber took from newspapers, mostly about military movements. While evidence of what he believed was happening with the war, the descriptions often were erroneous.

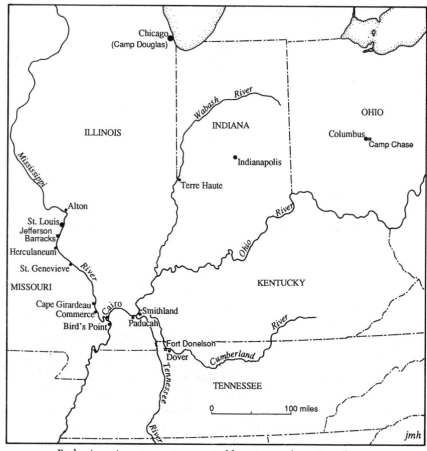

Barber's regiment was transported by steamer from Donelson to
St. Louis and then by railroad across Illinois and Indiana to
Columbus, Ohio, and the prison at Camp Chase.

After dark on Monday the *Tecumseh* started down the river
with her cargo of captives. I had previously dropped my Maynard
into the waters of the Cumberland, determined that it should
never be used against my country's cause. I had also received my
sword and pistol, and secreted them in my bunk on the lower deck.

Tuesday morning, the eighteenth, we were steaming down the
river, having on board the Third Tennessee and also the officers

of some other corps. The boat was exceedingly crowded and filthy and many of the men were taken sick.² It was a beautiful day. The sun shone brightly and the scenery on the riverbank was new to most of us. Sometimes when we could forget for a moment that we were prisoners we actually enjoyed ourselves.

During the day we met a boat loaded with Federal soldiers bound up the river. At Smithland we turned down the Ohio, stopped a few minutes at Paducah at the mouth of the Tennessee, and about 10:00 P.M. we arrived at Cairo. All along the route we were treated with respect both by soldiers and citizens.

On the morning of the nineteenth we left Cairo and steamed up the Mississippi. We passed Bird's Point and Commerce on the Missouri shore, wishfully looking westward and hoping that Jeff Thompson, the "Missouri swamp fox," would make his appearance on the bluffs and bring our boat to shore. But we looked and hoped in vain.³ We passed Cape Girardeau where there were Federal troops and fortifications, and when night overtook us we were still on the river.

On the morning of the twentieth we were still proceeding up the river, which now began to be obstructed by floating ice. We passed up by St. Genevieve and the lofty cliffs of Herculaneum and Jefferson Barracks, and toward evening found ourselves moored at the wharf at St. Louis. There was quite a large crowd on the wharf who manifested their sympathy for us in every possible way. The military endeavored to restrain this feeling by making arrests among the crowd, but when the men were compelled to keep silent the women and children openly avowed their sympathy and defied the soldiers. About dark our boat crossed the river and lay at the wharf at Illinoistown.

Next day, the twenty-first, we remained at our moorings. A private in my company died on our way up the river and I was permitted to take six men ashore and bury him. We carried him out in a rough coffin and in the woods of the Illinois shore we dug a grave. We were attended by a lieutenant and a guard who stood around us while we were at work. I walked a little way from the guards through the woods, but they watched me closely though no one said a word. The Federal soldiers were silent and respectful, and their feelings were evidently touched. We silently laid our comrade in the grave, raised a little mound to mark the spot, and returned to the boat.4

During the night we again started up the river, and on the morning of the twenty-second arrived at Alton. The first building we saw was the state prison, a huge structure situated upon the edge of a high bluff, and upon its walls and through its grates we saw some of our unfortunate companions in captivity. Here we met with the hardest trial of all. Our men were separated from us in order to be sent to Camp Douglas, near Chicago.

I stood upon the upper deck and watched our regiment, the noble but unfortunate Third, slowly passing over the planks to the wharf and along Front Street to the railroad depot. As they passed by where the officers were standing, company after company, led by their orderly sergeants, the officers lifted their hats and stood uncovered before those brave men whom they had led among the bullets and grapeshot of the enemy. Many a tear rolled down the cheeks of the weather-beaten soldiers, and many a heart which had manfully endured danger, defeat, and captivity now melted into softness.5

We were then transferred to the steamboat *Alexander Scott*, which we found already crowded with officers of other corps, and towards evening we dropped down the river. Next morning found us lying on the Missouri shore near St. Louis. As soon as the fog cleared away we dropped down to the city, and at the wharf we again met the crowd of sympathizing faces from which we had parted two days before. Here we were put on board the steamboat *Nebraska*, which was anchored out in the river off the Illinois shore. The *Hiawatha* lay alongside us, also crowded with officers. A strong guard was placed on board both boats and a guard line was established on shore to keep the sympathizing crowd at a respectful distance. The ferryboats were constantly filled with persons passing over from the city to get a glimpse of "the poor, ragged prisoners," and poor and ragged enough they were, for most of them had lost at Fort Donelson all their clothing except what they had on their persons, and their money, which was current enough in Dixie, was just so much worthless paper here. The charitable citizens of St. Louis sent us some underclothing, which did not come a moment too soon to save us from the additional epithet of "dirty."

Here we lay in sight of the fair city of St. Louis until the twenty-seventh of February, the monotony of our life broken only by the view of the beautiful city which lay before us, and by the crowds of visitors who came over every day to look at and to sympathize with us. But they were carefully kept outside the guard lines and even the ladies did not dare to wave their handkerchiefs at us without being insulted by the brutal sentinels and threatened with arrest by the officers. Even General Halleck himself, who was then at St. Louis, issued an order prohibiting any person from openly showing any sympathy with the prisoners under penalty of arrest.

We soon discovered that we although prisoners of war enjoyed almost as much liberty as did those noble citizens of the Federal states who felt a sympathy with our righteous and struggling cause. While here General Tilghman paid us a visit previous to his departure to Fort Warren.[6] The day of our departure Colonel Brown assembled the officers of his regiment and exhorted us to hold fast to our faith, never to disgrace ourselves or our cause by accepting of release upon dishonorable conditions.

On the morning of the twenty-seventh of February we received orders to leave the boat. We were conducted between two files of soldiers from the boat landing to the cars, and about twelve o'clock we set out on our journey eastward.

We passed through the beautiful prairie country of Illinois and next morning at daybreak crossed the Wabash and arrived at Terre Haute. Two sentinels were placed at each door of each car and we were not allowed to pass out even on the platforms. The people of the towns on our route manifested much curiosity to see "the Secesh" and talk with them, and sometimes showed some sympathy for our condition. We had passenger cars but were very much crowded.

On the twenty-eighth we passed through Indianapolis and on the morning of the first of March we reached Columbus. They gave us some breakfast on the cars and then marshaled us again between two files of soldiers through the streets of Columbus and along the turnpike four miles to our final destination, Camp Chase.[7]

Here we found huts of cantonments for several regiments of soldiers and a space enclosed by a high plank wall, the latter of which was to be our abode. We found here two Federal regiments, the Sixty-Ninth and the Seventy-Fourth Ohio, commanded by Colonels Campbell and Moody, the latter of whom had command of the prison.[8] At the gate of our prison our names were taken and our swords were delivered up to the authorities. The gate was opened and for the first time in my life I found myself immured within prison walls.

The first night was indeed a dreary one. Within the high, plank wall which separated us from the outer world we found two long wooden buildings with a street between. These buildings, constructed of plank put together in the rudest manner, reminded me very much of cabins built for the accommodation of visitors at watering places. They were divided by thin partitions into small rooms. Holes were cut in the planks for the admission of light and air. In each room was a small cylinder sheet-iron stove, and at the side were raised platforms to sleep on. Fifteen of us found ourselves in one of these small rooms. We procured a few cooking utensils, a little bacon, and some baker's bread, and commenced our prison life in earnest.

The day was quite cold, wood was scarce, a few stood round the stove cooking, and the rest stood back in the cold and damp. When night came we all lay down with our scanty blankets on the hard planks and shivered and dozed till morning. But our lot was far better than that of those poor fellows who were unable to procure lodging in the houses and who were obliged to remain in tents all night without fire, lying on the cold, frozen ground.

The next day we were better supplied with food and cooking utensils, but with our small conveniences and the large number assigned to each room we were obliged to be cooking all the time to supply the cravings of appetite. Many of our men were sick from exposure and a universal gloom rested upon the whole prison. We had heard of the capture of Nashville and of the retreat of Johnston to Decatur and the evacuation of Columbus by General Polk.[9] Everything seemed to be against us and many of our

Undated drawing showing crowded buildings within the walled compound of Camp Chase. Source: William H. Knauss, *The Story of Camp Chase* (Nashville, 1906).

weaker-minded brethren despaired of our cause. With us it was truly "the time that tried men's souls." When the thought came over me of my happy home and my beloved wife, left alone and unprotected in the midst of an enemy, I was entirely overcome for a moment. But hope soon came back and I felt sanguine of a speedy release and of my return to her who was to me more than all the world.

In a few days our condition was improved. We received some blankets from the Federal authorities; then came a cook stove with a full set of utensils; our room was renovated and bunks were erected, each for two persons. Our mess was organized. I was chosen to the responsible position of head of the mess. Captain Matthews was made chief cook, with Lieutenants Jones and McCoy as assistants. Captain Davenport and Lieutenant Long were placed over the wood department. Lieutenant Ellison was appointed water carrier. Lieutenants Lindsay and Giddens were placed over the provision department. George McCallum had charge of setting the table. Adjutant Tucker and Lieutenant Jennings were appointed dishwashers, and Lieutenant Hannah was directed to keep the house clean. Captain Herron was afterwards added to the list of cooks, and Lieutenant Samuel Ewing was made general "borrower" and errand boy on account of his great capabilities for public business. Ewing and McCallum were, however, both taken sick soon after our arrival and spent several weeks in the hospital.

We had very respectable fare. Our provisions were abundant and of good quality and our cooks did justice to their department. Bacon to any amount, beef occasionally, beans, hominy, flour, meal, coffee, sugar, rice, vinegar, and candles were regularly furnished, while we purchased from the sutler green tea, sassafras bark, molasses, butter, eggs, and occasionally fresh fish, as long as our money lasted. But funds were scarce. Tobacco and newspapers we were obliged to have, whether we ate anything or not, and we were compelled to be sparing of our purchases. We ate three times a day, went to bed early, and rose at dawn—at least most of the mess did; I was generally up by breakfast. Our health gradually improved.

A few weeks after our arrival our field officers were sent to Fort Warren and our quarters were improved by the erection of another prison. We had now three different enclosures, styled prisons number one, two, and three. Numbers one and two were only separated by a plank wall, while number three, the largest pen, was built at some distance from the rest. Number one was by far the smallest enclosure, comprising not more than three-fourths of an acre. We were sometimes allowed to pass from one prison to another to visit our friends, and once I was permitted to walk out through the camps accompanied by a sentinel.

Thus wore away the month of March. In the latter part of the month I was agreeably surprised by a visit from my brother who kindly furnished me money and whatever else I needed, and what was far more to me assured me of the sympathy of my relatives for my condition and promised to use every effort to have me paroled upon honorable terms or exchanged. During the first week in April, I received two letters from home, relieving my mind of a great load of anxiety, for they contained the first intelligence I had from thence since a letter received while in the trenches at Donelson. About this time the staff officers were sent from Camp Chase to Fort Warren. This order deprived our mess of two of its most valued members, Adjutant Tucker and Captain Herron, quartermaster of the Third.

During the month of March, Captain Wilkes, our regimental commissary, died in the post hospital, and his remains were carried to Columbus for burial. Lieutenant David Rhea, who was acting as nurse in the hospital, succeeded in making his escape, putting on citizen's clothes and passing out through the windows. Lieutenant Jones, Company G, Third Regiment, obtained a blank pass from someone and filling it out with the signatures of Governor Tod and Colonel Moody passed through the guards at the gate in open day, as a citizen of Columbus who had entered the prison on business. Some of the prisoners passed out along with the carpenters who were working in the prison. The system of forging passes became very fashionable and several succeeded in making their escape in that manner, but it was finally detected by the arrest of Captain Ephraim Gordon who was caught by Colonel Moody after he had passed through the guards and was outside the prison. Gordon was sent to the guardhouse and kept in close confinement several days and finally sent to the new prison at Johnson's Island.

We often received visits from distinguished individuals. Colonel Trigg, the agent of Andrew Johnson, on his way to Washington visited our prison, and standing upon the wall addressed us.[10] He spoke in a very respectable manner, pitied us as misguided men, sympathized with us as unfortunates, and promised to use every effort for the release of those who should return to their duty and allegiance. He carefully avoided saying anything that might irritate our feelings and politely answered questions that were publicly propounded by prisoners. He told us the Southern Confederacy was a failure, that the whole Southern country would soon be overrun, and that our only hope for safety was immediate submission.

Many of our number were homesick, and in ill health, and many were uneasy about the condition of their families at home, and several hundred sent in their applications for a release upon taking the oath of allegiance. It was so arranged that these applications could be made secretly, as it was supposed that the growth of Union feeling was suppressed in prison by the bitter "Secesh" who by argument, ridicule, or even threats might deter Union men from declaring their sentiments. Most of those who avowed their intention of taking the oath of allegiance excused their conduct on the ground of ill health or the condition of their helpless and suffering families. But a few openly declared their belief that the Federal arms would prove victorious and that it was useless struggling against overpowering force. The most prominent of these, Captain James A. Moore of the Forty-First Tennessee, wrote a letter to Andrew Johnson begging for release and pardon in the most abject terms. This letter was published in a Northern newspaper and some numbers of this paper found their way into our prison. From that moment Moore was treated by the prisoners with contempt and insults were daily heaped upon him. To escape these insults he finally procured a parole to the city of Columbus on the plea of ill health, where he was allowed to remain. Some months afterward a number of prisoners passing from Camp Chase to Johnson's Island saw him standing on the sidewalk as they were carried through Columbus, and all raised a shout of derision at the sight. Poor Moore! He suffered bitterly enough for his apostasy.

Sometime after Colonel Trigg had departed, Parson Brownlow paid us a visit.[11] He came out to Camp Chase after having been lionized by the abolitionists of Cincinnati and Columbus. In the morning he addressed the soldiers in the camp, was received with great enthusiasm, and promised the Sixty-Ninth Ohio Regiment (Colonel Campbell's) to go with them to Tennessee as their chaplain, stipulating only that he should be permitted to carry a musket until the Federal authority had been restored in east Tennessee.

While still under the influence of enthusiasm and self-glorification he determined also to address the prisoners. Colonel Moody first came forward upon the wall between prisons number one and two and asked us if we wished to hear Parson Brownlow. I was then at the request of the prisoners acting as superintendent of prison number one. I stepped forth and told Colonel Moody that we should listen to anything Brownlow might have to say if he addressed us in a respectful manner, but if he insulted us we would knock him off the wall with any missile that might be at hand. Colonel Moody replied that he was a countryman of our own and he presumed him to be a gentleman. Brownlow then came forward and commenced speaking. He began moderately but after a few sentences he spoke of "the hell-born and hell-bound rebellion." Upon this a universal shout of "Tory!" "Traitor!" and "Villain!" burst forth from the prisoners. Just then a Rebel with a basket of eggs passed by, on his way from the sutler's store to his quarters. Brownlow caught sight of the eggs and made a precipitate retreat into the guardhouse, muttering indistinctly some maledictions upon us. A reverend gentleman from Columbus who had accompanied Brownlow remained upon the wall and, turning to us, asked if we would suffer him to offer up a prayer to our common Lord and Savior. No objection being made, he proceeded to offer up his prayer, and was listened to with respect and attention. Colonel Moody then asked us if we wished to hear this gentleman preach on the next Sabbath. A unanimous "Aye!" arose from the crowd, and all dispersed in a good humor. I thought I saw a twinkle in Moody's eye which indicated that he was at heart well pleased with Brownlow's reception.

The Federal journals, on the authority of the officers of the prison and of our visitors, divided us into three classes: first, the intelligent traitors who were men of intellect and education and were utterly incorrigible; second, the "bushwhackers" who were extremely ignorant and rude in manner and equally incorrigible; and lastly, the men of middle class who had been deluded into the rebellion and who by defeat and imprisonment had become convinced of the error of their ways and were willing to return to their allegiance. Unfortunately the last-named class were quite numerous. Several hundred of our number were quite soft on the subject of the oath, and most of these were from that portion of Tennessee overrun by the Federal armies. You would easily distinguish them by their pensive, solitary look, by their lengthened faces, by their yellow-jaundiced complexions, and by their whining, desponding tone of voice. They were continually seeking interviews with the Federal officers and frequently holding private conversations with the sentinels. By their comrades in prison they were regarded with pity and contempt.

Colonel Moody of the Seventy-Fourth Ohio Volunteers was the governor of our prison. He had long been celebrated throughout Ohio as a Methodist preacher and an abolitionist. When the war commenced he became very prominent in urging it forward and finally obtained a colonelcy and a commission to raise a regiment. But he seemed to have no desire of leading his regiment into active service and preferred the more inglorious but safer course of remaining at home as jailer to the Secesh prisoners. Naturally his courage fell into suspicion among his own men and he became an object of contempt and ridicule to the Federal soldiers as well as to the prisoners. He visited us officially every Sabbath and brought us bundles of little tracts, which were sometimes rejected and sometimes received with ill-concealed disdain. He was treated with very scant civility by the prisoners but his obtuseness and ignorance of good breeding was such that he seemed to be unaware of the daily insults which were offered him. His manner was a compound of the pompous official, the boastful bully, and the unctuous divine. He talked loud and long of the vast power of his government and of "crushing out the rebellion," he turned up the whites of his eyes at a game of cards, and prayed over the sick in the prison hospital till great tears rolled down his cheeks. His lieutenant colonel, Von Schroeder, was a foreigner by birth, a professional soldier, and a gentleman. We saw very little of him as his time was occupied with his regiment. Major Ballard assisted Moody in the government of the prison and was tolerably well liked by the Rebels. Colonel Campbell of the Sixty-Ninth was but little known to us, but when he visited us treated us with more consideration than any other officer.

In the corner of our prison at the chief entrance next to the guardhouses was the sutler's store. This was nothing but a small shop with a small window on the side next to the prison, through which we transacted our business with the sutler and purchased such things as his shop afforded. These were chiefly vegetables, sweetmeats, pocket knives, combs, brushes, etc. Our newspapers were brought in every morning by newsboys from Columbus. Agents of the merchants in town frequently visited us and received orders for clothing or anything of value that we wanted. We were allowed to purchase anything except arms and tools that might aid us in making our escape. A little clothing of a coarse quality, such as the soldiers used, was furnished to those who had no funds. Money sent to us was deposited with Colonel Moody and we were allowed to draw five dollars at a time, and our drafts to the amount of our funds were honored when the articles purchased were named and not contraband. Our letters passing out and in were examined by a person appointed for the purpose, and all which were of an unreasonable length and all that contained contraband news and expressed contraband opinions were destroyed. A page of small-sized paper was fixed as the limit of letters passing out, but generally the examiner was a little more generous than his regulations. The letters were brought in every day by the Federal postmaster to the prison superintendent and by him distributed to the prisoners. Letters passing out were put in the box nailed to the prison wall.

Every second day we drew rations of provisions and wood. The provisions were brought in and delivered to the prison commissary, who gave them out to the persons appointed by each mess to receive them. They were abundant and except for the coffee of good quality. The cooks were by far the most important personages among us. They were absolute in their departments and would not permit the slightest interference nor listen to the most respectful advice. When they were in a good humor we lived on the fat of the land; when they were sulky we suffered accordingly. We had a long pine table, round which a dozen persons could be seated, and we took by turns the office of waiting on the table. Everything appeared quite as neat as at many a bachelor's table outside the prison, and from the jokes and laughter and cheerful faces and the excellent appetites around our board a looker-on would scarcely have supposed that we were pining in captivity. There were none of the oathtakers in our mess and indeed had there been any there they would have been ignominiously expelled. But the most ridiculous sight of all was the gentleman who washed the dishes. He put on his white apron, rolled up his sleeves, and dishcloth in hand went to work as gravely and deliberately as though he were advancing upon an enemy's battery at the head of his company.

The only outdoor amusements the confined nature of our prison would admit of were marbles and sham battles with potatoes. Neither of these suited my turn of mind and consequently I took but little exercise. Indoors we played cards, draughts, chess, and backgammon, wrote letters and diaries, read, and slept. We were allowed to burn lights as late as we pleased. The monotony of our life was broken by the daily newspapers and by the thousand rumors of the war which almost hourly came to our ears. According as these rumors were favorable or unfavorable, our spirits rose and fell. The battle of Shiloh produced a lively sensation. At the first rumors we were much depressed, but in a few days we discovered from the tone of the newspapers how severe a disaster it proved to the Federal arms. Prisoners occasionally arrived from the fields of Shiloh and Pea Ridge, from Island Ten, and from western Virginia, then a few stray men from Corinth, and then a few cavalry picked up throughout Tennessee, and from these we learned the particulars of all the battles and the sentiments of our people at home. Each man as he arrived was hailed as a treasury of news and was surrounded by an eager and inquiring crowd.

Occasionally one of our number would receive a parole for a few days or weeks to Columbus, either on account of his ill health or through the influence of some Federal friend. The wives of several of our officers came to see them, and in such cases Governor Tod granted them paroles. The violent Republicans of Columbus, however, severely censured the governor for his mildness and their newspapers had a great deal to say about the Rebel traitors walking at large through the streets of the city and insolently displaying their Confederate uniforms before the eyes of the loyal people. However, the citizens generally treated the paroled prisoners with respect and consideration. Many of the paroles were obtained by the influence of Mrs. Clark of Hamilton, Ohio, a Virginia lady by birth and wife of Judge Clark, a distinguished citizen of that state. She was truly an angel of mercy to the prisoners and spent much of her time and means in visiting our sick and providing clothing for the destitute. Clothing for distribution was also sent to us from Kentucky, St. Louis, and Baltimore.[12]

The Negroes who were found with our army at Donelson were carried to Camp Chase and treated as prisoners of war. The legislature of Ohio was much exercised about their persons. They ascertained that they still continued, while in prison, to wait on their masters without pay, and the cry was instantly raised that slavery existed on the sacred free soil of Ohio. Colonel Moody was accused of conniving at it and he was threatened with being exposed as a pro-slavery man and a Rebel sympathizer. He called the Negroes together and informed them that they were free so far as their masters were concerned, and that they ought to demand wages for any service they might perform. The Negroes listened, returned to prison, and were as much slaves as before.

About the beginning of April the new prison on Johnson's Island in Sandusky Bay near the city of the same name was finished, and squads of prisoners were sent thither from time to time, as the buildings were completed. The latter part of April it came the turn of our mess to go. We were all glad for it, for even a change of prison was a welcome relief to the monotony of our life.[13]

We left Camp Chase in the morning and traveled some on foot and others in omnibuses to Columbus under a guard. We there took the train for Sandusky City. On the way several men made their escape, some by jumping off the cars and taking to the woods, some who were clothed in citizen's dress by loitering behind the guards in Columbus and mixing with the crowd of citizens. We reached Sandusky in the evening and were immediately put on board the steamboat *Island Queen* and carried across the bay to our island, about two and a half miles from the city. We were marched between files of soldiers from the boat landing up to the gates of the prison, the gates were thrown open, and we walked into a large enclose of twelve acres surrounded like Camp Chase prison by a high plank wall. In this enclosure were built eight wooden blocks of barracks, four on each side of the street, each block capable of holding more than two hundred men. In the lower story of the barracks were large dining halls, and on the second floor were lodging rooms, each furnished with bunks to its

Johnson's Island. Source: Knauss, *The Story of Camp Chase.*

utmost capacity, from floor to ceiling. The first floor blocks were divided into small rooms, large enough to contain four or five persons. The other block each had three large rooms upstairs and one long room down, extending the whole length of the building. The lower room was furnished with bunks on one side. At each end of the block was a kitchen with a large cookstove and also a large boiler with a furnace under it. Our water was procured from wells or sinkholes in the street, dug down to the level of the lake.

Johnson's Island contains about three hundred acres, much of it heavily timbered, with a small cleared farm. Barracks for the officers and soldiers of the guard were built close outside the prison walls and in front of the boat landing. Most of the trees within the enclosure had been cut down, but on the west side beyond the wall was a thick forest which threw its shade over us in the evening. On the south our prison fronted on the barracks and parade ground of the guard. On the north was an open meadow, and eastward the waves of the lake almost dashed against the walls.

Officers' quarters on Johnson's Island. Courtesy of the Institute for Great Lakes Research, Bowling Green State University, Bowling Green, Ohio.

To a person facing the rising sun the scene was beautiful. Before him lay the smooth waters of Sandusky Bay, beyond which a long, narrow, thickly wooded promontory ran out from the mainland, terminating in Cedar Point. On this point were two lighthouses, one at a little distance out in the lake. On the right, two and a half miles away on the main shore, the city of Sandusky was visible, lying along the water's edge for more than a mile. To the left a long reef ran out from our island across toward Cedar Point, completely enclosing the bay and leaving only a narrow passage marked by buoys for vessels to pass from the bay out to the lake. When the water was smooth this reef was distinctly visible above its surface. But when the north wind blew, a long line of breakers, white with foam, marked it to the eye. Beyond the reef an unbroken sheet of water

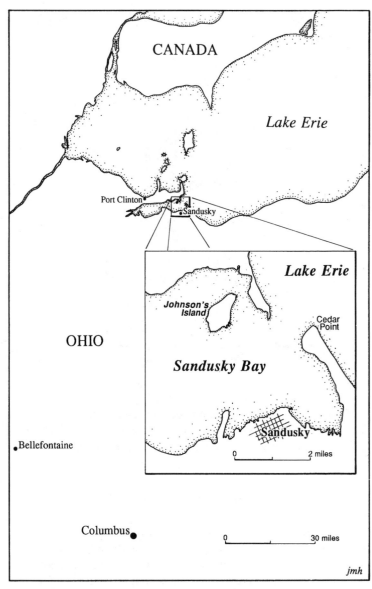

Johnson's Island

extended until it was blended with the distant sky. Steamboats, schooners, and various kinds of lake craft were continually passing in and out of the bay, and small fishing boats were lying about in the covers pursuing their avocation.

The view toward the lake was always novel to me. Sometimes the water was smooth as glass, again the waves were dashing furiously against the shore; sometimes half a dozen steamboats were ploughing their way in as many different directions, leaving behind them great trails of thick black smoke, again throughout the wide expanse of waters no moving thing could be seen except at the extreme edge of the horizon, and the bare masts of some schooner stood straight up against the sky like the skeleton of some phantom ship.

Our guards at this place were men who had enlisted merely for garrison duty and consisted of several companies called "the Hoffman battalion," under the command of Major Pierson. As soldiers they were much inferior to those who had guarded us at Camp Chase.[14] The regulations were much more strict. We had roll call every morning when we were all counted, and taps at 10:00 P.M. when all lights must be extinguished except in the hospital. Scarcely any visitors were allowed to enter the prison. We were not allowed either by night or by day to pass nearer to the wall than thirty feet. Several persons who passed within that distance were fired upon, and one, Captain Meadows of Alabama, had his leg shattered by a minié ball. An indignation meeting was held by the prisoners and a communication was sent to Major Pierson stating that if we were to be shot down in that manner we wished to know it, so that we could take measures for our own protection, and he was also assured that if such outrages were repeated we would break out and massacre the guard, even if all our lives should be the forfeit.

About thirty of us were placed in the same room, one to each bunk. We employed a prisoner to cook our rations for us, but whatever extras we bought we had to cook ourselves. We divided into messes of ten men apiece, raised mess funds, chose stewards, and got along very well for a while. We took it by turns in cooking our extra provisions. Our mess consisted of Lieutenant Hayman of Memphis, Captain Pointer of Spring Hill, Captain Fisher of Nashville, Lieutenants Martin, McDaniel, and Polk of Columbia, Lieutenant Saffel of east Tennessee, Lieutenant Matthews of Edgefield, Lieutenant Tidmarsh (an Englishman), and myself. Six of our mess were artillery officers, the rest infantry. Tidmarsh had formerly been an actor by profession and was a man of very distinguished and versatile talents and withal quite a poet.

Fresh prisoners were arriving every few weeks, some from Camp Chase, some from Pea Ridge and Missouri, some from Shiloh and Corinth, some from Huntsville, Alabama, some cavalry from Lebanon and other points, and some from New Bern, North Carolina. From these we were constantly receiving fresh information from the seat of war. Our weak comrades gradually grew stronger and soon the oath question ceased to be talked of. Those who had applied for the oath now were anxious to disavow their own acts and became more zealous in the cause than they had ever been. New buildings were erected until they had reached the number of thirteen, nine of which were used for prisoners' barracks, one for a hospital, and three were left vacant for future inmates, the results of future Federal victories.

About the middle of June three of our mess, Lieutenants Saffel, Matthews, and myself, procured a room in the hospital, but after remaining there a month we were compelled to leave it on account of the increasing number of the sick. We then procured permission from Major Pierson to occupy a vacant room in number twelve, one of the vacant blocks, the most desirable place in the whole prison. Five of us occupied the room: Matthews, Saffel, Captain Holt of our county, Lieutenant Schneider of the Twentieth Louisiana, and myself. We passed our time in quiet retirement, studying tactics, and reading.

From the first of June our spirits began to improve. The victories of Stonewall Jackson in the valley of the Shenandoah, the battles of Fair Oaks and of the Chickahominy, showed the power of our government and people. We all regarded the achievement of our independence as a fixed fact. Negotiations were opened and carried on for the purpose of effecting a general system of exchange of prisoners. These we watched with the most intense interest, and every morning the newspapers were eagerly examined to notice the progress of the negotiations. Rumors were constantly afloat that exchange had been agreed upon, and we were much elated at the idea. But it seemed to drag on from day to day, no nearer its completion. Our hopes so long deferred at length gave way, and we finally after so many disappointments despaired of any release until the end of the war. But after the battles before Richmond the united voice of the Northern people forced their government to renew those negotiations which had been so often broken off, and we at length heard with the highest emotions of joy the news that everything had been settled and that we were soon to be restored to liberty and to our friends and families. This news we heard about the last of July. We had all got tired of cooking and at length our mess hired a cook, a foreigner who had been captured in Virginia nearly twelve months ago and was regarded as one of the patriarchs of the prison.

We rose every morning about seven o'clock, ate breakfast very soon after, answered to roll call at eight. At nine the newspapers came in and the next three hours were spent in reading and discussing their contents. At twelve we had dinner, then we took our siesta, and lay about in the shade. At five we had supper, and from that time till dark we walked about, discussing the thousand rumors of war and exchange. At dark we had a lesson in Hardee's Tactics for an hour, and from that time till ten o'clock we gossiped, told stories, and talked about our absent friends. At ten, taps were beaten, our lights were all extinguished, and as we found sitting up in the dark very unpleasant we soon retired to bed and to sleep.

Such was our monotonous life, day after day and week after week. A letter from home was quite a serious and important event in our lives. It was anxiously expected, eagerly opened and read, and thoughtfully pondered over, and then occasionally re-read, until the arrival of a new letter threw the old one in the shade. Next after a home letter, in our eyes, was the telegram in each morning paper. At each report of the gallant deeds of our army at Richmond our hearts swelled high with hope and pride, and we envied those who were winning all the laurels of the war while we were cooped up within prison walls.

To no one can sleep be so grateful as to a prisoner. Every hour spent in its soft embrace is an hour gained—so much time killed, one hour nearer to that indefinite period to which we were all anxiously looking forward. But our pleasure in sleep did not arise merely from forgetfulness of our troubles but in dreams we took flight far beyond our prison walls to our homes in our own sunny land. Those homes we saw, not as many of them really are, laid desolate by a foreign soldiery, but as they were long ago when peace and plenty reigned throughout our land. And the forms and faces of loved ones, from whom we had long been separated and whom we might never see again, appeared vividly before us. The lover's first kiss, the wife's last embrace, thrilled through the sleeper's veins, and the mother's parting blessing was again whispered into the sleeper's ear. He starts, stretches forth his arms, and awakens. Alas! No wife or mother is there. The ceaseless dash of Erie's waves against his prison walls reminds him where and what he is.

July wore slowly away. After the stories of the battles before Richmond had been told and retold until they became monotonous, the news of Morgan's and Forrest's raids into Kentucky and Tennessee again aroused our attention and stimulated our sinking spirits, and the gallant defense of Vicksburg told us that in the Southwest all was not yet lost.

Then came the news that a general exchange had been agreed upon by the commissioners of the two belligerent governments, and we fancied that in a few days the doors of our prison would be thrown open and we would go forth free again.

But we soon discovered that an exchange was a work of time. First the privates confined in Fort Delaware were sent to Fortress Monroe and then up James River to Richmond. Then Generals Buckner and Tilghman and the officers from Fort Warren took the same road and also reached their destination in safety, but we were still in prison expecting every day our order to start. One day we would hear that we should receive our marching orders on the next, and the next day that the exchange had been entirely broken off. Thus we were constantly passing through all different phases of emotion from the highest exultation to the deepest depression. We thoroughly experienced the truth of the old adage, "Hope deferred maketh the heart sick."

August came and still found us here in spite of government agreements. At length we became distrustful of all hopes on the subject and came to the determination to believe nothing on the subject of our release until we found ourselves once more under the Stars and Bars of our beloved republic.

The prisoners within our walls viewed their release with very different feelings. Some, sunk in degradation, looked with dread to the day when their prison gates should be thrown open. They were enjoying animal existence and basking in the sunshine, with no uneasiness for the morrow. They knew their daily food and their nightly couches would be prepared for them without their own exertion, and they only wished to slumber away their lives until peace should be restored and they could come forth without risk of being compelled to take up arms and to expose themselves to the dangers and the fatigues of a campaign. They were unwilling to take the oath of allegiance to the Federal government, fearful of the consequences to themselves should the Confederate republic be established, and also ashamed of the odium which such a course would bring upon them in the eyes of their comrades.

Another class of prisoners looked forward with unmixed joy to the day of their release. Their homes were within the Confederate lines and from the moment of their exchange they could straightway rush to the embraces of their families and loved ones.

But there was still another class to whom this exchange would be a pleasure not wholly without mixture of pain. Their passage across the lines to Dixie would not be a return home. Their homes were within the lines of the enemy. While in prison they could correspond regularly with their families and friends, but as soon as they should be at liberty this solace would be at an end. Here, although powerless to aid their loved ones, they at least could know of their fate, but once beyond the lines all knowledge of their welfare would cease, and anxiety, worse than actual calamity, would prey upon them unceasingly.

August was already half gone, and still we were here. Then came the news of Stonewall Jackson's brilliant victory over Pope at Cedar Mountain, and for a few days we forgot our forlorn condition in the general rejoicing. Middle Tennessee seemed to be overrun by bands of guerrillas and although we rejoiced at their daring exploits yet sometimes we trembled to think of the dangers to which our loved ones were exposed in a land infested by roving, irresponsible bands of friends and foes. The impression seemed to prevail that we would be sent to the southwest, possibly to Vicksburg or Corinth, to be exchanged.

The monotony of our prison existence was broken by a cold-blooded murder. One evening about dark, Lieutenant Gibson of Arkansas was passing in front of block thirteen to his quarters. The prison regulations required us to be in our rooms after sundown, but this regulation had never been enforced and we were allowed to remain in the street till taps at ten o'clock. The sentinel on the wall near Lieutenant Gibson halted him and ordered him to retire to his quarters. Gibson replied that he was going there, at the same time pointing out where they were. The sentinel ordered him to go back in the opposite direction and took deliberate aim at him. Gibson then turned and proceeded in the direction indicated, but looking back over his shoulder he saw the gun still aimed at him. He then sprang towards a door of block thirteen, and as he was entering he received a musket ball through his body and fell on the threshold. The ball entered his right breast, passed through his lung, and out at his spine. He was entirely insensible and died in a few minutes. The sentinel was justified by Major Pierson, and no notice was taken of it.[15]

August 16. Today we have been in captivity exactly six months, the longest six months of my existence. Our cause looks bright enough but still I am in wretched spirits. A month has elapsed since the date of my last letter from home. I would give anything except my honor and my country's cause to be again with her who is more to me than all the world besides. May God protect her is my daily and hourly prayer. Day after day passes and no letter comes, and every arrival of the mail brings with it a fresh pang. Disappointment once a week might be endured, but disappointment every day is almost more than weak human nature can sustain. Will it never end? Shall I never hear from my beloved wife again? I am tempted to murmur against Providence.

August 20. Still we are here. The terms of the general exchange are such that our release, at least on parole, must happen before long. I suspect they are holding us back until the commissioners from Andrew Johnson shall visit us and try to induce us to take the oath of allegiance. They have already been at Camp Morton and have, it is said, persuaded many Tennesseans there to take the oath. Lieutenant Bledsoe of west Tennessee has gone out, as he declares, on parole, but as many persons believe upon taking the oath. A great revolution has taken place in the minds of many of our weak-minded brethren on the subject of oathtaking. They are now the loudest and most zealous for resistance to the end. Vicksburg is the point designated in the articles of agreement as the one to which the western prisoners will be sent, and if the vicissitudes of war shall render that place inconvenient, some other point as near as possible to it shall be designated. . . .

August 22. A month has elapsed since the cartel for a general exchange has been signed and still we are in durance vile. Last night it was reported that Major Pierson had received orders to send us forward but I do not credit it as yet. . . .[16]

August 23. . . . Exchange is going forward favorably. The list of prisoners here was called over and corrected today. . . .[17]

August 24. The prisoners' roll was partly made out yesterday, and so soon as that shall be finished we look for movements to be made for sending us off. The prisoners at Camp Morton, Indianapolis, are said to be started south in bodies of one thousand men per day. . . .

I am becoming very uneasy at the stoppage of my correspondence from home. God alone knows how much I suffer on account of my long separation from my beloved wife. I could endure it cheerfully if I could hear often of her welfare. She appears desponding in the tone of her letters, particularly about my reenlistment in the army after our exchange. God knows how ardently I desire to spend the rest of my days in peace and quietness at home, but it is impossible to do so with honor in the present condition of the country. Even if I were disposed to quit the army it would be impossible to remain at home without danger of arrest and imprisonment, so long as our part of the country is in the hands of the enemy. If the Confederates retake Tennessee it will be equally impossible for anyone of military age to remain at home, so that if honor and patriotism did not, necessity would compel me to join the army. I know if I could get home and have a short interview with her she would not be so unreasonable as to object to my rejoining our army.

August 25. Yesterday the roll of prisoners was finished. Today we learn that three thousand prisoners have been sent from Camp Morton to Cairo and four or five hundred who have taken the oath have been sent home. . . .

August 26. We have joyful news today. Colonel Hoffman has arrived here and notified us that we would be sent off as soon as transportation can be furnished, which will be in a very few days. Several hundred prisoners have arrived here from Camp Morton this evening and inform us that the last installment of exchanged prisoners leave that place today. . . .

August 27. . . . Three of our field officers left this morning for Vicksburg on parole. It is reported that we will all leave day after tomorrow at 6:00 A.M. and be guarded until we reach our destination. Our day of deliverance is fast coming.

August 28. Our departure is put off from day to day. There are still rumors that we shall leave tomorrow but we have as yet received no orders. The sutler is busily engaged in settling his accounts with the prisoners. Our delay is said to be owing to want of transportation. About half a dozen of our officers were released today upon taking the oath of allegiance, most of them natives of the Northern states. They were hooted and groaned at by their comrades who remained. The prisoners who came here a few days ago are partly state prisoners brought from Kentucky, partly guerrillas captured in the same state, and some soldiers and officers taken in various skirmishes brought here to be exchanged. We are all packing up and preparing for our removal. Every day seems longer and longer and if we are kept much longer in suspense every day will seem to be like a week. Still no letter from home. A few days ago I heard through a letter of another from Pulaski that the family were all well. That is some consolation but it is hard to remain month after month without a single line in that handwriting that I love so well to see.

August 29. When the last of prisoners were brought in, our little quiet mess were compelled to leave their room and to go back to their original messes. We are very much crowded but we can stand it for the short time we have still to remain. We are assured now that we shall start next Monday morning, but no orders have yet been sent to us. We are not allowed to receive any of our money outside but they promise to pay it over when we shall arrive at Vicksburg. . . .The excitement with regard to our departure has somewhat subsided. We are now certain of going and therefore we are taking it more coolly and as a matter of course.

August 30. . . . We have received orders at last to prepare our baggage for examination tomorrow. We will start day after tomorrow.

August 31. . . . This is our last day spent in prison. Our baggage has all been carried out this evening, to be taken over to Sandusky. Tomorrow morning 1,130 officers and men are to go. Those who recently arrived from Camp Morton are to be retained, as also a few others who did not belong to the regular Confederate army but were taken as citizens bearing arms or militia not mustered into service or suspected of being spies.

As the days of our captivity draw to a close, our thoughts instinctively turn to our homes, so far remote and yet so dearly loved. But in the tumult of feeling produced by our departure, and in the midst of continual bustle, it is impossible to write, and therefore I will close the chapter of life on Johnson's Island.

September 1. This morning we all formed ourselves in front of the gate of the prison and as we were called out alphabetically, one by one we passed out of the enclosure. As soon as a boatload had passed out we were transported over the bay to Sandusky where we were put on board a train of cars and awaited the arrival of the rest. It was late in the evening before they were all on board. Most of our cars were passenger cars but next to the engine were a few boxcars, in one of which I was so unfortunate as to be placed. We were furnished with three days' rations of hard bread and pork. We set out on the Cincinnati road, which we left at Bellefontaine, and next morning found us at Union [City] on the state line of Ohio and Indiana. Captain Follett who commanded our guard suffered us to leave the cars wherever we stopped and to converse with the inhabitants. News from the seat of war kept pouring in at every station. We learned that Pope had fallen back to Manassas, had lost much of his baggage and supplies, and the battle was still fiercely raging. We also heard that Kirby Smith had defeated General Nelson near Richmond, Kentucky, and was advancing northward. The people along the road appeared much dejected. They treated us with respect and occasionally someone would quietly express to us his sympathy with our cause.[18]

September 2. Today we passed through Indiana and in the course of the evening we reached Indianapolis. This city presented a far different aspect to what it presented when we came through it last winter. Then all were jubilant at the fall of Donelson; flags were flying and crowds were shouting. Now all were silent, depressed, and sullen. Some admitted their defeat but still professed to believe that their numbers and immense resources could ultimately give them the victory. . . . At Indianapolis we changed cars and were all put in a train of boxcars, one passenger car being reserved for the sick and another for the use of the guard. In the latter were also the ladies of two Confederate officers who were returning South with their husbands. When night fell, we were still in Indiana.

Daylight next morning found us at Mattoon, Illinois, at which point we took the branch of the Illinois Central Railroad for Cairo. We now found ourselves among a people still more strongly Southern in their feelings than any we had yet met. We passed through the beautiful and extensive prairies of the Wabash country and at every station we found sympathizing faces and the fair sex especially waved their handkerchiefs and kissed their hands to us. At Central City station we arrived at the main trunk of the Illinois Central Railroad where we found a regiment of the new levy encamped. From Centralia southward the secession feeling seemed to increase. At Tamaroa several arrests had been made by the Federal authorities a few days before, and as we moved out of town some ladies waved a Confederate flag, the first we had seen since we left our beloved Dixie. All through Egypt the Union men looked desponding and the Secesh jubilant. About 9:00 P.M. on the third we reached Cairo and were immediately placed on board the steamer *Universe* and anchored out in the Ohio River. The boat was crowded to excess, every part being filled, so that it was almost impossible to step from one part of the boat to another. We lay here until the eighth of September, having been transferred from the *Universe* to the *Chouteau*, waiting for the rest of the prisoners to assemble from various points.

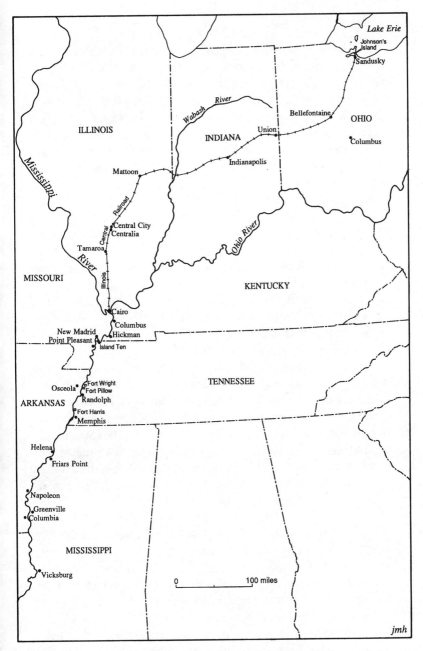

After the train trip across Ohio, Indiana, and Illinois, Barber took a
steamer downriver from Cairo.

Finding ourselves overcrowded, and not choosing to sleep out on the open deck in the weather without protection from the rain and sun, one hundred of our number hired a small steamer called the *Diligent* to carry us down the river, paying twenty dollars apiece for our passage. For rations we received from the government hard bread, spoiled hams, and a small quantity of coffee, which it was almost impossible to cook on account of our crowded condition. On board the *Diligent* we fared very well, at least in comparison with our former treatment.

At 1:00 P.M., September 8, our whole fleet, consisting of nine boats laden with prisoners convoyed by a Federal gunboat, weighed anchor and dropped down the river. In a few minutes we passed from the clear waters of the Ohio to the turbid flood of the Father of Waters. Our fleet presented quite an animated appearance, being more than a mile in length, the gunboat ahead. Toward evening we passed under the bluffs of Columbus, so long the Gibraltar of the Mississippi, but the Federal flag was waving over its fortifications bristling with many cannon. The ladies of the place, however, waved their handkerchiefs and cheered us, but the men were silent. The sight of Federal bayonets kept them from expressing their sentiments. All along the banks below Columbus the same thing was repeated, the men occasionally waving their hands when no soldiers were in sight. No guard was placed on our boat and we were in some measure regarded as on parole. At Hickman our reception by the ladies was even more enthusiastic, the windows and doors and the heights above town being crowded with them. At dark we dropped anchor a few miles above Island Ten and remained there till next morning.[19]

On the morning of September 9 we passed by Island Ten where some Federal troops were encamped on the Tennessee shore. The fortifications were mostly washed away or overgrown with weeds, so that it was almost impossible to distinguish them. When we arrived at New Madrid we were met by a boat from below and immediately our whole fleet hoisted white flags. At New Madrid was a garrison of Federals.

The day was fine and our voyage down the river was delightful, at least to me who had never taken the trip before. The banks were generally covered with a thick growth of cottonwood and a few cypress trees were seen today. We passed by Point Pleasant in Missouri and Osceola in Arkansas, and a little after dark we ran down by Randolph and under the batteries of Fort Pillow in Tennessee. All this part of the river from Cairo to Memphis has been made historic ground by the events of this war. Belmont, Island Ten, and Fort Pillow are all monuments of the bravery of our soldiers. During the early part of the night we passed by Fort Wright and anchored about ten miles above Memphis. The morning of the tenth we passed by the dilapidated earthworks of Fort Harris and our whole fleet stopped before Memphis where we lay till next day. The citizens and especially the ladies came down to see us and received us with the greatest enthusiasm. They were suffered to come on board our boat and all the Federal bayonets in town could not keep them from cheering and waving their handkerchiefs. We learned that a fight was going on twenty-six miles from town but could learn no particulars. Wounded men and some few prisoners were brought in.

On the eleventh we left Memphis and the same night anchored a few miles above Helena in sight of the town. All along the shore as far as the eye could reach stretched the tents of Curtis' army.[20] We dropped down on the morning of the twelfth in front of the town and remained there till evening. A large fleet of gunboats and transports lay in the river. The town appeared almost deserted. Few citizens were seen, and the shore lined with soldiers and contrabands. . . . We were allowed to go ashore and converse with the citizens.

In the evening we left Helena, passed Friars Point, and when night came, again anchored out in the river. We passed a body of Federals encamped on the Arkansas side about fifteen miles below Helena. Next day we passed Napoleon at the mouth of the Arkansas, which like all other parts on the river seemed almost deserted.

On the fourteenth we passed Greenville on the east and Columbia on the west side of the river and anchored at a point ninety miles above Vicksburg. No Federals were seen, but armed bushwhackers made their appearance at several points on the riverbank. They all seemed to understand the object of our expedition and waved their hats to our repeated cheers for Jeff Davis.

On the evening of the fifteenth we anchored a few miles above Vicksburg where we were met by the Confederate steamer *Paul Jones*, on board of which we found many of our friends.

On the sixteenth of September, just seven months from the day of capture, we were transferred on board the *Paul Jones* and landed at the wharf at Vicksburg, once more free men, beneath the flag which we all loved so well.

3 | Vicksburg

September 16, 1862–January 2, 1863

I SLEEP IN A CHRISTIAN BED. SWELTERING IN JACKSON. HOLLY SPRINGS. RECRUITING DUTY IN TENNESSEE. YANKEES LAND AT CHICKASAW BAYOU. THE FIGHT OPENS WITH A WHIZZING SHELL. A LONG ENEMY COLUMN DEBOUCHES FROM THE WOODS, THE GRANDEST SIGHT I EVER SAW. A SHEET OF FIRE FROM OUR BREAST-WORKS. THREE HUNDRED DEAD ON THE FIELD. A NIGHT OF POUR-ING RAIN. ENEMY WHITE FLAG TO BURY THE DEAD. GUNBOATS FIRE AS YANKEES WITHDRAW DOWN THE RIVER.

The day was rainy and cheerless, almost as cheerless as the one in which we were captured. Our feelings of joy and enthusiasm were somewhat dampened upon learning that we would not be per-mitted to return home but we were ordered to await the arrival of our regiment, reorganize, and then proceed at once to active ser-vice. We also learned that Colonel Brown had been promoted to be brigadier general and sent with Buckner into Kentucky.[1]

As soon as we landed at Vicksburg we were scattered through-out the town seeking shelter and food, both of which were scarce enough. After some trouble I found both at the rate of five dollars a day and for the first time in more than seven months I slept on a Christian bed.

The next day we went to Jackson on the cars and immediately upon our arrival went out to a camp which Lieutenant Rhea had prepared for us, close to a bayou setting back from Pearl River. The water was exceedingly bad, the worst I ever tried to drink; our provisions were rather indifferent; and we slept on the ground. Physically we fared much worse than in prison, but still not a word of complaint was uttered. Freedom was worth all the privations we suffered to obtain it.

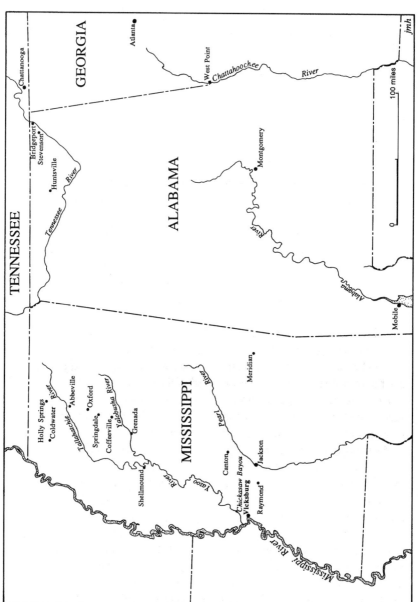

Vicksburg and environs, the scene of Barber's peregrinations in 1862–63

After waiting several days our regiment at length arrived and we organized by the election of Walker colonel, Clack lieutenant colonel, and Tucker major.[2] We then went into camp a short distance from Jackson. Our men were all sadly disappointed at not being allowed to go on to Chattanooga and join Generals Brown and Buckner, but we were compelled to submit to our fate however hard and to obey orders. We were placed in General Tilghman's division and our destination was supposed to be north Mississippi. About one third of the officers of our regiment were detailed on the recruiting service and ordered home to procure recruits to fill up our different companies, and by good luck I was placed upon the list.

September passed away and still we lay in camp, our men half mutinous because they were not sent on to their favorite commanders, and many of them sick. A universal gloom rested upon the entire regiment, both officers and men, arising partly from their peculiar position and partly from the depressing influence of the weather which was intolerably hot to us who had been living for some time in a Canadian climate. The companies of our regiment were consolidated, two being thrown to each captain who was retained, while the other officers who were placed upon recruiting service were temporarily relieved of their commands. I took lodging in town and was enabled to pass the time a little more pleasantly than in camp. The weather was warmer than at any time during our sojourn in prison and our men lay sweltering in their tents.

At length on the evening of the seventh of October our regiment received their arms and started up the railroad toward Holly Springs. The officers on recruiting service remained in Jackson until their papers could be made out. We were very restless, of course, but had no alternative but to obey. It was hard to part with our brave boys who were going to reinforce the shattered remains of General Price's army, not knowing whether we would ever see them again.[3] If my beloved wife knew how much I sacrificed at leaving my brave company on the way to the battlefield, she could estimate the strength of my affection for her.

We had just received the news of the defeat of our army, before our troops were ordered off, and their departure took place under

Capt. Calvin H. Walker (*left*) and his brother, James S. Walker. Calvin
became colonel of the Third Tennessee upon reorganization at Jackson,
Mississippi, in 1862. He was killed at New Hope Church, Georgia, in
1864; James survived the war. Courtesy of Herb Peck, Jr., Nashville.

very depressing circumstances. Separated from many officers under whom they had served so long, placed under the command of generals about whom they knew nothing, and in whom they had little confidence, they did not move like troops expecting a certain victory, yet they all went with an absolute determination to do their duty.

We who were left had a very disagreeable time of it. The town was crowded, noisy, dusty, and hot. We had nothing to occupy our time with but were expecting our orders to leave for home every day. Day after day slipped by and still we were here, anxiously hoping and expecting to start the next. Every morning we repaired to General Tilghman's headquarters and every morning we were doomed to disappointment. It was almost as dreary a life as that spent in prison, hoping and looking for release during many a weary month. We were doing absolutely nothing, our expenses were heavy, the paymaster refused to pay us off. We had no way to kill time except to eat and to sleep, and the latter it was almost impossible to do, for thinking about those homes which we were so soon to revisit. A few of our number who were sick obtained leave of absence and I almost wished myself for a slight chill that I might have some excuse upon which to found an application for a furlough. Our only consolation was that the day for our departure, although delayed, must surely be soon.

On the eleventh of October we received orders to report for orders with every prospect of getting away, but still we were doubtful and uncertain as General Tilghman was somewhat famous for countermanding orders. Our spirits were considerably revived, however, at the prospect.

[Six weeks of leave followed, on recruiting duty in Tennessee.]

On the morning of the twenty-fifth of November, 1862, I again left home for the army. I started in good spirits, for I firmly believed that I would soon return, to leave home no more. My wife and her mother accompanied me as far as Huntsville. At that place I took the cars, having in charge of four recruits for my company, the rest, about twenty in number, having gone on before by different routes. From latest advices we believed our regiment to be at Abbeville, Mississippi, General Van Dorn having fallen back from the line of the Coldwater to that of the Tallahatchie.[4]

The country from Huntsville to the Tennessee River looked desolate as though the hand of war had swept over it with no gentle violence. Houses and depots were burnt, fences were swept away, and but few living beings were seen. We changed cars at Stevenson and a little before night arrived at Bridgeport. The railroad bridge was in process of reconstruction and we crossed on a steamboat. Here I met Lieutenant Dick Saffel, now major of the Twenty-Sixth Tennessee, one of my old messmates at Johnson's Island. I also fell in with several officers of the Forty-Eighth Tennessee whom I had known in prison, going on with their recruits to rejoin their corps at Port Hudson, Louisiana, and made arrangements to travel in company with them as far as Jackson, Mississippi. We could not get our men on the evening train and lay all night on the island in the river, in a cornfield. Next day, November 27, our departure was still delayed and Captain Howlett and myself walked on the railroad track as far as Shellmound, getting our dinner at a farmhouse on the road. The train containing our soldiers came by in the evening but failed to stop and we were obliged to wait for the passenger train. We reached Chattanooga after night and I met Joe in the depot who piloted me to Dr. Stout's. The doctor was not at home but I found very comfortable quarters with Major Ben Roy.

At two o'clock on the morning of the twenty-ninth we left Chattanooga and the same evening arrived in Atlanta. Here we procured a special train which carried us to West Point by noon each day. We lay over at West Point till midnight and by daylight on the first of December we reached Montgomery. Not being able to get transportation for our men by railroad, Captain Howlett and myself left on the morning of the second and reached Mobile late the same night. We arrived at Tensas Landing a little after dark and made the last twenty miles by steamboat. We waited at Mobile for our men who were to come down the Alabama River by steamboat. On the morning of the fifth they arrived, and we all took the train on the Mobile and Ohio Railroad the same evening. By the morning of the sixth we were at Meridian, Mississippi. Here we found further difficulties in the way of getting forward. General Vaughn's brigade was moving toward Jackson and the trains were all occupied.[5] About noon on the eighth we

USS *Essex*, a typical river ironclad observed by Barber early in 1863.
Courtesy of the U.S. Army Military History Research Collection,
Carlisle Barracks, Pennsylvania.

again set forward and after a very uncomfortable and freezing cold
night we reached Jackson about three in the morning. Captain
Howlett and I slept on the floor in the parlor of the Bowman
House till daylight. Here we received certain information that
Van Dorn had fallen back from the Tallahatchie to the line of the
Yalobusha and that our regiment was near Grenada. On the
evening of the tenth we left Jackson and reached Canton by bedtime. We remained here till morning when we again took the
road and about noon arrived at Grenada. Here I found Colonel
Clack and nearly all our recruits, encamped close by town, while
the regiment was about six miles distant. I went on immediately
and arrived at camp the evening of the eleventh of December.

Things were in rather a bad condition in camp. On the retreat
from Abbeville nearly every tent belonging to the regiment and
all the clothing which Sergeant Beaty had carried with him from
home for the use of the company had been lost. There was only

one tent in the company and most of the men were living under brush arbors. Cooking utensils were very scarce and the supply of food was more meager than I had yet seen in camp. The men seemed much more cheerful and contented than they were when I left and General Tilghman was evidently gaining in popularity among them. All hopes of a speedy return to Tennessee were taken away, and the regiment seemed better satisfied with its lot.

General Van Dorn's corps, to which we belonged, lay along the south bank of the Yalobusha from Grenada eastward, and General Price's corps lay down the river westward of that place. Our cavalry extended along the front of our line as far as Coffeeville. The enemy's advanced posts were in the vicinity of Oxford. About the middle of December, General Loring assumed command of Van Dorn's corps and the latter was placed over the whole cavalry force in north Mississippi and immediately started on an expedition northwards.[6]

Immediately upon taking command of my company I commenced drilling the recruits. After a week's hard work I met with some success. Then came the old routine of company drill, which was only broken by a few attempts at battalion and brigade drill by General Gregg, our new brigadier. He appeared, from what little I saw of him, to be somewhat particular and exacting, and a little awkward. He had been a Texas judge; afterwards colonel of the Seventh Texas; had behaved with gallantry at Fort Donelson and served his apprenticeship in prison.[7] The monotony of our life in the pine woods of the Yalobusha was only broken by our being sent out on a foraging expedition north of the river on a very rainy day and our return late at night covered with mud and tired to death. My company and Captain Matthews' (A and K) were furnished with new rifles, mine made in Richmond, and supplied with the saber bayonet, and the others made at Liége, in Belgium. The men were all very proud of their new guns. Colonel Walker's health, which had been declining for some time, now grew rapidly worse, and he went home on sick leave, leaving the regiment under command of Lieutenant Colonel Clack. On the retreat from Abbeville our regiment had been attacked by surprise at Springdale and several men had been lost. From my company one was wounded and left in the hospital at Oxford, and two were missing, one of whom afterward came in, having dodged the Yankees. The other, William Scruggs, has not yet been heard of.

Jeff Davis and General Joe Johnston, commander of the Western Department, came to Grenada on the twenty-fourth of December and a grand review of the whole army took place on that day. In the midst of the review an order came for the Third, the Tenth, and the Fiftieth Tennessee to prepare to march. Our regiment was then consolidated with the Thirtieth Tennessee. On the night of the twenty-fourth we encamped a mile from Grenada and next morning got on the cars. When night came it found us at Canton, and next morning at Jackson. On the evening of the twenty-sixth we reached Vicksburg and pitched our camp, or rather raised our shelters of rails and cane, in a ravine among the Walnut Hills about two miles northeast of Vicksburg.

General Wilson commanded the post of Vicksburg, and General Lee had charge of the defenses on the north side of the town toward the Yazoo River.[8] On the twenty-seventh we were ordered to the front and took up our position in the road leading from the town up the Yazoo bottom along the foot of the hills. No signs of the enemy were seen except the smoke of their boats in the Yazoo River and an occasional shelling of the woods on the banks of that river. The same evening we returned to our camp. Next morning at two o'clock our regiment was again ordered to the same position. Feeling very unwell I did not start from camp till about 1:00 P.M. By that time the sound of cannonading became more frequent, and when I reached our men I found them lying in the road behind a bank and the enemy's batteries shelling them incessantly.

The Yankees had landed on the Yazoo, crossed the bottom, and mounted some cannon on the north side of Chickasaw Bayou, and were shelling the road and trying to drive us back into the hills. A line of breastworks hastily and imperfectly executed extended along the road for several miles, and an advanced line of rifle pits parallel to these but not continuous extended along the bayou four or five hundred yards in front of us. A battery was stationed on a mound between the two parallels. The enemy soon silenced this battery and drove off the cannoneers, who fled leaving one or two of their pieces. The bayou not being fordable alone

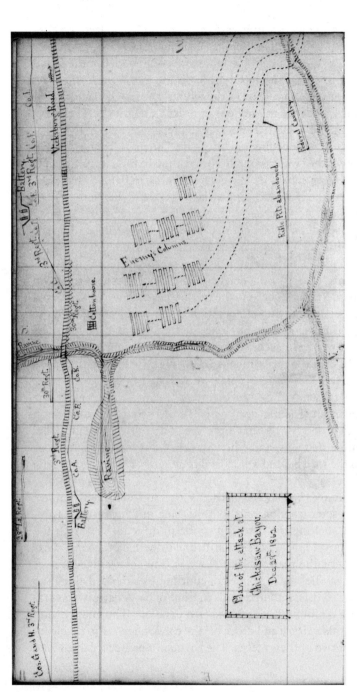

Barber's memory of the disposition of the Third Tennessee and supporting units at Chickasaw Bayou. Courtesy of the Lilly Library.

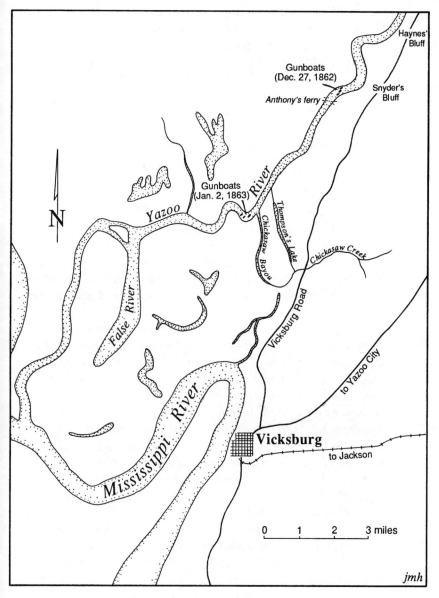

Haynes'
Bluff

Gunboats
(Dec. 27, 1862)

Snyder's
Bluff

Anthony's ferry

Yazoo River

Gunboats
(Jan. 2, 1863)

Thompson's Lake

Chickasaw Bayou

Chickasaw Creek

Yazoo

False River

Vicksburg Road

to Yazoo City

Mississippi River

Vicksburg

to Jackson

N

0   1   2   3 miles

jmh

Chickasaw Bayou

prevented them from capturing the battery. They then shelled a Louisiana regiment stationed in the advanced rifle pits and forced them to fall back to the road.

When night closed upon us we felt somewhat depressed. We had been fired at all day, without an opportunity of returning it, and though we had not suffered yet we knew that the enemy had gained advantages over us and forced back our advanced lines with some loss. Wounded men were occasionally carried by us, horribly mangled with shells, and we dreaded a repetition of the same mode of fighting for days. Nothing tries a soldier so much as to be under fire day after day with no chance of returning it. Two guns had been stationed in the road on our left but they seemed to have little effect on the enemy. We ate our cold meat and bread in silence and lay down in the road without fire to get such repose as we could.

At two o'clock on the morning of the twenty-ninth we were roused up by orders to move up the road about three miles and report to General Lee on the right. Our regiment was detached from General Gregg's brigade temporarily. We moved up near the extreme right. Part of the Third, consolidated with the Thirtieth, was posted in reserve behind a hill. The rest was placed in scattered detachments to support our two batteries on the extreme right. My company was offered to support a six-pound gun situated on an eminence on our extreme right. A portion having no breastworks I ordered the men to dig rifle pits with their saber bayonets. While thus engaged, daylight surprised us. The men worked diligently, throwing up the loose sand and earth with their long knives, expecting every moment to be fired upon.

At length the sun of the twenty-ninth of December rose clear and bright, and before our little work was completed a shell from the Yankee batteries came whizzing over our heads. Then the ball opened in earnest. Our batteries replied. For more than an hour the most terrific cannonade I ever heard was kept up upon our works. Much of it was aimed at a twelve-pounder on our left. Our little gun kept silent, I know not why, unless it was because they were unable to get the range of the enemy's batteries.

The shells crashed through the trees behind us and it seemed as though the whole woods was full of exploding missiles of death. Nothing we had ever seen at Donelson was equal to it in terrific grandeur. Occasionally some amusing incidents would occur and raise a laugh even in the midst of danger. Our surgeon, Dr. Bowers, had established his infirmary in a deep ravine, and to reach it, it was necessary to pass through the skirt of woods swept by the enemy's fire. Ridgeway, one of the surgeon's detail, was going along in the direction of the infirmary with a spade on his shoulder, in his usual leisurely gait, when whiz came a shell, exploding directly over his head, scattering its fragments far and wide. Ridgeway for once scared out of his usual equanimity sprang into the nearest gully without noticing its depth and rolled head over heels to the bottom. Our boys instead of sympathizing with his misfortune greeted his mishap with loud laughter. While one of my men, Isaac Pully, was busily engaged in his work a shell exploded behind us and one of the pieces glancing on a tree struck him in the short ribs. He gave a loud grunt, dropped his saber, and turning to his comrade pitifully asked him for a drink of water, with a paleness like death on his countenance. Upon examination not even the slightest bruise could be found, and the boys rallied him severely on his fright and especially on his sudden thirst. Another one, Osborn, was struck by a piece of shell on his foot, and on his attempting to limp off I ordered him to remain and in a few minutes he walked as well as ever. The boys were rather severe upon him for trying to shirk his duty.

We soon found that the enemy were not going to attack us in front, and soon a lull occurred in the terrible artillery duel. Just before the firing ceased, a shell from the enemy exploded a caisson in a battery on our left and killed Captain Hamilton of General Lee's staff, literally tearing him to pieces. The Yankees could see the mischief they had done and raised a loud shout of exultation. So far, everything had gone well for them.

Suddenly an aide dashed up to our rifle pits and brought an order to leave them and move to the left. We instantly moved back behind the hill and rejoined the regiment. Eight companies of our regiment and the Thirtieth were then moved down the road at a double-quick and thrown behind the breastworks to support two batteries. Companies G and H were left in the woods to our right. Companies A, B, and K were posted between the right battery and the bridge crossing a deep and narrow ravine. The rest of the Third were stationed beyond the bridge to support the battery on the left. The Thirtieth Regiment consisting of only four companies were posted behind the line as a reserve in a little ravine on the right of the bridge, and the Twenty-Eighth Louisiana, also in reserve, were behind the hill out of sight. On the left of the bridge there was a gap in the breastworks, leaving nothing but a rail fence between the road and the enemy.

My position was a short distance to the left of a battery of two six-pounders stationed by the side of the road. Immediately in front of us was a large corn and cotton field, much cut up by gullies and extending down to a rifle pit which had been abandoned by our men. Beyond this the trees had been cut down about two hundred yards on both sides of the bayou. Chickasaw Bayou makes out from the Yazoo River and runs parallel with the Vicksburg road for several miles at the distance of about half a mile from it. It could be crossed only in one piece, and that was nearly in front, a little to the left of our position. The nature of the crossing was such that only a narrow column could advance at once.

No sooner had we got behind our slight breastworks than the Yankees opened a furious cannonade upon us and seemed determined to silence our batteries. Our cannon returned the fire in a lively manner, but in the battery immediately on our right one of the guns from some accident became disabled and was of no service during the engagement. The air was full of balls and shells. The road immediately behind us was swept and torn up by terrific explosions. Some of the balls penetrated our earthworks which were very slight and low, in some places not more than three feet high, and without ditches. The sky which had been bright all morning became overcast with clouds, and the air became so filled with smoke that the artillery on both sides were forced to suspend their fire. When the air became somewhat clear a regiment of the enemy was seen winding its way four abreast along the narrow road leading out of the woods toward the bayou. Just then a shell from one of our guns struck the head of the column. It halted, wavered, and turned back in confusion into the woods. The artillery again renewed its fire and a dense cloud of smoke again filled the atmosphere.

The firing ceased, the smoke rolled away, and a most beautiful sight presented itself to our view, the grandest I have ever witnessed. A long column of the enemy debouched along the narrow road leading out of the woods through the fallen timber. Rapidly they advanced, crossed the bayou at a point where it was nearly dry, under cover of a high bluff. Our artillery opened upon them. Their batteries replied, and the woods directly in front of us seemed suddenly filled with sharpshooters. From behind every tree and log, and even from the tops of the trees, an incessant fire of long-ranged rifles poured in upon us. Whenever a head appeared above the breastworks a dozen bullets whistled past. General Lee rode up and down the road exposed to full view of the enemy, directing men to hold their fire. Not a gun was heard on our side. The enemy mounted the bluff on this side of the bayou and deployed into nine columns, and then marched straight toward the bridge, which was the weakest point of our works. Their artillery ceased and their long lines of soldiers advanced in perfect order, their arms glittering in the bright light, their officers waving their swords. It was a most beautiful but terrible spectacle, such a sight as a man sees but once during his lifetime. Nine regiments advancing against one, and not a tree or a bush to obscure the sight. Our men almost forgot their danger in viewing those beautiful columns advancing in such splendid order.

And yet how awful was the crisis. A few minutes were to decide the question whether Vicksburg and the great valley of the Mississippi was to be free or enslaved.

Just then a battalion of Federal cavalry came out of the woods on the left of their columns and formed a line in their rear. Onward they came, still straight toward the bridge. Their weapons and forms could more distinctly be seen. Our artillery almost ceased to play upon them, for they were so close that our guns, which were on high ground, could not depress their range sufficiently to reach them. Our men became restless and impatient and it required all the authority of their officers to prevent them from firing.

At length the order was given to the two rifle companies, A and K, to open. A sheet of fire burst from our breastworks. The advance columns of the enemy halted, faltered, and seemed ready to fall back in confusion. Just then a few shells from our batteries fell among their cavalry, which fled to the woods in confusion. The day seemed to be ours when a few brave officers rushed to the front and waving their swords restored order in their wavering ranks. A company of skirmishers rushed to the front of each forward column and throwing themselves flat on the ground kept a continued fire upon us. Under cover of these the enemy again advanced. The skirmishers would rise, run forward, throw themselves on the ground, fire and load, then rise and forward again. Behind this cloud of skirmishers the unbroken battalions still advanced.

Then came the order from General Lee for our whole line to fire. A terrible sheet of flame burst forth from our lines for nearly a quarter of a mile and converged upon the dense masses of the enemy. The effect was frightful. The dead and the dying lay in heaps. Half a dozen colors fell to the earth. In a moment, in place of nine distinct columns, nothing but a vast, confused mass could be discovered. Those in the rear and flanks began to scatter off toward the woods.

But again the voices and gestures of their officers urged them on. The colors were again raised and the struggling mass still advanced, though no longer in order. The incessant volleys of musketry continued from our breastworks. At length they halted, wavered, and commenced falling back, and were soon out of our range. There their officers formed them again and led them forward. During this breathing space of a few minutes we were supplied with fresh ammunition. The men took out their cartridges and laid them down by their sides, ready for the last struggle.

General Lee now rode up and down the lines encouraging the men and ordering them to hold their fire until the enemy came within full range. He seemed, as I thought, to manifest some uneasiness. As he was passing by my company he told the men to keep cool. They turned round and laughed at him. His face reddened a little and with a smile he remarked, "Boys, I believe you are cooler than I am; you need no encouragement." Someone told him he had better dismount or he would be shot. He replied that he had been in seventeen battles and he was not born to be killed by a d———d Yankee.

The enemy now came on for the final struggle. Our men could not be restrained and before they arrived within full musket range another volley was opened upon them. Still on they came, though with thinned and shattered ranks, marking their path by the dead and wounded. Volley after volley was poured upon them from the breastworks but it seemed as though nothing would stop them. At length the Thirtieth, which had been held in reserve in a ravine behind our line, was ordered across the bridge to take up a position behind the rail fence immediately on our left. They rushed forward gallantly and poured a fresh stream of fire into the foe directly in front of them.

But the advance column still kept on, though terribly thinned. It was as dangerous for them now to retreat as to advance under our fire.

At length the foremost color bearer, belonging to the Twenty-Sixth Missouri Regiment, reached a point one hundred and fifty yards of our works when he fell. That standard rose no more. The field was now full of our flying foe. No further attempt was made to rally. Many of the advanced columns threw themselves on the ground in despair, and many of their comrades who were fleeing across the field were overtaken by the swift bullets of the Rebel soldiers.

Just then half a dozen horsemen belonging to General Lee's staff dashed down into the field, followed by two companies of the Twenty-Eighth Louisiana, and many stragglers of our regiment, to secure the prisoners. The firing ceased, but we were ordered to keep our places in the trenches for fear of a renewal of the attack. Those of our men allowed to go on the field spread themselves far and wide, driving in prisoners before them, some single men driving a score. About four hundred prisoners were thus taken. As they were coming in the enemy's batteries again opened fire upon them, killing and wounding several of their own men, but not one of ours.

The field was now deserted by all except the dead and wounded, who lay thickly scattered over it. Those who could walk appeared, limping slowly, some back toward their own men, others toward our lines. Our soldiers with commendable humanity refrained from firing even upon those who were endeavoring to escape.

Just then a regiment emerged from the woods directly in front of us and marched out upon the field. Some distance ahead was a boy carrying a white flag. We all thought they were coming in to surrender, but our batteries opened upon them. They turned, fired a few shots at us, and fled into the woods. The flag came on to our lines and proved to have been sent by a wounded officer who lay upon the field, desiring assistance, and to have had no connection with the regiment following. The object of the latter we could never ascertain, but I still believe it intended to come in and surrender.

The battle was now over, our fugitive foe disappeared into the distant woods, and we had time to breathe and to look around us. But our self-congratulations were checked when we discovered our loss. Our victory had not been entirely bloodless. Two of our best and bravest officers had fallen. Major Tucker, when the enemy commenced their final flight, sprang upon the breastwork, waving his sword and cheering. He instantly fell dead, pierced by three balls, one through his heart. Lieutenant James Bass of my company was standing erect behind our low breastworks when he received a ball in his stomach which passed through his body and lodged in his back. He sank down on the ground, was carried to the rear, and died in the course of the night. A few of our men were slightly wounded but none so as to disable them for duty. In the Thirtieth Regiment (consolidated with ours) two men were killed and one wounded. The loss of life on our side was indeed small compared with the injury inflicted upon the enemy. Three hundred lay dead upon the field, four hundred were prisoners, and we were never able to ascertain the number of wounded which they carried off from the field. Their whole loss was estimated at from twelve to fifteen hundred.

There was but little firing in our vicinity during the remainder of the evening, but on our left a sharp skirmish took place between a Georgia regiment and the Yankee sharpshooters and the latter were driven back. The sky became overcast and before night a heavy rain commenced which continued throughout the night. As soon as darkness set in, our pickets were placed in the rifle pits in front of our lines and the infirmary detail was sent down on the field to bring up the wounded. They were followed by many soldiers who spread themselves over the field, either from curiosity or from motives of plunder. I did not go down myself for I could not bear the sight. The poor wounded wretches who lay on the ground writhing in pain, exposed to the pitiless soaking rain, implored our men to carry them to some place of shelter. The night was far spent before all the wounded within our picket lines could be relieved. Some were carried back to our infirmary in the ravine, and those who were worse mangled were left in an old cotton house directly in front of our lines where they were protected from the rain. But many of the wounded either fell or had dragged themselves beyond our picket lines, and all through that long and dreary night their groans and cries for help resounded in the ears of our guards. Many who were entirely unhurt had concealed themselves in the ravines and delivered themselves up as prisoners during the night.

Night came on, and the rain still kept pouring down upon our poor fellows in the trenches. No shelter, not even a fire, could be kindled anywhere. I stretched a few blankets on some poles and lay down under them on the wet ground. But the rain soon found its way through and the water from beneath soaked me to the skin. Literally and without exaggeration I did not have a dry thread on me. The detail carried up a dozen wounded men and placed them on the ground close by where I was lying. Their groans soon drove away what little propensity I had for sleep. About midnight the vehicles came to convey the wounded to Vicksburg but left two of the worst cases lying on the ground, regarding it as unnecessary to trouble their few remaining hours by removal. A lieutenant lay in a stupor, being shot through the bowels, and a St. Louis Dutchman shot through the lungs and diaphragm lay dying all night. He raved incessantly, sometimes praying, sometimes calling for water, sometimes imagining he was at home and calling on his mother and someone else, either his wife, sister, or sweetheart, whom he called Mary. When morning dawned both bodies lay cold, stiff, and lifeless. The sufferings of the poor wounded men on the field must have been terrible.

Next morning, the thirtieth, the sharpshooters of the enemy commenced annoying us as soon as it was light. But they found us better prepared than they anticipated. More than a thousand stand of arms had been taken from the field, Enfield and Belgian rifles mostly, and our regiment had fully equipped themselves.[9] No sooner did the sharpshooters make their appearance than our men commenced picking them off with their long-range guns. After a few essays they abandoned that business with disgust and troubled us but little more. A few cannon shots from our side failed to elicit any reply. We could now see their line of entrenchments in the woods beyond the bayou and the forms of men behind it.

Thus we lay all day, idly gazing upon the enemy and upon the battlefield of yesterday, over which the bodies of the slain still lay thickly scattered. Our detail went down upon the field and commenced carrying up these bodies for interment, but the enemy opened fire upon them and they were compelled to retire. Night again closed in and the field was soon covered with straggling soldiers gathering arms and stripping the dead. Our pickets could still, even on the second night, hear the groans and piteous cries of a few wounded wretches who lay just beyond our lines, impossible for us to reach, and who were still lingering in agony without help for nearly forty-eight hours after they had fallen. Some of the dead were shamefully stripped by our soldiers and by Negroes.[10]

Before daylight on the morning of the thirty-first the enemy in force attacked our pickets and drove them in, holding possession until daylight of a portion of the field. They did this to carry off under cover of darkness the rest of their wounded and as many of their dead as possible, and when day dawned they had retired into the woods.

This morning the firing entirely ceased. Scarcely a Yankee was in sight when about ten o'clock a white flag came out of the woods and crossed the field. It was met at the old cotton house by Colonel Clack and the communication of the bearer sent to General Lee. It contained a request that the Yankees be permitted to bury their dead. A truce was granted from twelve till five o'clock, at which hour hostilities were to be resumed. The enemy soon made their appearance on the field with litters, and one hundred and eighty-seven bodies were carried off. This was exclusive of those buried by our own men and those taken from the field previously by the enemy during the two last nights. The period of the truce was a sort of holiday to our men. The citizens and even the ladies came out from Vicksburg to see the battlefield and to get a glimpse of the bluecoats.

On the first of January a rifled gun on the hill behind us opened fire upon the enemy's entrenchments and camp and even upon the transports lying in the distant Yazoo. This was continued at intervals throughout the day. The enemy were evidently making preparations to retreat.

On the next morning the Second Texas and Third Tennessee were ordered out of the trenches and put in motion. We marched down across the battlefield, crossed the bayou at the same point where the enemy had passed it, and advanced along the road to their entrenchments, which we found entirely deserted. In their deserted camp we found a great number of knapsacks and cooking utensils and boxes of crackers and barrels of pickled pork, some of which they had thrown into the bayou. It was all recovered with little loss and proved a godsend to our hungry boys who had been living on one meal a day for nearly a week. In the woods to our right and at Mrs. Lake's Negro quarter, about twenty Yankee pickets were found who immediately surrendered. A large number of axes and entrenching tools were also found.[11]

We passed on down the bayou, keeping along the levee, the Second Texas in front. Shortly after we passed the Negro quarter we came in sight of the gunboats and transports lying in the Yazoo. The enemy had just embarked. Our regiments were thrown into line of battle and advanced across the open field, the Texans being deployed as skirmishers in our front. We continued our march until the skirmishers arrived near the levee on the banks of the Yazoo, when they threw themselves on the earth and opened a fire upon the transports crowded with troops. The gunboats instantly commenced shelling both regiments at a terrible rate. The Third was ordered to conceal themselves in a ravine and the skirmishers kept firing into the portholes of the gunboats whenever they were opened. The transports immediately moved off down the river. After the firing had been kept up some time the Second Texas was ordered to retire. They had only one man

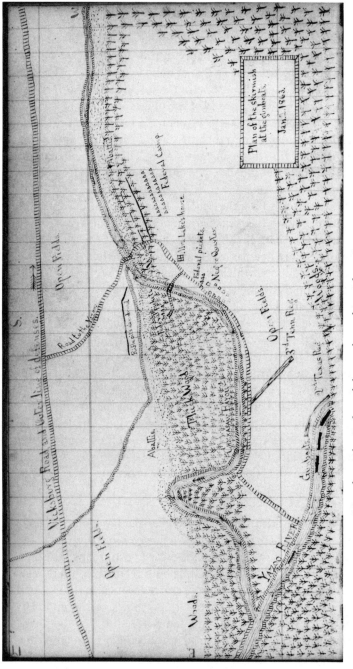

Map drawn by Barber of the gunboat skirmish on January 1–2, 1863.
Courtesy of the Lilly Library.

hurt, the lieutenant colonel, who was wounded by a shell. Our regiment was also withdrawn, but I was ordered to remain with two companies, A and B, as a picket to watch the gunboats. About four o'clock in the evening the last boat disappeared down the Yazoo. Our enemy had gone—foiled and disappointed after all his boastings—and Vicksburg still sat proud and free upon her impregnable hills.

4 Port Hudson

January 2–May 3, 1863

ABOARD THE *CHARM*. STRANGE AND UNUSUAL SCENES. PROMOTED TO MAJOR. SPRING ARRIVES. SIGNAL GUN FIRED DOWNRIVER. FIERY DEATH OF THE GREAT STEAMER *MISSISSIPPI*. YANKEE FLEET RETIRES. SHIPS ABOVE AND BELOW US LIKE SULLEN MONSTERS. ADIEU TO PORT HUDSON.

A rainy evening set in, and bade fair to give us a very disagreeable duty, but just before dark we were relieved by another picket and started on our way back. The regiment had been relieved from duty in the trenches and had gone back to camp, about seven miles from our picket post. I determined not to march back in the darkness, mud, and rain, and when we reached the Negro quarter I told the men to make themselves comfortable for the night. We had plenty of Yankee bread and pickled pork and good, dry shelter. I took up my quarters in the overseer's house where was a good fireplace, plenty of wood, and a fine, large cot.

We passed a very pleasant night and next morning by daylight we started for camp. When we reached the bayou we found it swimming. A flatboat lay on the other side and some of the men climbed over a fallen tree and lodged the boat in the middle of the channel. We crossed by dint of wading, walking over the boat, and late in the morning reached camp tired, wet, muddy, and hungry. Here we learned that the Federal fleet was lying at the mouth of the Yazoo and an attack was expected from the side of the Mississippi River. On the mornings of the fourth and fifth we marched down to the city before daylight but no enemy appeared. At length the joyful news arrived that the enemy had gone up the river and Vicksburg once more was safe.

In the evening of January 5 we again received marching orders and by sunset we were all on board the steamboat *Charm* lying at the landing.[1] Our whole brigade was moved with us and General Gregg made his quarters on our boat. Next morning we stopped at Natchez a few hours, passed the mouth of Red River before dark, and about 10:00 P.M. we landed at Port Hudson, Louisiana. We marched up into the woods on the top of the bluff and bivouacked till morning.

When the morning of the seventh of January dawned we found ourselves among strange and unusual scenes. The trees covered and almost hid by the long moss, the beautiful magnolia green in the midst of winter, the woods thick with luxuriant undergrowth, and verdant with rank cane, the land level as far as the eye could reach, yet intersected with ravines filled with dense, impassable thickets, all indicated an approach to a tropic climate, and to the shores of the Gulf. Port Hudson is situated on the east bank of the Mississippi River in the parish of East Feliciana, and about twenty-two miles by land above Baton Rouge. The country on the east side of the river is a tableland elevated about fifty feet above low-water mark and intersected in every direction by bayous which are but little about the level of the river. This tableland is so level that the drainage is very imperfect and in some places it is quite marshy. The bayous have banks nearly precipitous and are filled with a tangled thicket of cane and briars so dense that it is impossible to penetrate it without cutting paths. It is strongly fortified by excellent earthworks extending from the river below to Thompson's Creek above and by batteries commanding the river both above and below. Major General Gardner was in command of the post. The garrison consists of three brigades under Brigadier Generals Beall, Maxey, and Gregg, numbering about twelve thousand men.[2]

Directly across the river lay a low, flat country protected by levees from inundation. Our camp was soon established about a quarter of a mile back from the river and near the lower part of the fortifications, in an open cornfield. On each side of us was a deep bayou overgrown with magnolia and thick brush. We had brought some tents with us from Vicksburg, about half enough

Site of Port Hudson

for the comfort of the men. These were soon pitched and our residence for the remainder of the winter was fixed. The beautiful magnolia groves soon fell before the axe and the addition of rude cabins soon housed all who had no tents.

For the first few days we suffered for want of food. Nothing was served out except some cornmeal, unsifted and of the coarsest quality, and even of that the quantity was insufficient. Nothing could be purchased in the town, which was almost wholly deserted. The men complained much of hunger and for some days I did not get as much as I wanted to eat. But some beef was soon issued to us and then the other rations and after the first week complaints ceased. Our rations still fell short of the regulations but we had already while in Mississippi become so accustomed to that that few complaints were made. Our men soon commenced foraging throughout the neighborhood and supplied themselves partially with potatoes and other vegetables at very reasonable prices.

Captain Rhea and myself about the middle of January crossed the river into the parish of Pointe Coupee, late in the evening, and stayed all night with a French creole about four miles from Port Hudson. We found rather rough quarters but a plentiful table, the dishes all fixed up in Louisiana French style. After our scanty camp fare it was delicious, especially the gumbo soup. He lived in a creole settlement near the banks of False River. These settlements, or "cages" as they are called in the phraseology of the country, reminded me much of the settlements of the habitants which I had seen near Montreal, Canada. The farms were small, from twenty to sixty acres, narrow in front and running back from the road, along which the houses were built, resembling a continued village for miles. Thus the creoles were enabled to enjoy at the same time their passion for society and the pleasures of a country life. Their houses were small and built with but little regard to taste. Many of these creoles are extremely ignorant and associate with the free Negroes and the result is that their blood has come to be quite in a mixed condition. The man with whom we stayed was of pure blood but could neither read nor write but little above the capacity of a Negro. He had the portraits of some of his ancestors, however, hanging in the room and quite an elegant little library of French books for the use of his children.

Next night we stayed with Mr. Smith, overseer on a cotton plantation several miles farther up False River. The lands lying on False River are the richest and most beautiful I ever saw. The whole country is occupied by large sugar farms, all fronting on the river, with splendid sugar houses and near cottages for the overseers. None of the proprietors live upon the land. They reside in Europe, in New Orleans, or in some wealthy locality in the pine woods east of the Mississippi. The parish of Pointe Coupee has not much reputation for health.

After spending two days in that delightful region we returned to camp loaded down with provisions. Our saddles were garnished all around by chickens tied by the legs and our sacks filled with every variety of vegetables.

Thus quietly passed away the months of January and February. No enemy molested us and the monotony of garrison life became tiresome. Baton Rouge, the advanced post of the Federals, was twenty-five miles by water below us and the army at that place showed little disposition to approach nearer. We were constantly employed strengthening our fortifications and preparing for the desperate struggle which was soon to come upon us if the enemy were in earnest about opening the Mississippi River. General Banks commanding the Department of the Gulf was said to have an army of forty thousand men in lower Louisiana and was to co-operate with General Grant's Vicksburg expedition.[3] Several Federal gunboats had run past the Vicksburg batteries and two of them, the *Queen of the West* and the *Indianola*, were captured. The *Essex* made weekly trips from Baton Rouge to within sight of Port Hudson but carefully avoided coming within range of our batteries. Our pickets, infantry, and cavalry on both sides of the river kept vigilant watch upon all movements below.

At length, the latter part of February, it was rumored that the preparations of the Federals were complete and that their advance might be daily expected. On the twenty-fifth a force of fifteen hundred men started from here up the river, destination unknown but supposed to be a reconnaissance on the west bank of the Mississippi, as it was reported a body of the enemy were moving in that direction. The *Dr. Beatty* was fitted up as a gunboat at this place and participated in the action in which the *Indianola* was captured.

On the first day of February, I received the appointment of major of the Third Tennessee by promotion in place of the lamented Major Tucker who fell at Vicksburg. I had previously been acting in that capacity ever since our arrival at this place.

About the middle of the month Colonel Walker rejoined his regiment, his health having been recruited.

While I am writing, February 27, everything is being prepared for the enemy's advance, which is expected every day.

I have been neglecting my diary ever since my return to the regiment last December but am even with it now and hope to keep so hereafter. Thus far it partakes very little of the character of a diary but I expect to make it so in the future.

Our men here though ill provided for and many of them sickly are in good spirits and very sanguine about the result of a fight at this place. Our works are very strong, our men hopeful and even confident, and from what we can learn the enemy are far from being sanguine of success. I do not think their infantry will attack us with any spirit. A report has reached here that a Federal gunboat in passing the batteries at Vicksburg was so seriously damaged that she sank ten miles below. The *Dr. Beatty* has returned up the river to endeavor to raise and secure the *Indianola*.

February 28. Today is the last of winter. It rained very hard last night and this morning and all the waters are up and many of the bridges are swept away. Consequently this is an idle day in camp waiting for the mud to dry up and the waters to assuage. Louisiana mud is real mud; it keeps a man indoors. Today is my turn for field officer in charge and I must ride around the guards and pickets, rain or shine. I think the mud will stop the Yankees from coming up by land at any rate for a few days.

The news from Tennessee is not so hopeful. Rosecrans seems trying to turn Bragg's left and I am fearful that Bragg is not as strong as he should be to hold the enemy in check.[4] Everything from Vicksburg is encouraging. Peace prospects a little less bright than they were a week ago but I still think three months more of fighting will end the war. The ultra-abolitionists headed by

Greeley have declared themselves for peace, provided the spring campaign does not prove successful, and in May the term of service of three hundred thousand, two years and nine months, will expire, with no hope either of inducing them to reenlist or of filling their place by other enlisted men. These facts together with the increasing desire for peace on the part of the conservative party of the North make me sanguine, even to confidence that we shall have an armistice at least by the first of June. I may be mistaken but I never in my life felt so certain of anything in the future.

March 1. The first day of spring opened beautifully. The air was cool, fresh, and springlike, and the sun shone with a mild and genial warmth. No further news this morning. Everything seems at a standstill and all men are in expectation of some great event. Some look for a great battle in Tennessee, others for a grand combined attack on Vicksburg and Port Hudson, others for a desperate attack upon some point on the Carolina coast, either Charleston or Savannah. Others look for a speedy cessation of hostilities and think there will be but little more fighting. I am becoming somewhat tired of the monotony of a garrison life. Of all lives in the world it most resembles that of a military prison. Just one year ago today we were marched into Camp Chase and commenced our long and wearisome imprisonment. How much brighter our affairs look today than they did one year ago! One more effort and all our troubles and dangers will be over. The present Federal army is all that they can raise; destroy or cripple that and our work will be done. Their attempt to fill their rapidly thinning ranks with Negro soldiers will only respond to their own shame and confusion. That was evidently passed by the Republicans to render separation more sure and perpetual and to destroy the hopes of the Reconstruction Democrats of the North. So soon as all hopes of a reunion are taken away, the abolitionists will demand peace on the basis of an eternal separation from the slave states.

March 2. Another beautiful spring day. The railroad to Clinton has been so much damaged by the recent rains that we have had no train from above for several days and consequently no newspapers or letters. A report has reached here that the gunboat *Indianola* was blown up by our men for fear she would fall into the hands of the enemy. It appears to have been a very badly managed piece of service. No boat of the enemy has ever been below Vicksburg since the passage of the *Indianola*. The whole affair is a disgrace to our naval service. A flying rumor has reached us from below that the Yankees would visit us this week. Thus we live— no day without its rumor. We are very bad off for victuals just now. We dined today on a dish of rice and sugar, nothing more. No meat and no meal exists in our commissariat. The mill has stopped grinding on account of high water and the beef has given out in consequence of the neglect to supply our larder in time. We have been living on short allowance for a week and it has been getting shorter and shorter until we have almost reached starvation rations. Our commissary department at this place is very defective and our quartermaster not much better. General Gardner, I think, is quite deficient in his subsistence officers. Deprive an army of all news and put them on short allowance and they will very soon begin to show a mutinous spirit. But we live on hope.

March 3. Our spring seems to have opened in all its beauty. The railroad is not yet in running order and we have neither newspapers nor news. We are nearly starved on vague rumors, which are not worth repeating. Our rations have been very short for several days on account, it is said, of a quantity of provisions being sent to Clinton for a brigade of troops lately arrived at that place. Our dinner table yesterday presented a beggarly account of empty dishes. Our mess consists of eight whites and six blacks. The three field officers, the surgeon, the adjutant, the quartermaster and his sergeant, and the sergeant major. The Negroes do pretty much as they please, fix their own hours and dishes for meals, and we submit with some grumbling. We lived very well as long as we could forage in the country but that has become pretty well drained and we have gone back to army rations which are none of the most plentiful nor of the best quality. The days are now uncomfortably warm and the nights pleasantly cool. A fire is quite agreeable after supper. We cannot hear from home until the railroad from Port Hudson to Clinton is repaired and we are becoming very impatient and anxious. We are now isolated in a remote part of the Confederacy where we can see and hear but little either about our friends or our enemies. No news from Baton Rouge or Vicksburg, the two points that most concern us.

March 4. Weather still fine but cool. General Rust's brigade arrived here yesterday from Clinton.⁵ We have now about fifteen thousand men in this place. The Yankees are said to have twenty-six thousand at Baton Rouge and although it is constantly reported that they are coming to attack us I hardly think it is so. We are very short of provisions. Yesterday evening there was issued to our men corn in the ear in place of meal. The men loudly demanded fodder to eat with it. We have just received news of the passage of a conscript act by the Federal Congress, calling out the entire Northern fighting population with the usual exceptions. What effect this will have upon the duration of the war will be speedily seen in the course of a month. Within that time it can be seen whether the act can be enforced. If it can, the war will be a long and bloody one, the territory of the Confederacy will be laid waste, but I have no fears for the final result. If it cannot, it will truly tend to hasten a peace on the basis of a separation. Before the present month expires we can tell whether the war will be a long or short one. Today the Black Republican Congress will go out, and their power of doing mischief is over. They have done all that men possibly could do. I don't think that Lincoln will convene an extra session. If he does I look for peace speedily. We have been cut off from newspapers so long that we are entirely behind the times in point of news. The mails are not yet running to Clinton.

March 5. Another cool, pleasant spring day. The weather reminds me much of the time we went into camp at Cheatham. Last night the papers for the discharge of the non-conscripts came back from General Pemberton approved and they are in high spirits preparing to leave.⁶ They have been shamefully treated by men in authority, having been detailed more than two months over their time. Yesterday was my first essay at drilling the regiment. I found it not so difficult a task as I had supposed—only made one blunder. The men did remarkably well. Our rations have not improved in quality as yet. The beef drawn yesterday was too poor to eat and some of it appeared to have belonged to a diseased animal. I have been writing home so often of late that on attempting to write last night I was compelled to give it up for want of ideas. No news from below, or above either. We seem to be totally isolated. No mails beyond Clinton and no newspapers since the twenty-sixth of February. It will be a week tomorrow since the reception of my last letter from home. I am almost starved for news from home. In the present stagnation of affairs here I should like a letter every day. I do not think the enemy will move upon this place, though the fact of our receiving reinforcements would seem to indicate an apprehension on the part of our commanders. Perhaps it means an advance on our part, though I think that would be rash and ill advised.

March 6. A very rainy day. Everybody within doors. It is my turn as field officer in charge. I have the luck of serving on rainy days. Our non-conscripts are leaving today and with them Edward Hunnicutt, with whom I send a letter home. Yesterday came the appeal of the twenty-seven, containing the correspondence between the United States and French governments. Louis Napoleon actually made proposals of mediation in January last, but they were rejected by the Washington government and that too with some asperity. The French offer contains a doubt whether the Lincoln administration will be able to carry out its projects. Seward takes offense at this doubt, and his feathers seem somewhat ruffled. I think it is probable that France will renew the offer and probably hint at some ulterior measures which may be taken in case the offer is not favorably received. I believe Louis Napoleon sincerely desires the war to cease and separation to take place. We expect more news this evening, if the through mail from Jackson arrives. Great dissatisfaction and complaint exists in this brigade in consequence of the want of wholesome provisions. The men are actually suffering for want. The rumors from below are that the government has ordered Banks to advance on Port Hudson, but that he is unwilling to make the movement. We shall soon see. If they do not come soon, the river will commence falling and the gunboat season will be over.

March 8, Sunday. A beautiful Sabbath, the first real, soft spring day. We have news from Tennessee that Van Dorn has defeated the enemy at Franklin with the loss of one thousand killed and wounded, and twenty-six hundred prisoners. The Yankees have captured a wagon train near War Trace. Our mails are not yet forthcoming and we have no news directly from home. Everything quiet here and from all appearances likely to remain so. This beautiful Sabbath reminds me of some I have spent at home when a boy. What a vast change since then, and I fear for the worse, on me. But I have of late been trying to throw off the weight which presses me down and to do better. May God help me, for I can do nothing without His aid. I have become very remiss in my religious duties since I have been in the army and I have sometimes been led to think that it was impossible to be a Christian and a soldier at the same time. But the religion of Christ was not made for one period or for one occupation, but for all time and for every pursuit in life. My conscience does not rebuke me for being a soldier or for discharging faithfully all a soldier's duties. It rebukes me for not keeping vigilant watch over myself and not doing what good I can to others around me, for being too worldly in my views and aspirations, and not showing that godly walk and conversation which I ought to do toward all around me.

March 10, Tuesday. A rainy, cloudy day. The weather is warm, damp, and depressing. There are rumors and indications of a speedy attack from below. Nine deserters came in this morning. One rumor states that the Yankees had a fight among themselves yesterday in consequence of an order to advance. Another states that they drove our pickets back five miles this morning. I regard neither as reliable. But from some orders issued this evening I think our commander apprehends an attack very soon. General Rust's brigade is to occupy the extreme left of our lines, General Beall's next, General Maxey's next, and General Gregg's the extreme right. Our position will be much exposed to fire from the mortars and gunboats, as we are very near the riverbank below the town. Our position is very strong for an attack in front, as the ground is very broken and almost impassable in front of our entrenchments. Our right rests on the river batteries. The Third is the second regiment from the right.

I have had no letter from home since the one dated February 11 and am very anxious and uneasy. If a letter does not come tomorrow I shall be really vexed. I write regularly twice a week and feel provoked that I receive no reply. I know it cannot be my wife's fault, and yet the fact that others receive letters from our county proves that it is not the fault of the mails. I don't know to what to attribute the failure and it vexes me exceedingly.

March 11, Wednesday. A warm, sunny day. The news we received last night was quite warlike. It is reported that our pickets were driven in ten miles and that the Yankees are advancing. I do not credit the latter as yet, though I think they must advance soon if they ever intend to make a struggle for the river. There appears to be a great disinclination both on the part of Banks and his army to move on Port Hudson, although the movement is urged by the Washington government. Grant is said to be operating not only at Vicksburg but also by way of the Yazoo Pass to get into the Yazoo River above the raft and by way of Lake Providence to get into the bayous Tensas and Macon and thence into Red River. If he succeeds in the latter we at Port Hudson will have to sustain a siege from both fleets and armies and we will have a desperate struggle, but God being on our side we will assuredly gain the victory. We fear only one thing and that is starvation. Give us enough to eat and God for our helper and we can hold our works against the whole army of the West and Louisiana.

March 12, Thursday. Cold last night and warm today. It is reported that the enemy have advanced on the Baton Rouge and Clinton plank road and have surprised twelve of our pickets and with a force of forty thousand are endeavoring to get into our rear. I think their numbers are exaggerated. We had a grapevine telegram this morning to the effect that Van Dorn had captured Nashville with eight thousand men and ten million dollars' worth of supplies. Of course we are too old soldiers to believe grapevine telegrams, yet it puts us in a very good humor. His previous engagement instead of being at Franklin was at Thompson's Station and his prisoners have diminished in Brag's official report to twenty-one hundred. Three cavalry regiments and a battery escaped. All the infantry with nineteen wagons were taken. Our men in Kentucky have taken three steamboats on Barren River. The gunboats have come through Yazoo Pass and reached the Tallahatchie River. Kirby Smith is to take command west of the Mississippi. The army there is badly demoralized by desertion.

General Price reached here last night, whether to stay or not I do not know, but I suppose he will cross the river.

March 14, Saturday. Day before yesterday I went to the country with Captain Flautt to procure corn for the army and returned yesterday. We went out on the Jackson road ten miles. He succeeded in engaging five thousand bushels of corn. The people are generally very patriotic and willing to give up their surplus to the army. It is beautiful country, very finely improved and cultivated. Most of the planters on this side of the river live on their own plantations and consequently the country is highly improved.

When we returned, the whole post was in a fever of excitement. The Yankees had landed a force ten miles above Baton Rouge and brought up a large fleet of transports, gunboats, and mortar boats, and two sloops of war. Late in the evening the *Essex* came up a mile below our infantry picket and fired two guns up the river toward our batteries. Everything was got ready to meet the enemy and we lay down to sleep expecting to be summoned by the booming of cannon to take our places in the trenches. But the night passed away without alarm and this morning the *Essex* has returned down the river and everything is quiet up to the time I am writing. Last night a dispatch was received from Colonel Gantt that the enemy were advancing upon Tangipahoa. In a few days we expect to be surrounded and besieged and then comes the tug of war. Their force is variously estimated at from forty thousand to sixty thousand but in my opinion falls short of the smaller number. Ours is estimated at from twelve thousand to fifteen thousand. The former, I think, is about the correct number.

About 2:00 P.M. the enemy's mortar boats were in position and commenced shelling us. We were immediately ordered to the trenches. They kept up a terrific cannonade all evening. They had got the range of our trenches with great exactness and the huge shells frequently burst directly over us and fragments flew in every direction around us. Their distance was about two miles from us but out of our sight behind a point of woods. General Rust's brigade was stationed outside of the works and out two miles in advance of us. About sundown the firing ceased, there having been no reply on our part.

One-third of the men were retained in the trenches and the rest sent back to camp. I remained in command of that portion of the regiment in the rifle pits and after posting sentinels lay down to sleep on the ground.

At eleven o'clock a signal gun was fired down the river. I sprang to my feet but before I could hurry on my coat and boots shell after shell in quick succession mounted the heavens, looking like fireballs in the sky and rising to the zenith, then apparently remaining poised for an instant and then descending with the velocity of lightning. Sometimes they burst high in the air, sending the fragments hissing among us, and sometimes they struck the earth, penetrating to the depth of fifteen feet, then exploding and throwing a torrent of fragments and earth high into the air.

Scarcely had the mortars commenced their work when we were made conscious of the presence of a more dangerous enemy. Shell after shell and shot after shot came hissing over our heads from the direction of the river and completely in range of our trenches. We turned our heads in astonishment toward the river and there made visible by the blinding flashes of light we saw the tall spars of a huge war steamer slowly making its way up the river and delivering broadside after broadside upon our batteries. Alternately clothed in thick darkness and in vivid light, it reminded me of the old tales I once read of the Phantom Ship. It was followed by two others like it and an ironclad gunboat.[7]

Nobly our batteries responded. All along the bank for a mile a sheet of fire burst forth upon the enemy's ships. Still they advanced more than halfway along the line of our batteries, throwing shell, grape, and canister among us. The sight was the most terrific and grand I had ever yet witnessed. The grandeur of Donelson and Vicksburg was nothing compared to it. I can compare it to nothing less than that great day when the stars of heaven shall fall from their places. The whole air seemed full of the hissing globes of death, like fireballs in the sky, while the grape and canister ploughed up the ground and pattered like hail around us.[8]

But grand as was the scene, a grander still awaited us. The war steamer *Mississippi* was set on fire by hot shot from one of our

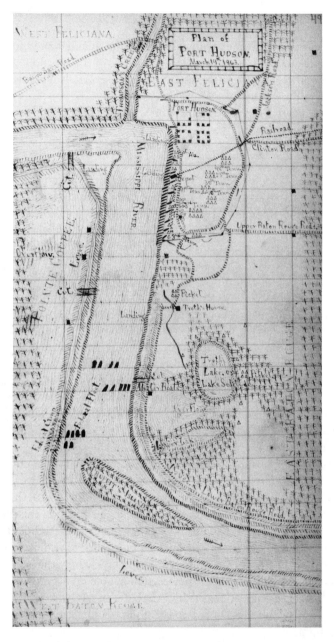

Attempted passage of the Federal fleet at Port Hudson on March 14, 1863, as witnessed by Barber. Courtesy of the Lilly Library.

batteries. The flames, at first low and almost smothered, grew brighter and brighter, then climbed the tall masts and cordage and mounted high above the burning ship, throwing a lurid glare over the river and the shore for miles. One of the steamers, supposed to be the *Brooklyn*, succeeded in making her way above the batteries; the others, terrified at the sight of the vessel in flames, and supposed to be badly disabled, dropped down the current out of sight. The *Mississippi*, now a mass of fire, her guns exploding with the heat, drifted slowly downward, burning lower and lower, until a terrific explosion was heard, the magazine was reached, and the remains of the noble vessel were raised high in the air and then forever buried under the waters of the great river whose name she bore.

The crew made their escape in boats to the Pointe Coupee shore and many of them were captured by our cavalry next morning.

The action terminated with the burning of the *Mississippi*. The firing ceased on all sides and in a short time I was again buried in sleep on my hard bed behind the breastworks.

Next morning everything was again quiet. Our loss during the engagement of the night was very small, only one killed and seven wounded, mostly in our brigade. The Third escaped unscathed.[9] Soon after daybreak a large frigate was seen anchored across the river above our batteries. A squad of Yankees were seen at the landing across the river guarded by our cavalry. About seventy-five were captured of the crew of the *Mississippi*, who reported that the two vessels above were the frigate *Hartford*, Commodore Farragut's flagship, of twenty-eight guns, and the *Monongahela* of nineteen guns.[10] We learned today that the land forces had retreated to Baton Rouge in great haste, throwing away their knapsacks and burning the bridges behind them. They were supposed to be almost seven thousand in number. On the fifteenth and sixteenth the enemy were quiet but on the evening of the seventeenth a gunboat ran up and commenced shelling our works at Troth's Landing two miles below us, where a battery and the Sixth Mississippi Regiment were stationed. No reply was made by our guns and toward evening the firing ceased. On the eighteenth stragglers from the Yankee camp came up on the west side of the river and set fire to a house just below our batteries. On the night of the eighteenth our lower gun shelled the woods on the other side of the river. Nothing more has been heard of the vessels which have gone above, except that they had been seen at Bayou Sara on the fifteenth. The cars have resumed their regular trips to Clinton since the retreat of the Yankees.

March 22, Sunday. We still have firing every day. The enemy try to shell our transports at the upper boat landing and make it too hot for them to remain there sometimes. In such cases they take refuge up Thompson's Creek. We have plenty of provisions now. The *Hartford* and *Monongahela* have gone up to Vicksburg and the Red River trade is now open to us. Yesterday I went to the boat landing with a detail to unload corn, but the place became too hot and the boats left. One shell exploded very near me, covering myself and horse with dirt. "Buckner" did not seem to mind it much. . . .

March 26, Thursday. A few shots have been fired by both sides for the last few days occasionally. The enemy have placed a battery on the other side of the river and below Troth's Landing. Yesterday this battery opened upon ours at Troth's house but met with no response. We have a regiment on picket at that place constantly. Nothing heard from the vessels above. Our Red River boats arrive as usual. Banks' official address highly compliments his army on their recent "gallant" advance from Baton Rouge. He says he could not draw the "demoralized Rebels" out of their stronghold but he is careful not to say that he was afraid to attack them. It is rumored that the Yankee fleet was badly riddled in their attack. Their land forces across the river are reported by a scout not to exceed two regiments. The rest are at Baton Rouge. The smoke of transports is seen today coming up the river. No letter from home since March 4. . . . I started Joe [apparently Barber's servant] home last Saturday on a furlough till the twelfth of May. He took with him a young alligator two and a half feet long, alive, as a present to his mistress. She will open her eyes very wide at its reception.

March 28, Saturday. All quiet for the last two days. The Yankee fleet is still below but their land forces and transports have returned to Baton Rouge. It is rumored that Banks is concentrating his forces at New Orleans intending to make an expedition up the New Orleans and Jackson railroad to Tangipahoa or up the Bayou Atchafalaya to Red River. The Yankee papers say that the two vessels which went above were the *Hartford* and *Albatross* with Rear Admiral Farragut on board. They are now below Vicksburg. Things look somewhat gloomy in Tennessee. . . . Yesterday was the day of fasting and prayer appointed by our president. By order it was observed in the army. Our chaplain, Mr. Deavenport, preached, and among other excellent things gave it as his opinion that the war would never terminate until we as a nation acknowledged our sins and humbled ourselves in the dust before our Creator.[11] I think our national character will be much improved by this war. Our pride has already been humbled by sufferings and reverses and much of our wealth has been destroyed. God send us a speedy peace.

April 1, Wednesday. The Yankee fleet has retired except one sloop which has taken the place of the *Essex* and is lying above the point of Prophet's Island. Baton Rouge is not evacuated as was reported a few days ago. The damaged vessels have been sent to New Orleans but the rest of the fleet and Banks' land force still remain. Our men have taken possession of Pontchatoula and driven the enemy back. The Yankees are still at work upon their canals above. Their fleet is said to be blockaded in Deer Creek by obstructions above and below. Greenwood seems to be an impassable barrier to them. Everything is uncertain in Tennessee. . . . Still no news from home since March 4. I am thoroughly vexed about it but that is useless and wrong, for I know my wife writes every week and the fault must be in the mails and not in her. It is said that Lincoln will not attempt to enforce the conscript law until June and till that is attempted we cannot tell whether the war will be protracted or not. I still think that its successful enforcement is doubtful, especially in the West.

April 6, Monday. On Thursday last we learned that Sam Mitchell had arrived at Osyka, Mississippi, with clothing for the regiment. On Thursday evening I rode out seven and a half miles through a beautiful country and stopped for the night at Mr. East's. Next day I went to Clinton eighteen miles farther where I met Sam Mitchell on his way to camp. He had left the goods at Osyka in charge of Captain Cooper. I thought it was unnecessary for me to proceed farther, as the wagon could bring the goods in charge of Captain Cooper, and determined to return to camp next day. Mitchell brought me two long letters from home. On Saturday, I returned to camp by way of Jackson. The parish of East Feliciana, through which I passed, is one of the most delightful countries in the Southern Confederacy. Many of the citizens and most of the Negroes have gone to a safer region and some of the farms are entirely deserted, but even in its desolation the land looks lovely. . . .

April 10, Friday. Both upper and lower fleets have retired out of sight. A few days ago the upper fleet made its appearance above and fired several guns across the point as signals. Next day three vessels made their appearance below near the head of Prophet's Island and shelled our pickets at Troth's. Day before yesterday they all vanished again. Farragut is said to have gone north and Colonel Ellet is reported in command. The *Hartford* is reported near Bayou Sara fastening cotton to her sides, preparing to run down past us. Our batteries have been ordered to concentrate their fire upon her and endeavor to sink her. The *Albatross* and the ram *Monarch* are her consorts. . . .[12]

April 18, Saturday. On the fourteenth a rumor was rife that the enemy were attempting to land a few miles below. On sending out two regiments to reconnoiter the rumor was found to be entirely without foundation. On the same evening the Third was sent on picket to Troth's Landing. We were stationed in a ravine behind Troth's house, running down to the lake, called Lake Solitude. Two companies were sent about two miles below as the advanced infantry picket. We all enjoyed our bivouac very much. It was almost like a country picnic to the inhabitants of a crowded city. We lay down on the green grass and rolled over with delight. Colonel Walker and myself and Dr. Henderson secured a little shelter built against a steep bank, out of poles, and covered with moss. We had moss for our bed also, on which we spread our blankets, and when night came we slept as well as the previous inhabitants of the moss, which were quite numerous, would allow us. Next day rose bright and clear and in a few hours our men were scattered under the trees all through the ravine. It was a most delightful spot and entirely secluded from the rest of the world, as we could neither see nor be seen by anybody or anything outside of the ravine. We spent the day in wandering about from one beautiful spot to another and when we became tired lay down in the shade of some gigantic oak festooned with moss.

On the sixteenth I went to visit the lower pickets. A mile of the road led through the cane forest. It was late in the morning, the sun was setting, and the tall trees interlaced their boughs over the narrow road and the moss so filled up the intervals between the branches that it became nearly dark at sunset. The tall cane rose like a wall on either side and shut out all view a few yards from the path. One picket post was on the banks of the overflow made by the river after the cutting of the levee. It commanded a view of Dr. Jones' farm, now nothing but a sheet of water which extended three miles westward, terminated by the dark line of forest beyond the Mississippi. On each side of this overflow lay the lakes, each surrounded by a girdle of cypress and magnolia, now standing six feet deep in water. It was supposed that the enemy might attempt to land in the overflow in small boats and our picket was there to give the alarm. When night came on, the alligators and frogs and fish and mosquitoes commenced a sort of fandango, accompanied by music and conversation, which continued till daylight. All sorts of noises could be heard, from the roaring of a bull alligator out in the lagoons, down to the humming of a mosquito close to the ear. Take it altogether, it was the noisiest place and the wildest too that I ever tried to sleep in. The escape pipe of a distant gunboat alone varied the monotony of the sounds.

April 19, Sunday. News has been rapidly pouring in for the last few days. More gunboats have passed Vicksburg, the number is variously reported at from five to eight. One is said to have been sunk. Farragut has quite a strong fleet above us now. Banks is said to be in Baton Rouge again. Rumors of a fight on Bayou Teche, but nothing certainly known about it. The movements of Grant's army are clothed in mystery. A part of it has returned to Memphis and the expeditions on the bayous east of the river appear to have been given up. I think we shall have another fight at this place shortly. The upper fleet is not in sight. One frigate of the lower fleet is in sight below. For the last few days we have heard much cannonading in the direction of Baton Rouge, supposed to be practicing. . . . The peace feeling in the North appears to be growing slowly but I do not think the peace men are in a numerical majority. If the attempt to open the river this spring shall fail, peace will become popular in the West. No attempt has yet been made to enforce the conscript act in Lincolndom.

April 20, Monday. A bright and beautiful day. A report has reached us of the destruction of the *Queen of the West* on Bayou Teche. The enemy's land forces were repulsed and returned to Baton Rouge. Banks is said to be massing a large force at that place. Since the passage of the boats by Vicksburg we expect an attack here soon.

Our regiment is well fixed up in their new quarters. They all have good shanties or good tents and our encampment presents a very neat and regular appearance. Our improvements at headquarters present a very neat appearance, and when they are finished we will have the nicest regimental quarters at Port Hudson. Adjutant Martin and myself are fixing up a mustard patch. The colonel's and quartermaster's quarters consist of four tents placed in a square with a bush arbor in front as a sort of lounging room for the officers of the regiment. Dr. Bowers' and mine will consist of two tents, one in front of the other, and an arbor in front. The rear tent will be our sleeping apartment and the front one the office. The arbor will do to lounge in during the cool of the morning and evening. Our kitchen built of logs is in the rear of our quarters and our stable will be in the rear of the kitchen. We are preparing to spend the rest of the spring and part of the summer in this post. General Pemberton says he will keep the Tennessee troops here till the river falls and if he sends any troops to Tennessee before that time they will not be Tennesseans.

April 21, Tuesday. Rumors have reached us today of the destruction of the gunboats *Queen of the West* and *Diana*. The rumors, however, come through the New Orleans newspapers. General Rust's brigade is again on its way back to this place; General Rust himself has been sent from this district to Arkansas. The movement of Grant's troops to Memphis is supposed to be a sham one, meant to draw our forces away from the Mississippi. Fort Taylor on Red River is reported taken by the enemy. They have succeeded in getting quite a fleet of gunboats and transports past Vicksburg and we look for active movements in this direction soon, as Banks is said to be in Baton Rouge with fifty thousand men. A frigate still lies below in sight as a sort of picket, I suppose, for the lower fleet. Signals are displayed from the masthead whenever one of Farragut's upper fleet comes in sight. There has not been a shot fired for five days. Dr. Bowers and Colonel Clack returned today from Jackson. Everything is so quiet in camp that we can hardly conceive that the enemy lies so near. General Rust gives it as his opinion that Port Hudson must fall into the hands of the enemy by starvation if they make an advance by land. Two months and a half must elapse before the river falls, and so long will our condition be precarious. The Mississippi looks like a wide lake extending into the woods out of sight on the opposite bank, and is, I think, still rising. Time moves very slowly. We are wishing for summer to come.

April 22, Wednesday. Rumors from below indicate that General Sibley has driven Augur back.[13] A black line of smoke was seen yesterday evening down the river but this morning nothing was in sight but the same frigate which has so long acted as picket for the Yankee fleet. A rumor came in on the cars today of a fight between Johnston and Rosecrans, in which we are getting the advantage. Today is my tour of field officer of the day. I am required to visit all the different regiments of the brigade, inspect their camps and guards, and also the grand guards on the breastworks, and our pickets down the river, and this too by night as well as by day. It is a very busy and laborious service and our brigadier is disposed to be something of a martinet without knowing much of military matters. This evening when the sun gets lower I must visit the pickets. Our brigade is in a tolerably good state of discipline. Colonel Walker, though not as good a disciplinarian as Colonel Brown, takes a notion occasionally that he will enforce the army regulations and we do pretty well until the careless fit comes on. He is not constant and firm enough to be a good commander of a regiment. He likes popularity and the good will of the privates too well to enforce strict discipline. I believe if he were more strict he would be more popular, at least that is generally the case with officers in the army. The men grumble sometimes but when strictness is united with justice it will win in the long run.

April 23, Thursday. We have bad news this morning. The boats *Queen of the West* and *Diana* have been destroyed. The Yankees attacked General Sibley in his entrenchments but were repulsed. They then succeeded in outflanking him, and his small force was compelled to retreat toward Red River. The Yankees have taken possession of Opelousas and I am fearful will be now able to get their transports through the Atchafalaya Bayou to Red River and to carry land forces to any point they choose on the river between Port Hudson and Vicksburg. We are going to have a terrible struggle yet between this time and the first of July for the possession of the Mississippi. They may succeed in starving us out of this place but I don't believe they can take it by assault. God be with us, the crisis of this war is fast approaching. Seven weeks more and this river will be safe, if we can hold it so long. General Kirby Smith is at Alexandria and no doubt an attack will be made on that place. General Price is in Little Rock and is re-organizing our scattered forces in Arkansas. If he and Smith unite their forces they will have a very respectable army and may still recover the ground lost west of the river. We are now anxiously looking for news from that quarter. The river is very high and the probabilities are it will not fall much before the June flood. The gunboat *Essex* is reported fast aground below here and several vessels trying to pull her off.

April 24, Friday. A pleasant spring day. The magnolia blossoms are beginning to appear and the forests will soon be clothed in beautiful white. The air is still soft and balmy but the middle of the day partakes more of summer than spring. The mornings are sometimes damp and chilly from the river fogs. A frigate still lies above us and another below, signaling to each other by flags from the masthead and completely blockading the river. Last night a gun was fired below, and the shell seemed to explode over the woods beyond the river. It is rumored that more boats have passed by Vicksburg. The enemy are getting quite a powerful fleet between us and that place. My belief at present is that they are trying to throw a force below Vicksburg and to invest it upon all sides without paying much attention to this place at present. The rumor about the battle in Tennessee has not been confirmed. Another rumor has reached us that Stonewall Jackson with his army had reached Chattanooga on his way to McMinnville. I hope this will turn out to be true and if it is true we may look out for stirring times shortly in middle Tennessee or Kentucky. I should not be surprised if Stonewall will soon be on the flank and rear of Rosecrans' army. I now feel quite relieved about Tennessee and all my anxiety is about the army of the Mississippi and of Red River. A good deal of anxiety is felt here on the provision question.

April 25, Saturday. Still warm and dry. Yesterday the enemy landed a plundering expedition on the other side of the river above us. A battalion of the First Alabama went over to meet them. They attacked them, killed six, took seventeen prisoners, and drove the rest to their boat. The gunboat then shelled the woods for several hours but without effect. No additional news from below or from across the river. An attack on Vicksburg is still anticipated. General Chalmers at last advices was in a critical position on Coldwater, Mississippi, nearly surrounded by the Yankees.[14] Today we, that is, Dr. Bowers and myself, have been busy improving our quarters. We have now two tents, one put up in front of the other. We use the rear one as a sleeping apartment and the front one as an office and public apartment. Our improvements are not yet complete and will not be so for some days, as we are neither of us remarkable for industry, especially in hot weather. We have a magnificent cane bed on a bedstead two feet high. Large pieces of cane are woven across like a cane-bottomed chair and on top of this is placed a bed of hay, on which are our blankets. It is railed all around to keep from rolling out. The doctor the other day bought a lady's traveling dressing case and I have just put up a stand made out of an old goods box to put it on. The doctor frequently is found in front of his elegant mirror surveying his countenance. We are now living in more comfort than we have done for a long time.

April 26, Sunday. Everything moves on as monotonous as usual and sometimes I feel like discontinuing my diary just from want of something to record. Sometimes a week passes by without furnishing an item worth the ink and trouble it takes to write it down. The ships lie above and below us like sullen monsters, showing no sign of life, and only occasionally firing a signal gun to show that they are still there. We sometimes forget that we have an enemy at our doors who may attack us at any moment and go on with our usual camp occupations just as we used to do at Camp Cheatham and Trousdale. We get newspapers every day, or the monotony of our life would be almost insupportable. The strange and beautiful climate and country was at first a perpetual source of novelty and enjoyment but that has worn off. We have grown tired of alligators and chameleons and though the beauty of the magnolia and the perfume of the China trees can never tire, yet we earnestly long for the magnificent poplar hills and beech groves of our own Tennessee, because among them dwell those whom we hold most dear and for whom we are now suffering all the privations of a soldier's life.

This little record, commenced among the pine hills of the Yalobusha and continued among the swamps of the Yazoo, now terminates on the cliffs of Port Hudson. May the next terminate in a place to me the happiest and most beautiful of all—home.

April 27. Today I commence another volume of my diary. I hope the present volume will record no greater disasters and at least equal triumphs to the last one. Greater ones I would scarcely presume to ask for. Fredericksburg and Vicksburg and Charleston could scarcely be improved upon. May God in His mercy grant that before this little book is filled I may be permitted to chronicle in its pages at least the cessation of hostilities, if not a permanent peace. When I commenced the last one in December, I thought that this spring's campaign would terminate the war. My hopes for that result are not yet entirely extinct, though probabilities are much against them. At the same time I am fully satisfied that the peace party at the North are very much stronger now than they were then and that they are gaining strength each day. By the first of July the campaign on the Mississippi will be over and if it is in our power to hold the river till that time, the peace party in the Northwest will be strengthened. Every moment of delay is in our favor if it is not attended with disaster to our armies. . . .

April 28, Tuesday. We had quite a hard rain last night but this morning is bright, clear, and quite warm. It is just like June weather in Tennessee. A rumor is afloat this morning that a force of twenty thousand Yankees have landed at Natchez and our telegraphic communications with that place are entirely cut off. Another rumor, purporting to come from Baton Rouge, states that the Yankees on the Teche have been badly whipped and lost many prisoners. Of course we shall believe neither report until confirmed. We have been in camp too long to believe anything we hear the first report. When the mail came in it brought further intelligence of the Federal raid into Mississippi. After leaving Newton the Yankees cut the telegraph and destroyed five miles of the road, then went to Enterprise and demanded the surrender of the place, but meeting with resistance they retired. Loring is after them but we have but little cavalry in that quarter. The Federals possess Okolona, Mississippi. They have made a raid upon McMinnville, Tennessee. No news of interest anywhere else. A shot was fired from our lower battery this morning down the river. The artillerists were trying their new Blakely guns and they succeeded very well. They threw shells to the lower blockading vessel. The creoles or Acadian French across the river have been discovered carrying intelligence from the upper fleet to the lower, and it is said that General Gardner sent a company across to dislodge or chastise them. The report about our captures over there the other day proves to be incorrect and we lost two men instead of taking the party.

April 29, Wednesday. Today several regiments were sent out in pursuit of the enemy's cavalry who had been heard of at Hazlehurst on the Great Northern Road. I started out with a wagon foraging for potatoes and went some twenty-five miles northwards to the Clinton and Woodville road without finding any, and put up with a Mr. Norwood who lived in great style. He seemed quite unwilling to entertain soldiers. Next day we crossed over into Mississippi and were successful in our expedition. We took dinner with a Mrs. Whittaker who was very clever to us and loaded our wagon. I returned the same evening to Mr. McLean's who talked a great deal about religion and quarreled with his family.

On the first of May, I reached camp about dinnertime. News had reached there that the Yankee cavalry under Grierson had visited Brookhaven and Summit on the Great Northern Road and were on their way to Baton Rouge.[15] On the evening of the first we were startled by an order for our brigade to march to Jackson, Mississippi. The enemy had landed near Rodney, driven General Bowen back, and occupied Port Gibson, and were threatening the rear of Vicksburg.[16] And so our sojourn at Port Hudson is at an end. We were almost sorry for we had just completed a little village for our summer quarters. But we were living almost too easy for Confederate soldiers and now we must take our turn at a little hardship. Our men were much discontented when we first went to Port Hudson but the beauty and richness of the country gradually gained their affections and I believe most of them were sorry when we received marching orders. Not a single cheer was raised for they all hated Jackson.

May 2, Saturday. I have received orders to remain and send off the sick and baggage of the brigade. This morning the whole brigade except the Seventh Texas which had gone several days ago started on foot. In the evening I commenced hauling the baggage up to the depot and pitched my tent for the night at the railroad. I felt quite lonesome, as all my mess were gone. About one hundred and fifty sick and convalescent men were left in my charge and many of them were quite troublesome. I had to quarrel with quartermasters in order to get wagons and then quarrel with drivers for being lazy and then with our convalescent men for being so lazy and unwilling to handle the baggage. I did not quite finish this evening.

May 3, Sunday. All morning we were busy hauling up baggage and loading it on the cars. About 2:00 P.M. I finished my task and started on horseback alone for Clinton. On passing through the fortifications I turned to bid adieu, as I fervently hoped, for the last time, to Port Hudson. Five months' stay had not endeared it to me. . . . [17]

5 | Marching through Mississippi

May 3–August 24, 1863

MAGNOLIA, BROOKHAVEN, RAYMOND. A GALLANT RUSH THAT DEC-
IMATES THE THIRD. CALHOUN STATION TO CANTON. NEAR YAZOO
CITY. PURSUING DESERTERS. BRINGING UP STRAGGLERS. STUNNING
NEWS FROM VICKSBURG. WE MOVE BACK. NEAR MORTON STATION.
MERIDIAN, ENTERPRISE. LOUNGING IN CAMP, GETTING FAT AND
LAZY. FURLOUGH.

May 3, Sunday. I had a delightful ride of ten miles on the upper
Clinton road and stopped for the night two miles from Jackson
with Captain Jones. The brigade had left that place early that
morning.[1]

May 4, Monday. Again I took the road and rode all day to over-
take the army. I dined in Clinton and overtook them fifteen miles
east of that place beyond the Amite River. East Louisiana is a
most delightful country, such a one as I would like to spend my
days in. The road from Clinton to camp was well lined with stragglers. Our baggage had reached Clinton and gone through safely.

May 5, Tuesday. Today we marched to a point five miles from
Osyka. I and Adjutant Martin rode on ahead of the army and kept
out of the dust. Just at the bridge over Amite River in St. Helena
Parish we passed the place where a skirmish had occurred a few
days before with Grierson's cavalry and visited the wounded Yan-
kees who had been left behind, among others Lieutenant Colonel
Blackburn of Illinois. The surgeon who had been left with them
told me that Grierson's command consisted of two regiments.[2]
Tonight we encamped in a beautiful pine grove just in the edge of
Mississippi.

May 6, Wednesday. This morning we marched into town and
encamped a mile above. The sick and broken down and the heavy

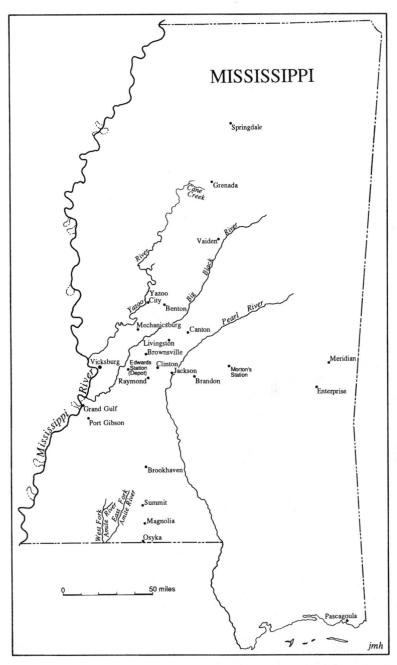

The campaign in Mississippi before and after the fall of Vicksburg, 1863

baggage were put on a train and sent up the railroad. Our men enjoyed very much the half day of rest which was given them and
employed the time in sleep and in replenishing their long-empty
stomachs. The commissary had failed to provide sufficient rations and the men often went supperless to bed. A shot out in the
woods, followed by the squeal of some distant pig, proved that
they were occasionally providing for themselves. Today we were
joined by the Seventh Texas Regiment.

May 7, Thursday. Again we started on our march and by 12:00
arrived at Magnolia, a beautiful little town surrounded by country seats where the wealthy people of New Orleans used to spend
their unhealthy seasons. Here the brigade took the cars, while
Phillips and Dr. Bowers and myself rode on horseback to Summit,
another pleasant village on the railroad. The Yankee marauders
had torn up the track between this place and Brookhaven and we
were obliged to march through the country. This evening when
the army arrived at Summit we encamped three miles farther up
the road. Here we heard the news of General Lee's splendid victory on the Rappahannock, and also learned that the Yankees
were occupying Port Gibson and Grand Gulf.

May 8, Friday. This morning we marched ten miles and arrived at Brookhaven about 12:00. We here took the cars and
reached Jackson before night. I had my gray, "Buckner," badly
crippled in putting him on the cars. At Jackson, I met Captain
Flautt just from home, who brought with him Joe and a long letter from home. We marched through the town and encamped a
mile and a half on the north side. I spent the time till bedtime
talking about home and reading my letters by the firelight.

On Monday morning, May 11, we again took up the line of
march on the Raymond road. The enemy were reported advancing from Port Gibson in strong force. I left my crippled horse at
the house of Mr. William Bracey, seven miles from Jackson, who
promised to take care of him, and purchased another, a very indifferent one, for $400. On Monday night we encamped half a
mile north of Raymond. News reached us here that the enemy
were still advancing.

May 12, Tuesday. This morning we heard that the enemy were
in force within five miles. About 11:00 they were within two
miles on the Port Gibson road. We marched out to the graveyard

on the south of town. The Yankees soon commenced skirmishing with our pickets and the artillery were soon engaged. About
12:00 our regiment advanced along the Gallatin road, then turned
to the right through the fields and formed a line of battle behind
a hill and in front of a thick woods occupied by the enemy. The
Seventh Texas was on our right and the Tenth and Thirtieth Tennessee on our left. The Third Tennessee and Seventh Texas were
ordered to drive the enemy out of the woods. General Gregg supposed them not to be in large force and promised to send the
Tenth, Thirtieth, and Forty-First to attack them in the rear. The
Third advanced to the brow of the hill and commenced descending the slope toward the woods in line of battle. They advanced
in most gallant style, yelling until the woods resounded. A hundred yards from the edge of the timber our skirmishers under
command of Captain Mitchell dashed forward and the enemy's
skirmishers opened fire upon us. Our line rushed forward at
double-quick and a short distance from the woods we received a
volley from a line of battle within the woods. Our men though
falling fast never faltered but still advanced and rushed into the
timber yelling like demons. The enemy's line was broken in a
moment and our men followed close at their heels, shooting and
capturing them. The undergrowth and briars were so thick we
could scarcely make our way through. The enemy again formed
a new line in the woods behind a bayou, but our men rushed
madly forward, jumped into the ravine, and climbed the steep
bank on the other side. Again the enemy gave way and fled entirely out of the woods in our front into an open field. We followed them to the edge of the woods and there beheld another
line in the field. A few volleys from the Third scattered them and
they retired out of range.

In the meantime we had passed a body of the enemy on the left
unseen, and as soon as we were past they opened a galling fire
upon our left flank and rear. Our men by this time had shot away
all their ammunition and a fresh column was advancing directly
upon us. No support appeared upon our rear or left and we had
been so terribly cut up and scattered in the thick woods that the
colonel thought best to order a retreat. We were barely in time,
for before our left wing could fall back the Yankees succeeded in

capturing some of our men who were exhausted. All the way back we were severely galled by the enemy on both flanks. We had to leave many of our wounded in the woods, not being able to carry them away, in spite of their entreaties not to be abandoned.[3]

We at length reached the place whence we had made the charge and again formed one line but 187 of our number were missing. But the noble old Third, though shattered and bleeding, and repulsed by overwhelming numbers, preserved her name unsullied. Officers and men all had done their duty. All our other regiments engaged were also driven back and the brigade suffered a loss of 530. We had twenty-seven killed, ninety wounded, and seventy missing, many of whom were supposed to be killed or wounded.[4] Our whole force then fell back to Raymond and immediately commenced their retreat. Tonight we encamped at Mississippi Springs, five miles from Raymond, where we met General Walker's brigade of Georgians.[5] We lay down in an open field and in a few minutes forgot all our losses and disasters. Dr. Bowers remained at Raymond with the wounded. Lieutenants Ridgeway of Company A, Darden of Company E, Farley and Rittenbury of Company I, were wounded, also Captain Walker. Captain Cooper was killed. Lieutenant Murphy and Captain Alexander were missing.

May 13, Wednesday. This morning we learned that the Yankees were in Raymond. We marched and countermarched half the day until we discovered that the enemy were in Clinton and advancing on our right. General Walker wanted to fight but Gregg refused, and in the evening we fell back to Jackson and encamped in the suburbs on the Raymond road. We had some rain this evening, which laid the dust. I laid down and slept soundly in my wet clothes, by the assistance of a dose of morphine which the doctor administered for a pleuritic pain which had annoyed me. Today General Johnston arrived at Jackson and we all expect an attack tomorrow. I left my crippled gray with Mr. Bracey to the mercy of the Yankees.

May 14, Thursday. This morning we heard that the enemy were still advancing. We lay on our arms till 10:00, then formed and marched around the edge of town on the west and north sides to the Clinton road. By this time I had discovered that we were evacuating. An incessant cannonade was carried on by the enemy against our advanced troops. Supposing we were going to fight in the trenches I sent my horse by a Negro back to the wagon train and lost him. Some Negro stole him from the train. An incessant rain kept pouring down and wetted us to the skin and the road became a deep mass of mud. I walked on several miles till I overtook Dawson with Dr. Bowers' "Selim" and I soon mounted him. We trudged along in the mud six miles and then struck camp. The rain ceased and we all laid down on the soaked ground, in high spirits because Old Joe was with us.

May 15, Friday. This morning broke bright and beautiful. We marched to Calhoun Station, nine miles from Canton. The enemy followed us no farther than Jackson. We have now about seven thousand men in our little army. Of our future operations of course we know nothing. Our men are very tired but still in good spirits and have the most unbounded confidence in General Johnston.[6]

Two years ago tonight I was married. What changes have taken place since then. Then I anticipated a lifetime of unalloyed happiness but one year ago found me within the walls of a prison and the present anniversary finds me in the ranks of a retreating army, defeated and driven back before an overwhelming force. God grant that the next one may find me in peace enjoying the society of her whom I love best of all on earth.

May 16, Saturday. Today we lay in camp at Calhoun Station. General John Adams was appointed chief of cavalry. We heard that the enemy had burned the statehouse, penitentiary, depot, and many stores in Jackson. Grant and Sherman were both there. Part of Maxey's and Gist's brigades are at Brandon and other reinforcements are reported at Meridian.[7]

May 17, Sunday. This morning we again commenced our march. We took the road to Vicksburg, made a pretty hard march and encamped ten miles from Clinton. The enemy have evacuated Jackson and gone towards Edwards Station. Our reinforcements are reported coming on behind. Our destination is supposed to be a junction with Pemberton's army but Old Joe keeps his own counsel. We passed through the little town of Livingston today.

May 18, Monday. We continued our march on the Vicksburg road to a point about ten miles from Brownsville where the enemy's cavalry were, and upon a report that they were advancing, our army remained drawn up in line of battle for several hours. We heard that a portion of our army had been defeated near Edwards Station and General Tilghman killed. Our loss reported heavy. No enemy appearing, we turned off to the right on the Canton road and encamped a few miles from Big Black River in the midst of a most beautiful and fertile country.

May 19, Tuesday. We made a short day's march through a most lovely country towards Canton and encamped a mile from Big Black. We passed through the little village of Vernon in which were only two inhabited houses. Water is very scarce and very bad. We have to drink out of mudholes and stagnant ponds by the roadside, and often drink water that our horses refuse. There are various speculations about our course. We seem to be retrograding today. Our men are not in so high spirits as they were but have entire faith in Johnston. There is great outcry against General Pemberton and many regard him as a traitor.

May 20, Wednesday. We marched to within six miles of Canton through the Big Black bottom, the finest portion of Mississippi I have yet seen. The country is just undulating enough to be pleasant. We have heard that our army on the lower Big Black was badly defeated. Loring left all his artillery in the swamps and made his escape to the vicinity of Jackson. Gist and Maxey are coming from Brandon with reinforcements. It seems to be Johnston's idea to collect the scattered divisions of the army and to act in the rear of Grant who is investing Vicksburg.

May 21, Thursday. We spent this day in camp. General Gist's Georgia and South Carolina brigade came in today. These troops have been in service a long time but have been stationed on the coast and have had little or no experience of actual warfare. They are eager for a fight, full of a soldier's first enthusiasm, but I fancy when they have been through the rubs as often as we have their ardor will cool down. Maxey's brigade is between Jackson and this place and Loring is in the vicinity of Jackson. It is conjectured that Johnston has at least twenty thousand men now within supporting distance of each other. Others are reported on the road from the east to join us. Our spirits though depressed by the reverses of our army on Big Black are rising at the sight of reinforcements. We all expect a terrible struggle and great loss of life but by the blessing of God we hope to conquer. Our regiment now enjoys quite an enviable reputation, won on the bloody fields of Vicksburg and Raymond, and earned by the blood of some of our best and bravest. When asked to what regiment we belong it brings a glow of pride to the face to answer, "The Third Tennessee." May we always sustain our dearly bought honors in all future engagements in which God, in His providence, may call us to take our part. May we never become so vain and boastful as to forget that we owe our reputation not to our own valor but to the mercies of our Creator. Our hardest trial at present is the absence of all news from home and in our migratory condition we cannot expect to hear any. We can still send off letters occasionally but receive none. Everything abroad is a blank to us.

May 22, Friday. We remained in camp today in a state of suspense, expecting to move every minute, hearing rumors from abroad of all sorts, favorable and unfavorable. General Johnston has made his headquarters in Canton. Captain Flautt started today for Jackson to collect the remains of our baggage which we had left behind and I purchased his horse for $500—a very good trade as I think.

May 23, Saturday. We marched this morning and encamped two miles west of Canton. Our whole army seems to be concentrating on the railroad from Jackson to Vaiden. Rumors grow thick and fast. Grant is said to have been repulsed in his attacks on Vicksburg with great slaughter and Pemberton is said to have taken two divisions out on Big Black. The enemy have possession of the Yazoo River. Lee is reported to have occupied Arlington Heights and preparing to cross the Potomac into Maryland, and Price is reported to have captured Helena. Some of our boys who escaped from Raymond hospital came in today and report the enemy's loss in our engagement there as much heavier than our own.

May 24, Sunday. In camp today. The Reverend Colonel Fountain E. Pitt preached today a very good sermon, the first I have heard for a long time.[8] The news of yesterday has been confirmed today, with the additional news that Price's men killed two thousand Negroes found in arms at Helena. It is also reported that the Yankees made an attack by land on Port Hudson and have been repulsed. It is said that Johnston will have thirty-five thousand men here in a week. Everything looks bright and cheering again—the clouds are beginning to break.

May 25, Monday. Still in camp. We are becoming very tired of lying still. When in garrison it will do very well but bivouacked in the woods it is very tiresome. We still have cheering news from Vicksburg. The repulse of the enemy with great slaughter is confirmed. Price is at Gaines' Landing and Marmaduke at Helena, according to report.[9] Banks is said to be at Alexandria.

May 27, Wednesday. Still in the same old camp. General Walker has been promoted to be major general and our brigade is in his division. It is reported that General Grant is retreating from Yazoo to Big Black. His loss is said to be immense. No confirmation of the rumors from the East. It is said that Rosecrans has been assigned to the Potomac and Burnside to the Cumberland.[10] No reports of an advance on our part as yet. We are ordered to change our camp tomorrow. Our brigade at present consists of the Third, Tenth, Thirtieth, Forty-First, and Fiftieth Tennessee, First Tennessee Battalion, Fourteenth Mississippi, Seventh Texas, and Hoskins' Mississippi and Bledsoe's Missouri batteries, in all less than 3,000 men.

May 28, Thursday. This morning at daylight our brigade commenced moving. We passed through Canton before the inhabitants had breakfasted and marched about two miles from town in a southeastern direction and encamped in a dense grove near a creek. We here settled down into camp where we expect to stay until General Johnston is ready for active operations. No further news today from any quarter. I read a *Mississippian* of the twenty-sixth today. Newspapers are very scarce now with us. The only items of interest are the discharge of the nine-months and two-years men of the Northern army and the statements concerning the death of Van Dorn by the members of his staff. They attempt to make it an assassination for political reasons.

May 29, Friday. We had a fine shower today and having no tents just stood and took it like ducks. We had an inspection and review of our brigade this evening and it presented a very fine appearance. A rumor reached us that we would move tomorrow. Breckinridge's division is reported to be on its way here.[11]

May 30, Saturday. This morning at daylight we were on the march. We passed through Canton and took a northwestern direction. Our division consisted of five brigades under Major General Walker of Georgia. We crossed Big Black River at Moore's Bluff on a pontoon bridge, traveled hard all day, and at dark encamped in a thicket twenty miles from Canton. We were on the road to Yazoo River. We passed through a beautiful country but water was very scarce. We heard today that Port Hudson had been invested by General Augur but that the enemy had been repulsed in their first attack.

May 31, Sunday. At daylight we again commenced our march. The day was warm and the road exceedingly dusty. About 12:00 we reached the town of Benton and the men dispersed through town in search of water. Our only chance for water on the road was mudholes and ponds. The inhabitants have cisterns but the quantity was insufficient for our division of fifteen thousand men. The country looked fair enough but dry as an African desert. All is one vast cornfield. Two men dropped dead in ranks from excessive fatigue. After night we reached the heights above the Yazoo River about a mile from Yazoo City and encamped.

June 1, Monday. An exceedingly hot and sultry day. We lay in camp all day resting from the fatigues of our march. When we arrived last night we had no supper except cornmeal, which delayed our bedtime till twelve o'clock before it could be prepared. Our horses stood all night without a mouthful to eat. This morning it was ten o'clock before we could get a little beef for breakfast and corn for our horses. We are seeing some of the sights of an active campaign. Today several heavy guns arrived, some of which were mounted instantly. The Yankee gunboats had visited this place but have been gone several days. All the government property has been destroyed. Yazoo City is 110 miles by water and forty-five by land from Vicksburg. Liverpool is ten miles below and the Yankees are still below that place. Breckinridge is reported at Canton and he and Loring are both on the march to reinforce us. We are encamped on a very high ridge which seems to be a continuation of the Walnut Hills of Vicksburg. Water is scarce and very bad. The best we can get comes from the river.

June 2, Tuesday. This morning at sunrise we again started on our march and about twelve o'clock reached camp on a creek about four miles from Yazoo City. Our general direction was southeast. The march was very badly arranged, very slow with halts every few hundred yards, more fatiguing than the march itself. The wagon train did not arrive for four hours after we reached camp. By far the best method of conducting a march is to start early and march steadily with but few halts until camp be reached about 3:00 P.M.; then rest till morning. We have heard cannonading all day in the direction of Vicksburg. A rumor has reached us that Banks' wagon train and a large number of Negroes had been captured by Kirby Smith and that he had raised the siege of Port Hudson and gone down the river, and also that Grant had made another assault on Vicksburg on the twenty-ninth of May and had again been repulsed. Their lines are now within eight hundred yards of our works. It is said that they have already lost fifteen thousand killed alone in their assaults and that the stench of the unburied dead has become very offensive. Pemberton is making a heroic defense. God grant that he may be successful. Breckinridge's division was arriving at Canton on the thirty-first of May.

June 3, Wednesday. We are encamped among the hills in a region so wild and remote from everywhere that I don't believe Grant has any idea where we are. This broken country looks very like middle Tennessee except that there are no rocks nor springs among the hills. The timber is very tall and heavy and indicates a very rich soil. We use the creek water which is good enough but very warm. The people in these parts are small farmers cultivating small patches of land in the bottoms and on top of the ridges. It reminds me much of the more broken parts of Giles County. We have not yet been in the Yazoo bottom, which is said to be of extraordinary fertility. The grapevine today is working beautifully. There are rumors of a cavalry fight near Mechanicsville in which our men had the advantage. It is said that Grant has lost forty thousand men since his entrance to this state and that the troops of McClernand's division have refused to sacrifice themselves any longer in fruitless assaults on Vicksburg.[12] Rumors from Port Hudson state that it was Sherman instead of Banks who made the assault on that place and that the enemy were repulsed with the loss of three thousand men and Sherman was killed. Kirby Smith is said to have commanded our troops. The news of the capture of the enemy's wagon train is confirmed. Everything is going on finely in the Southwest. The enemy is exhausting himself against our strong fortresses and Joe Johnston is organizing an army which we hope will complete their destruction. The failure of the enemy on the river will bring on a speedy peace, as I believe, and at any rate involve our speedy return to Tennessee.

June 4, Thursday. We were kept under arms all day. After twelve o'clock an incessant cannonading was heard down the river and late in the evening we marched back to our old position a mile from Yazoo City. It was dark when we arrived and Colonel Clack laid down to sleep close by a pile of decaying beef. He snuffed a good deal, grumbled a little, but was too tired to change his position and went to sleep. Phillips laid down on the ground like a log and never turned over till morning. I had a restless fit and had to light up a fire and take a smoke and talk to Dave Martin an hour before I felt sleepy. I heard from home today.

June 5, Friday. All day we were hearing rumors about the advance of the Yankees from below and talking about going back to Tennessee after Grant was whipped. In the evening we received orders to move and marched about three miles down the Yazoo River and encamped on a beautiful spot on the banks of a creek. Part of our baggage was left behind. We still hear cannonading below.

June 6, Saturday. We spent this day in camp. It was very warm and we lay in the shade lounging in idleness. After a succession of marches a camp presents the most idle spectacle in the world. The colonel and Phillips were attempting to play chess, both almost too lazy to say "check." Clack was lying on his back under a tree trying to read a novel. Captain Flautt was sound asleep. Occasionally a lounging soldier would pass by our "tree," on his way to the spring, apparently bending under the weight of a single canteen. Here and there could be seen some inveterate talker with his back against a tree retailing, between the puffs of his pipe, the latest grapevine to auditors who manifest the greatest indifference to him and to his news. As the sun sinks low in the west, everything becomes changed. Every face becomes eager. Smoke arises from five hundred fires and around each one stand men with sleeves rolled up, frying and boiling and baking and running to and fro, carrying water and wood and fresh beef.

June 7, Sunday. In camp all day. Sunday in camp does not differ in any appreciable degree from any other day except that perhaps more letters are written than on any other day. It was a very warm day and in the evening Colonel Clack and myself went down the creek to a quiet place and wrote letters till sundown. We heard cannonading nearly all day in the direction of Vicksburg. We heard today that the enemy had retired from Mechanicsville southward. General Loring was in town today. His command is in the vicinity of Benton. Breckinridge is on our extreme left.

June 9, Tuesday. Last night a good many deserters were reported from the brigade and I received an order to pursue them across the Yazoo River. Mounted officers were sent out on every road. After twelve o'clock I crossed at the ferry at Yazoo City and went up the west bank of the river. At Colonel White's place I received news of three stragglers from the Negroes. I took dinner with the overseer who set me over the bayou in a skiff, my horse swimming. At Dr. Woodbury's place I could hear nothing. After leaving that place I struck out from the river and soon became entangled in an impenetrable morass. The whole face of the earth was covered with palm leaf plant and the swamps were filled with cypress knees standing in a green, loathsome-looking water. I again came out on the river and proceeded up the bank. Towards evening I reached Andrew's place where I remained all night. His whole white family consisted of himself and nephew. They lived in considerable style and I had a fine supper and a splendid bed. The change was too sudden, however, and I did not sleep half so soundly as on the ground with hunger and fatigue as opiates.

June 10, Wednesday. This morning we had quite a rain and as soon as it was over I went on up the river. I met with an old gentleman named Paine who gave me some information and went with me through the swamp to Wolf Lake. Here we found a camp which some deserters had formerly occupied but the men were gone. About dinnertime we came out on the river at Mr. Paine's place, ten miles above Yazoo City. He lives in very fine style, has a beautiful house, well furnished, and gave a dinner got up in superlatively fashionable style. We had two kinds of wine at dinner. He is a retired New Orleans merchant and lives as well as he used to do in the city. After dinner I gave up on the pursuit and started back to camp. When I reached Yazoo City, I reported to General Walker and after being bored by his excessive loquacity I made my escape and reached camp about eight o'clock, when I found three letters from home awaiting me.

June 12, Friday. Today we received orders to be ready to march. The men cooked their rations by twelve o'clock but at sunset we were still in camp. Tomorrow morning we shall likely receive the order to march. We have not the slightest idea where we are going, as we have no reliable reports from below. This morning we still heard guns from Vicksburg. Bragg seems to be making an advance upon Rosecrans and our men are at Franklin. The Yankees appear to be quiet at every point except Vicksburg, and there the whole interest of the war is culminating. Everyone North and South has his eyes fixed upon the hills of Vicksburg.

June 13, Saturday. This morning at daylight we started on the march. Myself with Majors Robinson and Van Trandt were detailed to bring up stragglers. The column moved two miles toward Yazoo City and then turned to the right on a big road. I rode on to town and came out the plank road toward Benton, then turned off to the right and wandered through the woods and hills and plantations for several hours and finally came out on the Dover road but could hear nothing of the whereabouts of the army. I then got a citizen to pilot me through the country, who brought me to where the head of our brigade was resting on the Scott's Ferry road. We had a long and tiresome march of more than twenty miles, and picking up and urging forward stragglers was anything but a pleasant occupation. We passed about two thousand on the road. About sundown we went off from the road a mile, got our suppers, and after dark overtook the rear of the column encamped on the west side of Big Black at Scott's Ferry. We crossed on a bridge made of flatboats and about ten o'clock reached our command encamped in a cornfield on the edge of the Big Black swamp. I laid down between two corn rows and was oblivious till morning.

June 14, Sunday. We lay in camp till 3:00 P.M. and then started in the heat of the day. We passed in sight of the little village of Vernon and before dark reached our old camping ground at the brick church, the same ground we had occupied on the eighteenth of May. It is the most beautiful bivouac I ever saw. Our news from Vicksburg still continues cheering, with the exception of a scarcity of ammunition. Kirby Smith is reported as annoying Grant on the other side of the river. Banks has Port Hudson closely invested. Grierson has been repulsed in an attack on Clinton, Louisiana. It is reported that Grant is calling loudly for reinforcements and everything indicates that he must soon raise the siege.

June 16, Tuesday. Still in camp at Mound Bluff Church. Last evening I received an invitation from Mrs. Judge Tarpley whose family is related to my wife, to call at her house. I went this morning with Colonel Clack and spent the day very pleasantly. A dinner in the country is quite a treat to a hungry soldier. We had quite a hard rain this evening. The corn had begun to suffer and was needing it very much.

June 17, Wednesday. A damp, drizzling day. By stretching out blankets we managed to keep dry. Our news from Vicksburg is composed entirely of unreliable rumors of which the camp is constantly full. Only one thing is certain. Vicksburg is still safe. Nothing seems to be stirring in other departments. Walker's division is here, Loring's at Canton, Breckinridge's near Jackson, Kirby Smith and Taylor across the river opposite Vicksburg.[13]

June 18, Thursday. Still bivouacked at the church, with a prospect of remaining some time. All our wagons were taken today except half a one for each regiment, to carry cooking vessels alone. Our baggage is reduced to the lowest compass possible. Privates and company officers must carry everything on their backs. Field officers must carry their baggage on their horses. Old Joe must intend to make foot cavalry of our men. The news of the defeat of the enemy at Milliken's Bend by General Marshall Walker is confirmed. No news from Port Hudson, which is closely

invested by the enemy. Accounts from Vicksburg represent the
garrison as having two months' provisions. It has been just a
month since we were encamped on this spot before and it seemed
a very short month, not more than half as long as the weary
months at Port Hudson. Ever since we have been in service it has
been our lot until recently to discharge garrison duty but now we
are paying for our long months of ease.

June 19, Friday. The sun again made its appearance this morning after several days of rain and damp weather. Everything in the
news line has become stagnant and the monotony of our camp
has become distressing. So long as we are not doing garrison duty
and are allowed none of the conveniences of garrison life, we
would prefer being constantly on the move, with halts only long
enough for rest. I would like to travel at least two days every
week. I have been thinking today of the eventful life to which our
regiment has been exposed since it first entered the service—
more eventful perhaps than that of my other regiment in the
Confederacy. Camp Cheatham first received us all fresh and in-
experienced in military affairs and full of warlike enthusiasm,
and ridiculously verdant as to all the duties of soldiers. There we
learned the routine of our profession and there disease commenced its work of lopping off the feeble and hardening the
strong. Camp Trousdale next received us but the destroyer still
followed us and many a vacant file and many a grassy mound at-
tested his power. Then Bowling Green—and the cold, clear waters of Barren River flowed by our camp for many a month. Next
the muddy streets of Russellville held us "stuck in the mire" for
many a weary day. Thus far we had never seen an enemy and our
"active service" was confined to expeditions on Green River in
which no enemy made his appearance. But the smooth, even current of our lives was soon to change. We had envied those regiments who had been sent to Virginia and who had participated in
the glories of Manassas and Big Bethel, even those who had suffered in the disasters on the Upper Kanawha. We left the soil of
Kentucky and Donelson received us within its walls. The excite-
ments of three days' fight passed like a dream and we awoke to
find ourselves prisoners and on our way to a foreign prison. Then
came seven long months of weary captivity—humiliating, op-

pressive, monotonous to the last degree. From that prison we came forth veterans and upon our exchange found ourselves in the midst of new levies and conscripts, fully entitled to the epithet of "old soldiers." The toilsome campaign of north Mississippi followed, with its forced marches without a battle. Then Vicksburg and Chickasaw Bayou where we gained an immortal name for the regiment at a very small expense. Then the long months of sojourn at Port Hudson under the shade of magnolias by the rushing waters of the Mississippi and then the toilsome marches through the pine forests of south Mississippi and the bloody and disastrous day of Raymond, and the rapid retreat, and ceaseless marches along the banks of the Pearl and Big Black and Yazoo, complete the chapter to the present time. But many another toilsome march and many another bloody day must doubtless elapse before the book of our history is finished.

June 21, Sunday. We made a fine breakfast on the provisions brought in by my "kinsfolk" yesterday. They are very kind and clever. Good biscuits are very refreshing to a soldier who has lived so long on cornbread and beef. We have news that our army has captured eight thousand prisoners under Millroy at Winchester, Virginia, and also that Banks after being badly whipped at Port Hudson raised the siege and retreated to his boats at Bayou Sara. Cannonading yesterday and today in the vicinity of Vicksburg, but no news from that quarter. General Marshall Walker defeated the Yankees at Milliken's Bend and drove them to the cover of their gunboats.

July 1, Wednesday. I have been out of camp at Mrs. Tarpley's, chilling it for the last week, but finally succeeded in getting rid of them [apparently the chills], thanks to the kindness of Mrs. Tarpley and her family. I shall never have a word to say against the Mississippians again. This morning we heard that our army was moving down Big Black and after dinner Dr. Bowers, Captain Nelson of Walker's escort, and myself started for camp which we reached before sundown. We found our division about five miles west of Brownsville encamped at a pond. Loring's division was just behind us and French's on our left near Brownsville.[14] We hear that Price has taken Helena, Taylor has whipped the enemy at Berwick's Bay, and Bragg has fallen back to Tullahoma.

July 2, Thursday. This morning we were again on the road and after an exceedingly hot and dusty march encamped on Cane Creek, three miles from Big Black and twelve miles north of Edwards Depot. The enemy are said to be in force across the river seven miles distant and it is believed we shall cross over and attack them. Our whole army is here except Breckinridge's division which is said to be seven miles below us. News from Virginia is cheering. Our forces have advanced into Pennsylvania and occupied Chambersburg and Gettysburg. The Yankees have captured Shelbyville.

July 4, Saturday. We are still in camp at Cane Creek. No news from the front. We still hear the cannon at Vicksburg, which is about twenty-five miles from us in an air line. The news of the capture of Helena is confirmed but still I think it doubtful. Taylor has made a raid in lower Louisiana and taken Algiers with a Connecticut regiment and a large quantity of commissaries. Banks is still investing Port Hudson. The raid into Pennsylvania still goes bravely on. Ewell is said to have taken Carlisle and to be threatening Harrisburg. The militia of that state are said to be very slow about turning out.[15] The Yankees are concentrating a force at White House and threatening Richmond.

July 5, Sunday. Last night the terrible news of the fall of Vicksburg came like a thunder stroke upon us. We could not believe it—it was too improbable and stunning. At first everyone loudly avowed his disbelief, but still doubt sat on every face, and the terrible truth gradually made its way.[16] The enemy were encamped in strong force on the opposite side of Big Black and shelling and firing of pickets took place last night. At 2:00 in the morning we started and about 6:00 we turned to the left on the Jackson road and bade adieu to the swamps of Big Black and with heavy hearts and weary limbs took up our retreat for the capital of Mississippi. All along the road we received reports confirmatory of the fall of Vicksburg on the third, but the more sanguine still disbelieved. Tonight we encamped at a large pond three miles west of Clinton. The enemy pressed us hard all day but Jackson's cavalry kept them back. The day was so hot and our march so rapid that some of our men dropped from exhaustion.

July 6, Monday. Another hard day's march and we encamped near the fairgrounds at Jackson. As we passed through Clinton we learned the particulars of our great disaster from some paroled prisoners who had come out. Everybody is leaving home and fleeing eastward and western Mississippi is fast becoming a wilderness. The enemy are following us and are occupying Clinton and Raymond.[17]

July 7, Tuesday. We lay in camp all day enjoying that rest which we so much needed, the enemy still slowly advancing, our cavalry contesting every inch of ground. We hear from Tennessee that Bragg has fallen back across Tennessee River and middle Tennessee is once more abandoned to the mercies of the Yankees. God have mercy upon our friends and families for man seems to have forsaken them. Lee has defeated the enemy at Gettysburg, Pennsylvania, and captured many prisoners.

July 8, Wednesday. This morning at an early hour the whole army was ordered into the trenches. Our brigade occupied the line about midway between the Canton and Clinton roads. In our front were open fields and in our rear an open, level expanse of country liable to be swept by the enemy's cannon. All day the sound of fighting was heard on the Clinton road, approaching nearer and nearer. The enemy are reported advancing from Livingston, Clinton, and Raymond. All the ponds have been drained and they must suffer much for water. Loring occupies the right, Walker and French the center, and Breckinridge the left. Our army is desponding but confident of their ability to whip the enemy in the trenches.

July 9, Thursday. Today our cavalry were driven in and infantry pickets were thrown out. The enemy advanced within sight on the Clinton road and threw a few shells within our works. The siege has fairly commenced. The weather is excessively hot and water has to be hauled around our works for the men. We have no shade and have to erect shelter of rails and brush to keep off the intense glare of the sun. Our men are getting sick fast from exposure. The inhabitants have nearly all deserted the town, leaving their furniture and effects exposed, and a wholesale plunder is going on by the soldiers. The Seventh Texas is out on picket today.

July 10, Friday. Last night the enemy erected batteries and cannonaded us occasionally through the day. Several houses in the suburbs have been burned as interfering with the range of our guns and affording shelter for sharpshooters. The enemy attacked Buford's brigade on our extreme right but were completely repulsed.[18] This evening they attacked Breckinridge on the left and were likewise repulsed. They shelled the town venomously. Our wagon trains have been ordered across the river and our rations are sent to us in the trenches. About dark the Seventh Texas pickets were driven and I was ordered to go out with two hundred men and reoccupy the grounds. I posted my picket after dark as well as I could, in total ignorance of the ground, and found no enemy.

July 11, Saturday. At daylight while advancing my posts we were suddenly attacked and almost surprised by the enemy. Some of the men ran back to the breastworks but I made a stand with the rest and finally succeeded in repulsing them. All day they kept up their attacks and would sometimes compel us to fall back a hundred yards, but in every instance we regained our ground except on the right where the situation was so exposed that it was impossible to hold it. I had to send back twice for reinforcements, and was very glad when night came and relieved us. General Gregg sent his compliments and thanks to myself and men for holding the position so stubbornly. We lost three killed and eleven wounded. Returned to the trenches at 8:00 P.M. after spending twenty-four of the most anxious hours of my life. We slept under a rail shelter and were frequently aroused from sleep by the bullets striking the roof.

July 12, Sunday. The enemy's sharpshooters are annoying us very much. Several men have been struck behind the works, among others Lieutenant Colonel Moody of the Seventh Texas and a lieutenant in the Third.[19] Occasional cannonading through the day and night. More houses were burnt and the town looks as though it were sacked.

July 13, Monday. Skirmishing going on all around the line. A constant uneasiness is felt lest the enemy may cross the river and get into our rear, and an evacuation is looked for every night. On the twelfth General Sherman who is in command of the enemy sent in a flag for permission to bury the dead. We get very little news from abroad and all we get is of a discouraging character. Lee's victory at Gettysburg turned out not to be such a victory as we anticipated. His loss was very heavy and he fell back to Hagerstown. Charleston is again attacked and Bragg's army is at Chattanooga. Farewell to our Tennessee homes for a long time to come.

July 14, Tuesday. Sharpshooters still annoying us constantly. A person cannot step out of the trenches without danger. Men are shot every day and every hour. The troops are becoming dispirited and exhausted. This evening Lieutenant Colonel Clack was ordered out with the pickets.[20]

July 15, Wednesday. Today the enemy attacked our pickets and drove them in and advanced quite close to our breastworks. We opened fire upon them and repulsed them and captured several prisoners. Our regiment lost a dozen prisoners taken on picket.

July 16, Thursday. Another uncomfortable day. At dark we received the order to be ready to march at 10:00 P.M. We slowly and silently filed out of the trenches, passed through town, and through the Pearl River swamp, crossed the river by pontoons, and daylight found us far out on the Brandon road. Everything was brought off and the evacuation conducted in perfect order.

July 17, Friday. We had a very hot day and tiresome march, passed through Brandon and encamped three miles east. Many of our men straggled from heat and exhaustion and the rest were worn out and dispirited. We heard the news of the fall of Port Hudson and the repulse of the Yankees at Fort Wagner. Many of our men are reported deserting, especially Mississippians. It is very hard work for those officers who do their whole duty to keep the men from becoming entirely discouraged.

July 18, Saturday. Another very fatiguing march eastward. No news from the enemy. We hear from Tennessee that Rosecrans is endeavoring to cross into east Tennessee and that our portion of the country up to the eleventh of July was free from the enemy. Our spirits rose immediately. We marched through a very heavy rain and knee-deep in water and about ten at night, perfectly exhausted, reached our camp four miles from Morton Station on the Jackson and Meridian railroad.

July 19, Sunday. Rested in camp. Our regiment received two months' pay, being nearly twelve months in arrears.

July 20, Monday. We moved four miles and bivouacked on a small creek near Morton Station. The day was so hot that many of our men gave out even on that short march. We hear that Lee has retreated across the Potomac and again resumed the defensive. No news from the front. There seems to be a prospect of our army resting a few days. General Hardee has arrived and is reported to be about to take command of our army.

July 21, Tuesday. Rested in camp. Our men are evidently in very low spirits but struggle to keep up. They are a noble, brave set of fellows and are suffering much both in mind and body. We do all that we can to encourage them and keep up their spirits. This is indeed a gloomy hour. This evening at 6:00 a Georgian of Wilson's brigade was shot for desertion. I did not witness the execution. It took place in the presence of our whole division. The culprit is said to have met his fate calmly. He was a substitute and his case was an aggravated one.[21]

July 22, Wednesday. Another sultry day. We are encamped by the side of a small branch in a dense thicket of undergrowth with here and there a tall pine. Hills rise on each side thickly wooded and during the heat of the day scarcely a breath of air reaches us. Water is good and our rations are unusually good and plenty. A great number of our men have been poisoned from some species of a noxious vine which grows here very luxuriantly. Their faces and bodies swell until they become very disfigured. Good news from Charleston. The enemy have been repulsed with great loss at Battery Wagner.[22]

July 23, Thursday. Busy all morning writing letters to send home by Mr. Ferguson. There is no mail and we have to depend upon odd chances to send letters. It has been nearly a month since I have received any. We are leading a very lazy life now. A soldier's existence constantly shifts between extreme labor and extreme indolence. One day toiling along through dust and heat until tired nature refuses to take another step and the next reclining under some shady tree lazily smoking a pipe, too indolent to look up at the approach of a comrade. Such is a soldier's life.

July 24, Friday. We have had quite a succession of rainy days. The weather is sultry and I look for malarial fevers soon to begin their work. It is currently reported that General Hardee will take command of our army. The field officers of the Tennessee regiments of our brigade have addressed a communication to General Johnston requesting him, if any troops shall be transferred to Bragg's army, to send our regiments. It is reported that the Yankees have evacuated Jackson and are retiring toward the river, doubtless to make an attack somewhere else. Mobile is the point generally designated. Morgan is returning from his raid into Indiana and Ohio.

Our troops are much discouraged though I cannot call them demoralized. I believe they will fight desperately whenever called upon. Desertions still occasionally occur, even since the execution of the Georgian. They are well clothed and fed, however, and have just received two months' pay, so that they have no real grievance to complain of. We have just heard of a cavalry raid into Giles County in the vicinity of Lynnville. Ferguson started home yesterday but I fear he will be too late to carry our letters through to their destination. My anxiety about the situation of my wife amounts sometimes to torture. If she were in some secure place within our lines I could breathe more freely. I can only trust in God who is the protector of the helpless and persevere in trying to do my duty. Peace and happiness must come at last.

July 25, Saturday. We have received orders to be ready to march at a moment's notice. Our destination is said to be eastward. The enemy have retreated toward Vicksburg and evidently given up the idea of invasion from that direction. Part of their forces are said to be going up the river. Mobile is supposed to be next in danger. A detail has been ordered to be made to return to Tennessee and recruit our thinned regiments. Captain Matthews and myself are the officers from the Third. Our wagon train started this evening for Enterprise. The troops are to go on the cars.

July 26, Sunday. This morning at sunrise we were in motion and marched two miles to the railroad station. About 12:00 the Third and Tenth got on the cars and reached Meridian after dark in the midst of a hard rain. We here changed cars and about midnight reached Enterprise, fifteen miles south of Meridian. We learned by a citizen directly from Giles that the Federal cavalry from Fayetteville had advanced to Pulaski. Huntsville and all points eastward are also occupied.

July 27, Monday. We moved out to our encampment distant a mile from town on the banks of a beautiful creek. Our quarters are in a pine grove. About 2:00 our wagon train arrived, having made almost as good time as the cars. We are in a poor but beautiful country with fine running water.

July 28, Tuesday. We learned today that the rest of the troops on their way hither have been ordered back to their old encampment. The enemy are reported landing at Pascagoula, Mississippi. There are none this side of Big Black. News from Tennessee is terrible. The enemy are desolating our homes, leaving our families to starve. God reward them for their evil deeds. How long shall we suffer the yoke of tyranny? Lee has reoccupied his old position behind the Rappahannock. I received a letter by Mr. Mitchell but it was dated July 2 and contained no news of the Federal occupation.

July 29, Wednesday. There are no troops at Enterprise except our brigade and some conscripts and we are all pleased with our camp. No further news from abroad. Johnston is at Mobile and Hardee at Morton. It will be a month before the Vicksburg paroled prisoners can be exchanged and reorganized. They are now scattered all over Mississippi and Alabama.

July 30, Thursday. An order has been made known to the brigade that one enlisted man out of every twenty-five and one company officer out of three will be furloughed home for fourteen days. My chance of going is very much lessened, indeed is almost hopeless. Another disaster in Virginia—a brigade cut to pieces at Manassas Gap. Verily the evil days are upon us—defeat after defeat follows in quick succession. Morgan's command in Ohio seems to be perfectly scattered.

July is nearly over. It has indeed been a month of disaster to us. Last year it was a month of success. If August continues to be as much our enemy as July our cause will be at a low ebb when autumn sets in. We have met with disaster everywhere from the banks of the Great River to the shores of the ocean. Port Gibson, Raymond, Baker's Creek, Vicksburg, Port Hudson, Jackson, Helena in the West, and Gettysburg in the East and Tullahoma in the center, all disastrous. It is true, Charleston still holds out, but our faith has grown so weak that we would not be surprised to hear of its fall at any moment. Mobile only awaits a vigorous attack to succumb. Rosecrans is pressing Bragg in Tennessee and Lee seems with difficulty to sustain himself behind the Rappahannock, even with all the prestige of two years of victory. Abroad the European powers seem as indifferent as ever, apparently well pleased to see Americans exhausting and ruining each other and liberty depreciated and destroyed in its native home. Our homes are desolated by the hands of tyrants and soon will be homes no longer. Our families are insulted, robbed, oppressed, and driven out in penury to seek shelter in the woods. How long, oh God, how long wilt Thou suffer such tyranny upon the earth? We have deserved all we have suffered but spare the rod of Thy anger before we are utterly destroyed. Chasten us, but do not entirely destroy us. I hope our misfortunes will not harden our hearts.

July 31, Friday. No news today but an extraordinary stir in camp arising from the new furlough order just promulgated. The privates of each company drew lots to see which should reap the benefit of the order. Officers were also busy settling with each other who should go and who remain in camp. My only hope of going is to be detailed to Tennessee to collect men. I have still hopes of seeing home on that business. I wrote home yesterday by Mr. Mitchell. Even if I do not succeed in going I can write again by some person on furlough. So long as I can write and receive letters I can bear separation from home with fortitude but should all means of communication be cut off I fear my fortitude would soon give away. I have no hopes of a speedy redemption of Tennessee, scarcely before the close of the war, which may be years in the future.

Last year at this time the doors of our prison house were opened widely enough for us to see deliverance approaching us afar off in the shape of exchange. Our spirits were elated at the idea of returning to our young, victorious Confederacy, but now all is changed. We are free, it is true, but the elastic step of hope has been exchanged for the slow tread of doubt and despondency. We still have courage and resolution left but we are fighting more because we know our cause to be just than because we are sanguine of success.

August 1, Saturday. Another month has commenced by bringing news of fresh disaster. Morgan has been captured at New Lisbon, Ohio—a disaster not unforeseen nor unexpected by us. In Virginia the opposing hosts seem to be gathering on the upper Rappahannock and in the valley of the Shenandoah and among the passes of the Blue Ridge. Grant has not yet superseded Meade but it is supposed that he soon will. The hero of Vicksburg will endeavor to become the hero of Richmond and to lay the fame of McClellan in the shade. Donelson and Vicksburg have already obliterated the disaster of Shiloh in the minds of the Northern public and a victory in Virginia would render Grant the idol of the populace and the soldiery. Our government is straining every nerve to recruit its armies, with what success time will show. All the fighting population of the Confederacy have been called to the field. The spirit of our soldiery is resolute and determined, yet scarcely hopeful. The spirit of the large property holders in the cotton states is broken. They would gladly accept peace on any terms which would guarantee them even a partial protection of the estates. The middle classes are still as determined as ever and nothing but a series of crushing defeats will subjugate them. The sky becomes darker and darker—not even a small or partial success to relieve the gloom of successive defeats.

August 2, Sunday. Last night we had a violent rain and the whole camp was flooded with water. We had to sit up and the water came into our tent and covered the whole floor. Today was spent in drying our clothes and blankets.

August 3, Monday. Our regiment was on guard today and for the first time since our arrival in camp, I went over to Enterprise. There is a small conscript camp near this place where the Mississippi conscripts are assembled. No news of any importance yet. Lee and Meade are confronting each other on the Rappahannock. Our forces are evacuating the valley. The bombardment of Charleston still goes on without effect. Nothing is doing in the West. The Yankees are confined to the river and seem to be doing nothing.

August 6, Tuesday. Evans' brigade went down the road yesterday on their way eastward and other troops are said to be ordered from Morton to the east.[23] We hear that the Yankees have left our county, after stealing a few Negro men and many horses and mules. Meade is reported as having crossed the upper Rappahannock to Culpeper. The enemy seem to be making no headway at Charleston. The whole North is in a ferment on account of the attempted enforcement of the draft. In many places it is meeting with forcible resistance and most of the drafted men are purchasing exemption.

We have been long enough in our present bivouac to feel at home and to know something about the country around us. There are but three tents in the regiment, ours, the doctor's and the commissary's. Ours is rather a forlorn and tattered concern and the rain does not pay much respect to it. We have it well ditched and thrown up as the level of our camp is under high-water mark as we discovered the other night. A tall pine stands directly in front, the shade of which answers very well for an antechamber. Under this tree stands a box with a chessboard on top, around which is an almost constant group from morning till night. The interior of the tent contains a strange mixture of valises, carpetbags, saddlebags, blankets, and bundles of dirty clothes. A basket of peaches or apples and a watermelon or two adorns one corner. Over a pole hang various coats and nondescript articles. The soldiers live under shelters built of pine poles and covered with pine leaves and some improvise a tent by stretching a blanket over a pole. In daylight you can see hundreds of loungers lying about in the shade and as soon as night comes each man crawls into his den, in none of which it is possible to stand upright. Watermelon and peach wagons and Indian squaws are the great subjects of attraction throughout the day, and to the soldier night and sleep come together.

August 8, *Saturday.* Still lounging in camp, getting lazy and fat. Every day we listen for news, hoping that something favorable will turn up but it has not "turned up" yet. Everything is quiet in every quarter. The president has issued an address to the soldiers. In Tennessee, Rosecrans is massing his forces on his left wing and withdrawing from north Alabama. On the first of August, Fayetteville was his most advanced post southward and from the most recent advices he seems to be evacuating that place and Shelbyville and moving his army toward McMinnville.

After a month's suspense I received a letter from home dated July 31 by Mr. Trentham. All is well and our county has come out much better than I expected from the Yankee raid. General Johnston has ordered one officer from each brigade to be sent to collect stragglers and deserters and yesterday General Gregg promised to send up my name. I expect an answer in the course of a week. I consider my chance of going home as better than ever, although I do not build much upon it yet. Trentham and Scruggs arrived here on the seventh and will remain until the middle of next week and perhaps I may return with them. We are daily looking for a desperate battle in Virginia. If Lee is defeated our affairs will look gloomy indeed. If Meade is badly whipped the courage and war spirit of the Confederacy will be up as high as it ever was.

August 11, Tuesday. Yesterday the furloughs for the men and officers of our regiment were returned approved and today they are beginning to start home. The quartermaster is engaged in paying off the regiment up to the first of July and everything is in a stir. Trentham and Scruggs started home this evening and I have hopes of being ordered to follow them in the course of a week. Stealing seems to be the order of the day now and not a night passes without either money or provisions being stolen in the brigade. It has become such an intolerable nuisance that it will be necessary to organize a secret police before the rogues can be arrested. They have stolen our flour and General Gregg's bacon and indeed have stolen everything that was left exposed. The morals of our men have become fearfully deteriorated in the last six months, owing to the inattention and even to the example of some of the officers. Discipline is very lax and something must be done or inefficiency will surely follow. Many of our officers seem to think because the regiment has gained so much credit for its fighting qualities that there is no use trying to keep up its former state of drill and discipline. It would be very easy to keep it up as our men all know their duties and are sensible of the importance of discharging them. Even our privates are well posted in military affairs and it is sometimes amusing to hear them criticizing the movements of our ablest generals.

August 13, Thursday. Last night five of Captain Matthews' men deserted. One of them was mutinous before his departure and was put under guard but made his escape, carrying the others with him. Captain Matthews started about an hour behind them with six men in pursuit. Last night a courier started for Morton and my name was sent up as the officer detailed from the brigade to Tennessee to collect stragglers. If this business is done as slowly as usual I may look for the order and instructions about the twenty-first, or in nine days. There is a great deal of desertion going on among the Tennessee regiments of Maxey's brigade, which is encamped two miles from us. Still no news of any importance. . . .

August 14, Friday. There is a continued succession of hot days and it has been long enough since we have had a cool breeze in daytime. The latter part of the night is tolerably cool, bed covering is very pleasant after midnight. Sickness in camp is slowly increasing. In a week I hope to be on the way home. No news of any importance afloat.

August 15, Saturday. Last night it turned a little cooler but today is as warm as ever. An ominous calm pervades the whole country. In the West positively nothing is stirring. Banks' short-term troops are being discharged and the Federal army of the Mississippi is rapidly wasting away by discharges and disease. No reinforcements are reaching it except a few regiments of Negroes which are being organized. Our people are reoccupying western Mississippi and repairing the railroads from Jackson to Grenada. In Tennessee everything is quiet. The Yankees are reported as reinforcing Corinth. Rosecrans is occupying the first plateau of the Cumberland Mountains. Meade and Lee are watching each other on the Rappahannock. The siege of Charleston proceeds slowly and apparently the enemy make no progress toward its reduction.

August 16, Sunday. My prospects of going home seem somewhat less than they have been. Lieutenant Colonel Beaumont of the Fiftieth Tennessee has gone to Tennessee to collect stragglers and that may prevent my application from being successful, though I have scarcely had time to get an answer from headquarters. When I heard of it last night I was very much vexed and imagined that Captain Hall, the general's adjutant, had tricked me out of it. He is a strong personal friend of Beaumont's. If he has, he shall hear of it. In three more days my permit will come if it will come at all.

August 17, Monday. We had quite a rain yesterday evening and last night and the weather is much cooler. There is quite a revival in our brigade, which has been going on for a week. There is preaching every night in town and the church is constantly crowded. Last night Colonel Clack started to Mobile and will be absent probably a week. I have not heard from my case but expect an answer in two days if an answer ever comes. We hear that Rosecrans is at Cumberland Mountain and that there are no Yankees in our region of country since the raid of July. It is said that our cavalry are crossing the Tennessee at Bainbridge.

August 19, Wednesday. We have rain nearly every day and our camp is so narrow and confined that it has become quite filthy and I fear will soon become unhealthy. There is a general stagnation of news from every quarter. Corinth is reinforced and the enemy are making raids into north Mississippi. No answer yet from my application. If I do not get one today I will apply for a furlough.

August 21, Friday. News of a Yankee raid in north Mississippi in which all our rolling stock at Grenada was destroyed and Chalmers defeated. My application has come back disapproved and yesterday I sent up a simple application for leave of absence for twenty days. I have but little hope of its success but if that fails I will find some other way of getting home and will not rest till I accomplish it.

left Port Hudson	May 2, 1863
left Jackson, Mississippi	May 11, 1863
battle of Raymond	May 12, 1863
arrived at Yazoo City	May 31, 1863
left Vernon, Mississippi	July 1, 1863
siege of Jackson commenced	July 8, 1863
evacuation of Jackson	July 16, 1863
arrived at Enterprise	July 27, 1863

August 24, Monday. Everything is still quiet. Fort Sumter has been reduced to ruins by the Yankee guns and it is the general opinion that Charleston will fall after a while. Some of our troops at Morton have been ordered eastward and are now at Meridian, destined it is reported to Chattanooga. They belong to Walker's division. No return yet from my application. I am expecting it to-day or tomorrow but my hopes of success are by no means sanguine. General Pillow has applied for three officers and three sergeants from each regiment to be placed on the recruiting service and Colonel Walker offers to send up my name. If my furlough does not comes back approved I shall probably be placed on the list.

6 | Georgia

December 3, 1863–March 28, 1864

DALTON. INSPECTOR ON GENERAL BROWN'S STAFF. GLOOMY NEW
YEAR. NEW REGULATIONS FOR THE ARMY. INSPECTION BY GEN-
ERAL JOHNSTON. SUDDEN MOVE TO KINGSTON AND THENCE TO
ROME. THE FLUX. WE PROCEED TO DALTON. NEAR TUNNEL HILL.
LIEUTENANT GENERAL HOOD TAKES COMMAND. FIRST MAIL SINCE
NOVEMBER 13. A SNOWBALL FIGHT. RELIGIOUS REVIVAL IN THE
BRIGADE. RETURN TO DUTY.

Thursday, December 3, 1863. I again commence another volume
of my diary. The last one was commenced at Enterprise, Mississippi, last August.[1] Since then how many changes have taken
place! I have once more looked upon the face of her whom I love
best on earth. I have again encountered danger on the battlefield
and perils by the wayside but the providence of God has brought
me safely through all. Victory has again perched upon our ban-
ners and disaster has again trailed them in the dust. We are lying
still at Dalton, Georgia, refreshing ourselves after another retreat. . . . Desertions are frequent and a gloom rests upon the
whole army. Lee and Meade are again confronting each other on
the Rappahannock. Every account from home confirms the tales
of desolation and insult and robbery inflicted upon our once
happy and prosperous middle Tennessee. Truly we have much to
bear. May God give us strength and courage to bear it. How long,
oh how long, shall we suffer? Is there no end? Oh God! Our cause
must succeed but after how much suffering? But if we would enjoy liberty we must pay the price, be it great or small.[2]

December 7, Monday. Longstreet is retreating toward Virginia
and Burnside is now at liberty to cooperate with Grant. Our army
is encamped in the vicinity of Dalton and Tunnel Hill but I think

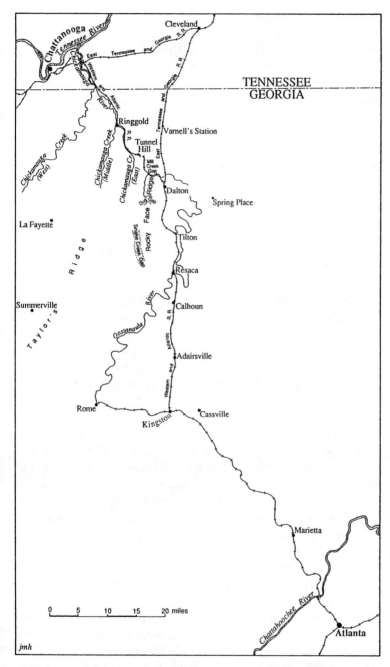

The Atlanta campaign

we will eventually fall back still farther. The Yankees have evacuated all west Tennessee and Mississippi except a few military posts at Natchez, Vicksburg, and Memphis. Corinth is said to be free from the enemy now. From home we learn that they are repairing the railroad from Columbia to Decatur and every soldier they have in the West is concentrated at Chattanooga. This is the only army we have to fear. Meade has fallen back from the Rapidan. They are weak everywhere except right here and all we have to do is hold our own a little longer and the backbone of the invasion will be broken.

December 10, Thursday. There are reports from Tennessee of still more and greater ravages committed in Giles County. General Gregg, our old brigadier, is in town and complaining bitterly that his old brigade has been broken up. He is trying to get it up again.

December 17, Thursday. Ever since last Saturday, I have been staying in the country two miles from Dalton trying to get well of the jaundice, but thus far with indifferent success. Mrs. Tillman, my landlady, is an incorrigible wretch, feeds badly, and charges enormously. Captain Rhea is with me and Dr. Bowers' quarters are nearby. Everything seems to indicate that the campaign is over here for the winter. . . .

December 24, Thursday. I am again in camp entirely recovered. Our troops have gone into winter quarters and are building comfortable cabins. Our mess is living in a tent with a chimney. We have had [illegible] excessively cold weather but have managed to keep comfortable. Christmas is near at hand—how different from the Christmas of peaceful times. I think there will be no fighting this winter to break the monotony of camp life. No news from family. . . .

December 27, Sunday. A dreary, rainy, desolate day. . . . News from home informs us that General Dodge has made his headquarters in Giles County and is desolating the whole county.[3]

December 28, Monday. The rain has ceased but the sky is still gloomy and threatening. An order has been issued granting furloughs throughout the winter to one enlisted man out of every thirty; to one company officer out of every three; and to one field and staff officer when all are present. It is Colonel Clack's turn this time. Colonel Walker is absent at Cassville with his wife but will return in a few days. Our mess are fixing up for winter quarters. We have a very snug tent with a good chimney but it is too small for all of us, and Adjutant Martin and I have determined to hive out. Our stable is finished and our horses are comfortable at last. We expect to begin our house so soon as the ground dries a little. No news. Joe Johnston has not arrived yet but is daily expected. An attempt has been made to send our regiment to Atlanta on provost guard duty but it seems to have failed through the influence of General Brown. Nothing from home lately.

December 29, Tuesday. A beautiful winter morning.

December 31, Thursday. The last day of the year. Yesterday I commenced my duties as inspector on General Brown's staff. My appointment is only temporary and will continue only till Captain Lowe's return. The year closes in gloom although it opened so brightly. Then the enemy were repulsed at every point and held in check—now they are jubilant and as determined as ever. Virginia is the only place where [we] have held our own. In that state they have not gained a foot of soil this year. But they have overrun Tennessee and Arkansas, driven us from the Mississippi River, and gained a foothold in Texas. All we can do is to fight on and hope and pray for better times next year. Submission has been made impossible by the conduct of our insolent foe; and the only tolerable alternative left us is resistance to the bitter end. We must fight, we can do nothing else, if necessary forever.

January 3, 1864, Sunday. On Friday morning the weather turned bitter cold and in the evening our brigade was ordered to move down toward Resaca to work on the road. A little before night we reached the point indicated, Dr. Sullivan's, five miles from camp. Colonel Searcy was in command of the brigade.4 The men were encamped in the woods and I procured a room in the house for Colonel Searcy and his staff. It was a bitter cold night but the men kept off the cold by building great log heaps. About nine o'clock Lieutenant Colonel Butler who stayed in our room sent out for his fiddler and there being four young ladies in the house Butler, Searcy, and some of the lively members of the staff got up a dance and kept it up till the small hours.5 In the midst of the excitement I laid down on the bed in the ballroom and slept soundly till morning. The cold was still so severe that we could do no work and about noon we were ordered back to camp as the weather was too severe. Last night we had another freezing time of it, almost the coldest weather I ever felt. General Brown sent for his staff to meet him at dark. We found there plenty of eggnog and several guests among whom was General Reynolds and his quartermaster, McCormick.[6] Several of the party imbibed too much whiskey in the course of the evening. We had an excellent stringed band composed mostly of officers of the Forty-Fifth Tennessee.

The New Year has opened gloomy enough for our cause but yet I cannot feel despondent. Hope still dwells securely in my breast and I believe would still exist there even if our affairs should become still more desperate. Thank God that He has made me of a sanguine temperament, otherwise I should have suffered unendurable miseries.

January 4, Monday. The weather has abated and it has drizzled rain all day . . .

Tonight I went over to General Brown's quarters and met Lieutenant Colonel Rogers, my old partner at Giles College. We went up to the general's room and had a social chat till bedtime. Both Brown and Rogers seem despondent, far too much so, I think, about our affairs. It is the duty of every patriot to cultivate a hopeful spirit and he who lets fall desponding expressions is really injuring our cause. Confidence and hope alone will add much to the strength of an army.

January 7, Thursday. The weather for the last two days has been excessively cold. On Tuesday we had a brigade inspection and I was kept very busy all day but laid down to sleep at night better satisfied than I had been idle, as I usually am when on regimental duty. The major of a regiment when all field officers are present and the regiment is stationed in quarters has next to nothing at all to do. I am not very fond of work but I am very thankful General Brown has given me something to do as it keeps my mind from brooding over unpleasant things. I don't believe a man can be virtuous or happy without having most of his time occupied in some kind of business and I prefer some pursuit in which I can be useful to my country to passing my hours in making pipes or rings or in playing cards or chess—although I regard them as very harmless amusement. Rose this morning earlier than usual.

January 8, Friday. This morning bright, clear, and cold. The ground covered with frozen rain. Yesterday I was very busy examining muster and payrolls and another day's work of the same kind lies before me. This has been quite a busy week with me. Lieutenant Jones has started to Courtland and promised to use his endeavors to send a letter home for me . . .

January 9, Saturday. The weather still excessively cold. Last night I could scarcely keep warm. This winter bids fair to be a very severe one. The enemy are reported to be building a bridge over Chickamauga at Red House Ford. Their forces in Knoxville are suffering for want of provisions. Congress is debating the currency question and the repeal of the laws allowing exemptions. The whole press of the country is violently opposed to the universal conscription as in that case many editors and printers would be forced into the ranks. I hope their clamor will not terrify Congress out of that measure. We ought by passage of these measures to bring one hundred thousand fresh men into the field next spring. There is a whisper passing round now that we may soon send an expedition against Knoxville to cooperate with Longstreet.

January 10, Sunday. Weather still very cold, the coldest that has been known in these parts for a generation. There is almost a dearth of news in the papers. Nothing of importance going on in the field. The Congresses of both republics are talking a great deal and doing very little. Our Congress is engaged on the bill repealing exemptions and on the currency questions. John Morgan has reached Richmond and issued an address calling his old soldiers into the field to rendezvous at Decatur, Georgia. The Yankees are busy conscripting our men who remain within their lines in Tennessee and Virginia. It really seems that Lincoln is struck with judicial blindness for he could adopt no measure which will more effectually stop desertion from our army than that one. Many men would willingly leave our army if they could live in peace at home even under Yankee rule but they are not yet prepared to put on Yankee uniform and serve against us.

January 11, Monday. Weather still freezing this morning. I have scarcely ever seen such continuous cold weather since I have been a resident of the South. Our soldiers all have warm cabins, however, and are not suffering at all, though they have very few blankets or clothes. A veteran will soon make himself entirely comfortable if he is furnished with an axe and set down in the woods. Many are nearly barefooted and could not march over the frozen ground at all and if they had to bivouac there would be much suffering. Still there is but little complaint and fewer murmurs than when we were all well provided at Bowling Green. They have learned to endure privations, to laugh at suffering, and to regard hardships as their natural lot. But off, as they are, from home, they consider themselves as "in for the war," and not knowing how long the war shall last they enjoy each day as it passes, "having no thought for the morrow."

January 12, Tuesday. Last night the ground was frozen but this morning is damp and drizzling. The severity of the cold has abated. I have found my place no sinecure since I have been on General Brown's staff. One day each week is devoted to general inspection of men, arms, accouterments, camps, papers, mules, wagons, and stables, and a very hard day's work it is. Last inspection day I wore the skin off my fingers examining guns. Besides this I am required to inspect the stables, transportation, and camps once a week myself. Then I have all the muster and payrolls of the brigade to examine, more than two hundred in number, and to correct countless errors and omissions. Once in three days I have to see to the posting of the picket guard and every day other odd ends of business turn up to my share. Finally I have to make out monthly a voluminous inspection report of everything.

January 13, Wednesday. The weather continues soft and the roads are beginning to become muddy. Captain Lowe, General Brown's inspector, returned to camp last night and I suppose I shall soon be relieved of duty on the staff. Our camp now presents a singular aspect. The cabins are built very irregularly and if the encampments were extensive enough a person would lose himself in the narrow and tortuous streets. It reminds me of what I have heard of the suburbs of towns on the continent of Europe and it is not as cleanly as it ought to be. From four to six men occupy each cabin, which contains a chimney, a door closed by an oilcloth, or rather open always, no window, a straw bed, and guns sitting up in the corner. There is not much variety in architecture; one cabin is just like another, except in point of cleanliness, and those men who have lived in clean houses at home are not always the most cleanly in camp.

January 15, Friday. The weather has become quite mild and I hope the vigor of winter is over. Yesterday Adjutant Martin and myself moved into our new quarters. We have a very comfortable tent with a chimney and a bed of broom sedge, much more comfortable than our old quarters which were overcrowded. Colonel Walker is left by himself since Colonel Clack has gone to Alabama. I have now a quiet place to read or write. A crowd always did annoy me and even in the army I never could become accustomed to it. This morning finished reading *Silas Marner* by Miss Evans of London. Read it not because I liked it but because I had nothing else to read. Captain Lowe, General Brown's inspector, has returned, but the general requests me to remain on duty a few days longer until Captain Lowe has entirely recovered from his wound. I am now engaged on road building.

January 19, Tuesday. A few days ago I received a letter from my sister Sarah, sent through the lines at City Point by flag of truce. All were well at my old boyhood home. I am much rejoiced that I can hear from some of those that I hold dear. Not a word from home for more than two months. My anxiety would almost kill me, were it not that I see around me hundreds of others who are in the same condition and who bear their misfortunes and their privations so heroically that I am compelled to do the same for very shame. . . .

January 20, Wednesday. A slight snow fell yesterday morning but melted soon after sunrise. The weather is now very fine but the roads bad. No news of any kind from the field. A few days ago our regiment agreed to reenlist for the war upon condition that they should be permitted to reorganize, if Congress should extend that privilege to the rest of the army. The Thirty-Second Tennessee followed suit next day. Vaughn's Tennessee brigade had previously agreed to the same terms and from the newspapers I see that Strahl's Tennessee brigade have also offered their services.[7] It is a great gratification to Tennesseans to see our troops taking the initiative in this important matter. Much anxiety has been felt both in the army and country about the reenlistment of troops for the war, whose three years' term of service will expire next spring. A large majority of the men wish reorganization and a majority of officers do not. A very natural state of things.

January 21, Thursday. Today a new era commences in this army. A series of new orders have been issued for the discipline of the army, which brings everything up to the army regulations, and are more stringent than ever have yet been enforced. If these orders are faithfully carried out they will reinvigorate our somewhat demoralized troops and give a brighter aspect to our gloomy prospects. I do not now think that our army will be reorganized by the election of new officers but that the same organization will be preserved, though the men are clamorous for that privilege. The higher officers of the army are decidedly opposed to it. Our regiment is still on guard duty in town. The Third, Thirty-Second, Twenty-Sixth, and Newman's battalion have mostly agreed to enlist for the war. Most of the Eighteenth and Forty-Fifth have refused and I suppose prefer being conscripted when the time comes.

January 22, Friday. The weather has become very mild and pleasant. The regiment is still in town. Today General Joseph E. Johnston inspected our brigade. Our camp is cleaned up, regular guard lines and regulations established, and everything is being put in good order. No news from abroad today. Parson Deavenport, our chaplain who went home from Port Hudson, Louisiana, has returned to camp and brings doleful news from Giles County. General Dodge's command are still there and are stripping the country of everything. He says the people are as firm and hopeful as ever and still believe in our ultimate success. They bear poverty quietly and meekly and look to the army for deliverance. How long shall they suffer, oh God? Stretch forth Thine arm and spare them. I could cheerfully serve ten years in the army if I only knew that she who is dearer to me than life was secure and happy.

January 23, Saturday. Weather mild and beautiful. Went to town this evening and dined with our mess in Colonel Walker's room in the courthouse. Mrs. Walker, who is now staying in Dalton, honored us with her company at dinner. We had cornbread, biscuits, coffee, and two kinds of sugar spread out on a bench. Rough was the cook. The same room served for kitchen, drawing room, and dining room, and bedchamber. Part of our regiment is quartered in the courthouse and part in some vacant private houses. Their guard duty is very severe, the men being on every other day. Received a letter from my mother dated December 31. She had received a letter from my wife dated November 20, a week later than the last one I have received. The flag-of-truce authorities are very liberal to allow a letter to pass through the lines directed to an officer in the Rebel army.

January 24, Sunday. Another beautiful day. The regiment will probably remain in town on guard duty all week. . . .

January 25, Monday. Day beautiful as ever. Rumors are abroad that the enemy are advancing in force toward Ringgold and Rome but I do not credit it. Most of our cavalry are below Rome on our left flank. The Yankees are working on the railroad from Bridge-port to Chattanooga, and from Chattanooga to Knoxville our army and our people are recovering from the depression which weighed them down at the close of last year. Both sides are strengthening themselves for the terrible struggle in the spring, the struggle which both sides agree will finish the war. Three years of unceasing warfare have pretty well exhausted both parties. Men are difficult to procure to fill up the wasted armies; enthusiasm has entirely subsided North and South, and dogged determination alone remains. I feel very sanguine that this is the last year of the war.

January 26, Tuesday. Weather fine. Yesterday the regiment returned to camp from Dalton and the day was mostly spent in cleaning up the camp and grounds. We have not commenced drilling yet. This morning a Yankee flag of truce made its appearance at our picket lines half a mile from camp. It had come all the way from LaFayette without meeting a single Confederate soldier until it reached our picket lines. Certainly our front is not well guarded. The enemy made a dash into Summerville, Georgia, and captured a few home guards. . . .

January 28, Thursday. Weather still fine. The newspapers have nearly ceased croaking and the tone of public opinion is far more hopeful than it was a month ago. I don't believe our good people of the Confederacy have faith enough to make them sanguine. I wish they had a little of Yankees hopefulness without Yankee credulity. Our nation has been almost ruined once or twice from want of faith and hope. If the Yankees had ever been half so much depressed by their defeats in Virginia as we have been by a single defeat, and only a partial one at that, the war would have ceased long ago. I really think that we ought to cultivate a hopeful national spirit. At the commencement of the war we were unreasonably boastful, even more so than the Yankees; that spirit has entirely disappeared and an equally unreasonable depression has taken its place.

January 30, Saturday. It rained a little last night but this morning was very pleasant. On the night of the twenty-eighth we were ordered to be ready to march at a moment's warning. The enemy attacked Cleburne's pickets near Tunnel Hill but were repulsed.[8] Yesterday everything was quiet. We had a review of Hardee's corps by General Johnston. The troops looked well and in fine spirits. Some citizens who had been sent through the lines from Nashville recently were very much surprised at our appearance, they having heard that we were ragged, dirty, and half starved. From all accounts the garrison of Chattanooga is more nearly starved than we are. The Yankees are reported as having ten thousand men there and the rest of their army in east Tennessee and north Alabama. This is my thirty-fourth birthday. Last one was spent quietly in Port Hudson; the one before at Russellville, Kentucky, and the one before in peaceful avocations.

February 1, Monday. Rained last night—this morning bright and beautiful. Yesterday we had an excellent sermon from our Chaplain Deavenport. This morning our regiment was paraded and Colonel Clack addressed them on the subject of reenlistment for the war. Nearly the whole regiment manifest their willingness to reenlist but nearly all have a strong desire to reorganize and elect officers over again. General Johnston offers a furlough to one out of every ten men who agree to reenlist. A few days ago I heard that nearly all the Negroes in our neighborhood had gone to the Yankees and that at home there were only a few left. This is no more than I have expected for some time and I am not at all surprised. Yesterday I received a letter from Mrs. Tarpley, at whose house I was sick while near Mound Bluff, Mississippi. She now lives in Columbus, Georgia, and seems as kind as ever. I am getting very anxious to get a letter from home.

February 2, Tuesday. Weather fine; inspection this morning by the brigadier general. Inspections and reviews are quite numerous now and this fact taken with several others, such as the cutting down of transportation, the delivery of stores by the regimental quartermasters to the division quartermaster, all indicate I think a speedy move and that forwards. Yesterday our regiment legally offered their services for the war; comparatively few refused. One furlough is granted for every ten men reenlisted for the war. Colonel Clack made a very telling speech to the regiment on the subject. Last night nearly the whole brigade went over to General Brown's and called him out for a speech. He and Colonel Clack and General Deas all spoke and the crowd dispersed in high good humor and with much enthusiasm.⁹ The state of feeling among Tennessee troops is excellent now, better than it has been since the commencement of the war. The old war spirit seems revived in full vigor.

February 3, Wednesday. Weather turned cold last night and to-day is bright and boisterous. The newspapers have changed their tone very much since the first of the year. Then all was despondency and gloom and at the North all was exultation and joy, now although nothing of importance has happened to change the military position, public sentiment on both sides has undergone a change. Here hope has revived and union and firmness has made its influence thoroughly felt. There a doubt has begun to spring up, more from seeing our resolution than from any other cause. Some Northern papers are beginning to speak out and to declare their belief that the South can never be subjugated and they attribute it to the false policy of the president. They profess to believe that the Union could have been restored if conciliatory measures had been employed but they seem to despair of the Union now.

February 5, Friday. Weather still fine. A grand review took place today of the whole army. The troops were drawn up in three lines extending I know not how far, as one end was out of sight.

The general rode along the lines and the army then passed in review before him. They made a very fine appearance, especially the Tennesseans and Kentuckians, all well clothed except shoes, and looking healthy and contented. The news today is encouraging. The reenlistment of our army still goes bravely on and the men are more hopeful and better contented than I have ever seen them since our return from prison. All seem to hope that Tennessee will soon be redeemed and they feel quite confident that our army can whip Grant. If the newspapers tell the truth, the Yankees are very backward about reenlisting for the war, in spite of the great bounties offered them. Our men have gone in without hope of fee or reward.

February 6, Saturday. Last night after dark we were astounded by an order for our brigade to be ready to move at a moment's notice. At 9:00 P.M. we received orders to be at the depot by eleven o'clock, leaving our wagons and baggage behind. We got on the cars about midnight and by daylight this morning we found ourselves at Kingston. We lay over at that place until about noon when we took the cars for Rome at which place we arrived at 3:00 P.M. Before night the other regiments were encamped a short distance from town and the Third was placed in quarters in some storehouses in town. We secured an office for our headquarters—three good ones, one for office, one for kitchen, and a sort of antechamber. We enjoyed our fine quarters hugely, as we expected to have lain on the cold, wet ground. We had a good bed to sleep on, although of course it was on the floor.

February 8, Monday. Weather has become very fine again. I hope the rigor of winter is over. We are having a very pleasant time in Rome. Our men are all quartered in comfortable places and we have an excellent room for headquarters. We expect every day to be sent out of town, however. The rest of the brigade is about a mile off across the river. No enemy reported nearer than the Tennessee River. A considerable force is on this side the river at Guntersville and Larkins' Ferry and a movement in this direction is anticipated, but I do not think such a move will be made before spring. We are living much more abundantly than at Dalton. Provisions are cheaper and much more abundant. The town though thinned in population has yet many respectable inhabitants left in it and is not like Dalton, utterly deserted by all except the most worthless population.

February 12, Friday. Weather delightful. We are being repaid for the cold days of New Year's. We are still snugly quartered in our pleasant barracks, but expecting every day an order to go into the country and take the cold ground instead of the hard floor. The other regiments of the brigade seem to be quite jealous of our quarters in town and we shall have to move perhaps today. There is no enemy in our front nearer than Tennessee River. Longstreet is still advancing southward and it is reported that the Yankees have evacuated Knoxville and are falling back toward Chattanooga. Every report from middle Tennessee is encouraging. The enemy's force is much weakened by furloughs granted to men reenlisted for the war. Dr. Conwell from Elkton reached here a few days ago but brought me no letter nor word from home. I was considerably provoked at not getting a letter.

February 14, Sunday. Weather threatens rain. Yesterday we had brigade review. Everything is quiet in Rome. It is reported that General Johnston is preparing for an advance. General Cleburne's and Walker's divisions have been sent forward, one toward Ringgold and the other toward Cleveland, and the pontoons have been sent forward to Dalton. . . .

February 19, Friday. The weather is still quite cold. I had quite an adventure the other day. A secret police detective named Joseph Hall came into our quarters partially drunk and made some insulting remarks about our regiment. I ordered him out and as he was rather slow about going, had him arrested and sent to the provost marshal. Next morning he sent me a written challenge. I sent Colonel Walker to make some inquiries about his standing, but receiving a rather unfavorable report took no notice of it. The affair seems to have got wind, however, and our men could hardly be restrained from taking him out and ducking him in the river. I have kept them quiet so far but have heard nothing further from my challenger. . . .

February 21, Sunday. Weather still cold. . . .

February 25, Thursday. I have gradually been becoming worse with the flux, and this morning I feel very much like going to bed. . . . Two of our regiments, the Eighteenth and Twenty-Sixth, left here yesterday for Calhoun, and we expect an order to move every hour. I fear the Yankees have outgeneraled Old Joe in inducing him to weaken his army here. We look for stirring times very soon in this department. General Roddey's cavalry is said to be near this place.[10] We shall likely remain in Rome so long as Johnston is above Kingston.

February 26, Friday. Yesterday evening we were all surprised by a sudden order to proceed to Dalton. The enemy were reported advancing from Tunnel Hill in strong force upon that place. We took the cars last night and this morning at daylight the Third and two companies of the Forty-Fifth found themselves at Dalton. The rest of the brigade with the general were behind. We marched out to a gap in the mountain in front of our old camp and were placed in Polk's brigade, Cleburne's division. We learned here that the enemy had been driven back from the mountain toward Tunnel Hill. We bivouacked on the side of the mountain. Most of our blankets and all our baggage had been left in town and the night was cold, so that our chances of sleep were rather doubtful. The cold wind sweeps down the side of the mountain and makes us shiver.

February 27, Saturday. This morning we all rose very early; indeed men are generally very early risers when they bivouac in the woods in cold weather. About ten o'clock we were ordered (that is, Polk's brigade) to hold a gap in the mountain farther to the right. Before we reached our new position an order was received sending us back to our own brigade which had arrived at the front. Late in the evening we took our position in Stevenson's division on the right wing of the army this side of Taylor's Ridge and to the right of Tunnel Hill.[11] A cavalry fight had taken place there two days before, between the two railroads, in which the enemy were repulsed. We bivouacked again in the woods but today our horses had arrived and our stock of bedclothing had been replenished, so that we were now comfortable. The enemy have retired beyond Tunnel Hill.

February 28, Sunday. This morning at sunrise we were ordered back to reoccupy an old camp. The enemy have retired from Ringgold in the direction of Chattanooga and our little campaign seems to be over. The whole movement on the part of General

Thomas was doubtless a reconnaissance in force to discover whether Johnston had sent most of his army to Mississippi to meet Sherman, and if he had to make a real attack and occupy Dalton and perhaps push into Kingston. But he found no one absent from here except Cheatham's division and that we were too strong to be driven from our positions on Taylor's Ridge.[12] This morning found us again in our old quarters. Our mess is again confined to one tent and we had quite a crowded time of it. Our cabins have been left untouched and everything is just as we left it. No news from the front or indeed from any quarter. Cheatham's troops are arriving constantly and we shall soon have our old army together again. It is reported that Johnston will assemble a large army here to make a forward movement so soon as the season and the state of the roads will admit of it. He has about thirty-six thousand men here. Loring is to come with seven thousand, Longstreet is said to have thirty thousand, and fifteen thousand to come from Beauregard's department, making eighty-eight thousand men. I cannot help thinking this estimate is extravagant, especially in the number of Longstreet's troops, but hope it may be true.

March 1, Tuesday. Spring has again visited us, but with quite a frowning face. According to the old proverb, March will go out like a lamb. The third year of the war is drawing to a close but peace still seems as far off as ever. Last year at this time we were housed in our comfortable quarters at Port Hudson looking for Banks and Farragut. Two years ago we were entering the dreary walls of Camp Chase prison, downcast and almost brokenhearted. Three years ago we were full of life and confidence, preparing for a dissolution of the Union. We have accomplished our object, at any rate, but at a fearful sacrifice of human life and suffering and loss of property. Yet no one can now sincerely believe that the Union can ever be restored. Subjugation is within the limits of possibility, but restoration never.

March 4, Friday. Today we have a grand review. Lieutenant General Hood assumes command of his corps in which our division is placed.[13] I have not been able to do any outdoor duty for some weeks as I have a lingering case of flux, which medicine does not seem to alleviate. . . . The enemy have entirely disappeared from our front and Cheatham's division has returned to Dalton. . . .

March 6, Sunday. The weather is still cool but bright and pleasant. I am not getting along very well with my disease. It is now three weeks since it has commenced troubling me and I fear it is gradually assuming a chronic form and that it will finally compel me to go to the rear for treatment and diet. I have done scarcely any duty for three weeks except work at the colonel's regimental record, which is still far from being complete. Last night I wrote home by Dr. Lewis Freeman who is making an effort to visit home. We have brigade inspection this morning and while I write our camp seems almost deserted. Colonel Walker is absent on a visit to his wife and General Brown has also gone to see his new bride. No signs of any movement of this army for the present, though everybody expects a lively time when the spring opens.

March 7, Monday. Weather cold and unpleasant. No news today. The spirit and confidence of the troops is unimpaired. The whole country seems to be awake to the importance of the struggle for existence which is going on and is straining every energy to furnish soldiers and to supply the armies in the field. The reenlistment of the soldiers in the field first excited the enthusiasm, which spread from the army to the citizens throughout the whole country. An hour of deep depression had just preceded this uprising and had infected not only the citizens and soldiers but even our generals of the highest rank. Some of the latter had become so demoralized that they began to lose confidence in the soldiers and believed that they would leave the army when their term of service expired, and they began to look around for desperate means to save the republic.

March 8, Tuesday. We had quite a hailstorm yesterday and a shower of rain last night, but today is bright and cool. . . .

March 9, Wednesday. The weather is quite springlike and active operations must soon commence. Sherman has returned to Vicksburg and by this time is on his way to Memphis. His grand effort to turn the flank of the Confederacy has failed signally and we have gained two months of time. This army is in as good fighting trim as it can be put with the resources at our command. Our transportation is deficient yet, but that deficiency is unavoidable. Our private horses are very poor and indeed I am afraid I shall lose mine this spring, as he seems to be diseased. I am hard at work every day on the regimental record for Colonel Walker and have been so ever since the middle of January. I think I can complete it this month if we are allowed to remain undisturbed in our quarters. It will be a valuable work when completed, as it furnishes a complete record of each individual.

March 10, Thursday. Weather becoming quite warm. Had a violent rain last night. General Stevenson had a division drill today. The impression prevails that the time for movement has nearly arrived and that we will move very soon. I think myself that General Johnston will not commence the campaign but will wait until the enemy advances upon us, which is likely to happen so soon as Sherman's army reaches Chattanooga. I think then that Johnston will fight at Dalton, though I do not feel at all certain that he will not transfer the battlefield more to our rear, to the Oostanaula or perhaps even the Chattahoochee. The latter would, I think, be the safest plan, though a retrograde movement might discourage some of the least intelligent of our soldiers and cause some desertions, especially among the Tennesseans and Georgians. A month will decide this matter.

March 12, Saturday. Weather pleasant and springlike. . . . The Yankees in our front have an infantry force at Ringgold and their pickets are this side of the gap in Taylor's Ridge. Another infantry force holds LaFayette. . . .

March 13, Sunday. A warm, pleasant day, inviting us to take the field. Rumors of skirmishing in front of Tunnel Hill. Our usual brigade inspection and review took place. I wrote home this morning requesting my wife to come out through the lines if she desired. I have given up my hopes of a speedy advance into Tennessee, and now believe that Johnston will wait here until the enemy advances which will not be till next month. The draft which was to have taken place March 10 has been postponed. Why, no reason is given. Governor Brown of Georgia has got up one of his peculiar messages, quarreling with the Congress and the Confederate government, and advocating his strange, obscure peace policy, through the intervention of states, a policy which no one whom I have yet seen seems able to explain or even to comprehend. He is savage on suspension of habeas corpus.[14]

March 14, Monday. Weather bright but cool. The reign of winter is not yet quite over. The Currency Bill passed by the last Congress is creating quite a commotion and even great inconvenience, but no complaints in the army. Privates' pay amount to nothing and officers' pay will not support them in comfort and decency. Any measure which looks towards raising the value of Confederate money, even if the present issue should be entirely repudiated, is hailed with joy by the army. They have never hoarded up any money and consequently have nothing to lose. The loss will fall on the producing and trading community and no soldier cares whether they grow or not. Indeed if money does not go up or prices come down I do not see how those officers can live who have no method obtaining remittances from home. They can barely obtain food and coarse clothing, and if his horse is lost he is bankrupt.

March 15, Tuesday. Colonel Walker returned this morning. The weather has changed and become freezing cold. News has reached us of a Yankee raid into Decatur across Tennessee River. Nothing yet heard from Sherman. This morning I rode to town to attend the military court of Hood's corps as witness in the case of W. D. Suttle of Company G, our regiment. It was evening before the case came on and I was detained nearly all day. When I returned in the evening I felt as much exhausted as though I had made a hard day's march. This is the first exercise I have taken since coming into camp at this place. Captain Alexander reached camp this morning from prison. He was captured at Raymond, has been confined at Johnson's Island in the [illegible] with Captain Jim Rivers, and was sent to Point Lookout and thence to City Point.

March 16, Wednesday. Weather still very inclement, indeed we feel the cold as sensibly as at any time during the winter. I bought a horse this morning from Lieutenant Jones for six hundred dollars, a tolerably high price but horses are dear, money is low, and I want to send my other horse to the rear to recruit him. There is some news today. Grant has been made lieutenant general and takes Halleck's place as commander-in-chief under the

President. Sherman succeeds Grant and McPherson succeeds Sherman.[15] I think there will be active operations early in the season on either side and perhaps the initiative may be taken by us. Our army is anxious to move forward into Tennessee, yet it will remain still without complaint if Johnston so orders. They have implicit confidence in him, and it will take some gross blunder to shake this confidence.

March 17, Thursday. Weather has moderated, but is still cool. Very little news today. The enemy are said to be raiding down Tennessee Valley from Decatur to Courtland, making desolate the garden spot of north Alabama. I suppose they have finished poor old Giles by this time and reduced it nearly to its primitive condition of wilderness. So far as enclosures and valuable property is concerned, the stock is nearly all taken or destroyed. The fences are broken down or burnt along and near every thoroughfare. The able-bodied Negro men are forced into the Yankee army. The Negro women and children have followed them and are hanging around the outskirts of the Yankee camps, victims of exposure, disease, and debauchery. Such is the physical condition of our country and the moral condition seems to be even worse.

March 18, Friday. Weather still cool but pleasant. Very little news. . . . There are rumors of foreign recognition again but no one believes them. Our people have gained enough wisdom to cease building hopes on any foundation except their armies, their efforts, their power of endurance, and above all upon a just and merciful God.

March 19, Saturday. Everything quiet in camp today. No drills, inspections, or reviews. Saturday seems to be the soldiers' Sabbath. Newspapers barren of news. Quite a revival is going on in the brigade. There have been several professions of religion in our regiment, among them one officer. I think there is more religious feeling in our army than there has been for a long time. A great abundance of religious newspapers and tracts are now circulated throughout the army. Our chaplain made the rounds of the regiment today and found about 140 men without Bible or Testament, and I think the deficiency will be found equally great if not greater in other commands. There is a great deal of profanity in the regiment but in other respects I think its morals have improved. The calamities which have fallen upon our state have, I think, worked good to Tennessee troops in the field.[16]

March 20, Sunday. A cool, bright spring day, but it does not much resemble a Sabbath at home. This morning while I write the sound of martial music and the columns drawn up for review in the field in front of our camp tell but too plainly that war in its spirit is decidedly anti-Christian. Oh how I long for those quiet country Sabbaths, whose privileges I once enjoyed! No, I should rather say once abused. I could not then appreciate their calm and blessed stillness. But three years of war and privation have learned me many things. They have made me a wiser and I trust and hope a better man. If the war must still continue longer and my life is still spared, God give me grace still to improve, and to learn new patience from every suffering both of body and mind, and a firm and abiding faith in His promises.

March 21, Monday. Last night just at dark as I was sitting before the fire, sadly ruminating upon the happy days of the past and the gloomy ones of the present, Lieutenant Jones suddenly entered the tent and thrust a package into my hands. Matthew Beaty had just returned from home and brought me a letter! The only one I had received since November 13. All were well, at least as well as they could be under the circumstances. The Yankees have taken everything they could conveniently carry off. Most of the Negroes have gone to them and many of those who remain seem disposed to follow. Joe and Washington are the only able-bodied men who remain faithful. Most of those who remain are insubordinate. Henry especially. I shall remember him when I have an opportunity. A perfect reign of terror prevails. Tories and Negroes roam over the country, plundering at their will.

March 22, Tuesday. This morning we were very much surprised at finding the ground covered with snow and the snowstorm still continuing unabated. Our boys were soon enjoying the luxury of a snowball frolic. Pettus' brigade came over to attack us this morning, but our boys repulsed them and drove them to their camp. Uniting with them, they made an incursion against Deas' and Manigault's brigades. After exhausting themselves in the combat they returned to camp with the colors of the

An engraving based on Alfred R. Waud's sketch of the "snowball frolic" near Dalton, Georgia, on March 22, 1864, in which the Third Tennessee took part. Source: Joseph M. Brown, *The Mountain Campaigns in Georgia* (1890).

Tenth South Carolina. Officers and men mixed freely in the fray. General Pettus came out on horseback with several mounted officers. A spirit of fun pervaded the whole army and it was the first real holiday I have seen for a long time. Toward evening the storm subsided and the weather turned quite cold. The whole country is covered with snow.[17]

March 23, Wednesday. The snow is beginning to disappear, but the weather is still quite cool. No movements of any kind along our extended lines. Kentucky seems to be in a ferment about Lincoln's abolition measures and the governor and *Louisville Journal* seem considerably exercised, but I do not think there will be an outbreak in that state. She is irreversibly lost to the Confederacy by the action of her own citizens, unless our successes in the field enable us to reconquer her. I do not believe her citizens generally will take any part for or against us. . . .

March 24, Thursday. Weather still cold and unsettled. Our spring is remarkably late. Everything quiet in front. The enemy occasionally advance toward Tunnel Hill and then retire to Ringgold, to which place it is said they are running the cars from Chattanooga. . . . It is generally believed that the campaign will begin in north Georgia.

March 25, Friday. Last night we had another snow but it is melting rapidly this morning. The newspapers are even more than usually barren of news. The only item of military movements is that Sherman has returned to Nashville. Reports are conflicting as to whether the Yankees are about to make their grand advance on Richmond or on Atlanta. I believe myself they will advance upon our army, but unless they reinforce very greatly we can meet them with the utmost confidence. Our army is said to be increasing by conscripts and recruits quite considerably. Of course the Tennessee troops have not that advantage. Lieutenant Matt Beaty thinks that if we should reoccupy middle Tennessee we could get a vast number of young men recently arrived at conscript age. Those who are more advanced in years would not profit us much.

March 26, Saturday. Weather still quite cold. This morning we commenced building a log house. Four of us live in a small tent and it is too small and too much crowded for a sleeping apartment, office tent, and living apartment. Colonels Walker and Clack will occupy the house and leave the tent to Dave Martin and myself. No report of any military movement in the newspapers but it is said that our scouts report the enemy sending troops from Chattanooga toward Nashville. Opinions are yet undecided whether the Yankees will attack here or in Virginia first. The whole army and people of the Confederacy are very hopeful and even confident. They anticipate hard fighting but look for victory to crown their efforts with the utmost confidence. I have never seen affairs in better trim than they are now.

March 27, Sunday. Weather bright and beautiful. Our usual brigade review takes place this morning, and while it is in progress I am quietly writing in my tent. I have not done any outdoor duty for six weeks, partly because I have been considerably weakened by dysentery which is not yet cured, and partly because I have been almost constantly engaged in arranging our regimental record at the request of Colonel Walker. I am getting tired of sedentary life, however, and as soon as the weather becomes fine I intend to take plenty of outdoor exercise. The religious revival still goes on in the brigade, and several of our best young soldiers have manifested a deep interest. Indeed I think there is quite an improvement in point of morals throughout our whole army.

March 28, Monday. This morning I rode with Colonel Clack over to visit Dr. Bowers and took dinner with him. We returned in the rain and passed by a division drilling earnestly in the midst of the storm. This is my last holiday and if I feel as well tomorrow as I do today I will report for duty in the morning. Saw the general this morning on my way to town. No news of any kind. It is now the general belief that the campaign will open in Virginia by Grant massing a large force and attempting to take Richmond. If that be the case it is not probable that the enemy will make a serious attempt upon Atlanta until the Virginia campaign is over. They have not men enough to organize two great armies of invasion, while I think we can give Lee enough men to repel an attack in Virginia and still retain our position everywhere else.

7 The Last Attack

March 29–May 15, 1864

STORMY WEATHER TURNS PLEASANT. GENERAL HARDEE'S SHAM
BATTLE. APRIL A COQUETTISH MAIDEN. NEW CAMP AT THE BREAST-
WORKS. IN CHARGE OF SKIRMISHERS, BUT ENEMY RETIRES TOWARD
RINGGOLD. SMALL ARMS FIRE ACROSS ROCKY RIDGE. WORK ON
FORTIFICATIONS. EXECUTION OF FOURTEEN DESERTERS, IGNORANT
NORTH CAROLINA MEN. ENEMY REPORTED ADVANCING. WE SEE
THE FIRES OF YANKEE CAMPS ALL OVER THE VALLEY. ENEMY FAILS
TO CUT THE RAILROAD AT RESACA. WE ARE PERFECTLY WORN OUT
BY FATIGUE AND LOSS OF SLEEP. THE END NEAR RESACA.

March 29, Tuesday. Weather stormy and rainy. We had a very
hard rain last night. I reported myself for duty this morning, the
first time for six weeks. The rains have put a stop to any military
movements, even if any were contemplated on our part, which I
do not think is the case. Very little in the newspapers. Rumors
have reached us that Longstreet's army is divided and that Lee is
to be reinforced from that quarter, while Buckner is in command
of what is left. I think now that both the Federal army and ours
will be concentrated in Virginia while our poor old state must be
patient and suffer another season. At present I see no signs of an
advance on our part, nor of any movement at all, until the Virginia campaign is finished. I think a part of our army will be sent
to Virginia so soon as Grant and Burnside make their advance.

March 30, Wednesday. Weather still too cool and stormy to be
pleasant. Yesterday Mr. Andy Mitchell arrived here from Giles
County and brings us the same terrible accounts of robbery and
terror. Hancock of Company G has a furlough of thirty days to go
into Giles County and will start tomorrow. I shall be able to send
another letter home. The newspapers contain vague accounts of

operations in west Louisiana, with various success, but nothing is certainly known about it. Grant is in Washington to take immediate command in Virginia and the Yankees must soon take the field for the spring campaign. We anticipate a bloody campaign but not a long one and perhaps by midsummer it will be decided. Grant must take Richmond or the Yankee nation will lose heart. The first mutterings of the political storm in the North are beginning to be heard.

March 31, Thursday. Weather cool and still savoring of winter. It is reported that our division will move in a few days to Crow's Cove in the direction of Tunnel Hill. We are not sorry, for we are becoming tired of our old camp where we have lain inactive four months. . . . It is reported that Dr. Jim Thompson who left us for Tennessee more than a month ago was captured near Tennessee River. Hancock started this morning. Inspection this morning, division drill this evening. The manner of life here begins to grow monotonous. The men are anxious for a chance to go to Tennessee, to Virginia, anywhere to keep stirring.

April 1, Friday. Rain last night and weather still unsettled. . . . Stevenson has not gained the confidence and affection of our brigade. His habits are suspected to be intemperate and he has no prestige to his name like Cheatham and Cleburne. I believe our men like Walker best, although they used to laugh at him and call him Old Hell Fire, while under him in Mississippi.

April 2, Saturday. A gloomy, cloudy day, very much more like winter than spring. . . . The Copperhead newspapers and orators of the North have all turned loose with the bitterest invective against Abe Lincoln, the administration, the manner of conducting the war, and the war itself. No terms are too harsh to apply to their government and they seem desirous of peace upon any terms. A desperate political struggle for the mastery is about to occur, but I think at present, with the army and the treasury, he is too powerful for his opponents.

April 3, Sunday. Weather is still cool but more springlike than usual. We had our usual regimental inspection and review this morning. After review I went to church in the brigade. Chaplain Chapman of the Thirty-Second preached. The revival is still going on and producing some good fruits. Desertions have ceased and the soldiers seem better satisfied than they have ever been before, although their discipline is stricter than usual. They seem happy and contented with their rough fare, though a shade of sadness passes over their countenances whenever a thought of their downtrodden state enters their minds. All believe that we shall soon see our beloved land from which we have been exiles so many long months. We can never be conquered so long as our men have their present spirit.

April 4, Monday. Weather very rainy and disagreeable. We have no newspapers today and consequently no news from abroad. Major General Walker's division is reported as having gone off on the cars to someplace unknown, supposedly Virginia. It is the almost universal belief here that we will maintain an army of observation at Dalton and send part of our force to the assistance of General Lee. There are as yet no indications of an advance upon the part of the Yankees into north Georgia. I wrote home today by a man on furlough who sewed the letter in his clothes. I have plenty of chances to send letters home but I fear but few of those that I start ever reach their destination. I wrote home yesterday by way of City Point and flags of truce and have left no opportunity slip of communicating with home. My conscience is clear on that point.

April 5, Tuesday. Weather still quite cool. . . . The Northern opposition to the administration is daily assuming a more embittered form, but Lincoln holds the reins with a bold hand and seems utterly unscrupulous as to the means employed to crush out any spirit of insubordination. We watch and wait for the coming election.

April 6, Wednesday. Weather very fine, the most pleasant day of the season. We had recitation an hour this morning on Evolutions of the Line, commenced at the beginning of the book. Also brigade drill this morning, and division drill this evening. The day has been a very busy one to me and I feel quite tired, being unused to be on horseback for the last two months. . . .

April 7, Thursday. Weather pleasant. Today General Hardee's sham battle came off. His corps was drawn up in two lines, one consisting of Cleburne's and Walker's divisions, the other of Bate's and Cheatham's, on opposite sides of the valley through which runs Resaca and Dalton road.[1] The troops were supplied with half a dozen rounds of blank cartridges and after maneuvering several hours they opened a fire of musketry and cannon on each other. The noise was terrific and the excitement intense, but nobody was hurt, so far as I could see, except perhaps one of the cavalrymen who was dismounted while charging a square of infantry. Many of the fair daughters of Georgia came up from below to witness the show, and there was quite a quantity of crinolines.

April 8, Friday. Weather rainy and disagreeable. This has been set apart by our Congress and President as a day of national fasting, humiliation, and prayer. We had divine service at eleven o'clock and prayer meeting in the morning and evening. Parson Chapman of the Thirty-Second preached. Subject: the influence of individual sin upon our national success. The day seemed to be very generally observed throughout the regiment and brigade. Many of our men ate nothing until late in the evening and some abstained not only from food but also from drink and tobacco [illegible] meal until 4:00 P.M. The revival in the brigade goes on with unabated zeal and success. There seems to be a powerful awakening and seriousness, more than I have ever seen in the army.

April 9, Saturday. Weather pleasant but threatening rain. This evening we organized a Christian association for the brigade for the suppression of immorality in the brigade and General Brown presided at the first meeting. I am now on detached duty again, being a member of the examining board to examine officers applying for promotion. We meet every day except Sunday and sit about six hours per day. The business is quite laborious. We examine lieutenants on the first volume of Hardee's Tactics and captains and field officers in both volumes. The examination of the latter must be reduced to writing and forwarded to the War Department. No news today of any kind and the rainy weather has stopped operations everywhere. Dr. Jim Thompson arrived last night from his scout into Tennessee and his Decatur prison.

April 10, Sunday. Weather variable with occasional rainstorms. Spring has not yet favored us with a single one of her sweet smiles. The usual brigade inspection and review took place today but my detached service saved me from the infliction.

Divine service as usual. Forrest has published his official report from Dresden, west Tennessee. He says his loss was only twenty-five killed and wounded. The Yankee cavalry have been whipped in several skirmishes in west Tennessee. General Rousseau, commander of the Nashville district, has issued an order for the protection of the people of middle Tennessee, and stops the further impressment of Negroes and stock, and encourages the loyal citizens to raise their crops and improve their farms.[2] An attempt is making in north Alabama to inaugurate a state government.

April 11, Monday. Weather quite pleasant and springlike. The trees are beginning to put out. The season is very late and vegetation is backward. The only vegetable we can produce of our table as yet is water cresses, which are gathered on the laurel branches. The peach-tree blossoms have nearly all disappeared and grass is springing up in the meadows. We are in the midst of a region which would be delightful were it not for its desolation. As far as the eye can reach there is no sign of an enclosure. What few houses there are stand [illegible] stripped of all their beautiful surroundings. The hills are stripped of every tree and bush except here and there a tall pine left standing unfit for food and the face of the country looks as though shaved by a razor.

April 12, Tuesday. Weather rainy and gloomy. April is as inconstant as a coquettish maiden. One day all smiles and caresses, the next petulant and frowning. The Atlanta newspapers have suspended publication on account of a printers' strike for higher wages. *The Rebel* published at Marietta is our only newspaper today and it brings nothing new.[3] Several regiments (two and a battalion) have arrived from General Polk's department and a full brigade is expected. Whether this betokens any movement or not we are in the dark. Late remarks and opinions indicate a forward movement but I do not believe them. I still think Virginia will be the theater of the spring campaign. The Yankees in Tennessee seem inclined to remain on the defensive and Grant in person is with the Army of the Potomac.

April 13, Wednesday. Weather very fine. No drills and the camp quiet. Everything in this army and the army in front of us betokens the most quiet, but any movement may find us all astir. Such is a soldier's life. He, above all other men, cannot tell what tomorrow may bring forth to him, and he, above all others, should be constantly prepared for whatever may befall mortal man. Our army is fortifying at a point between the Cleveland and Ringgold roads. General Wheeler is said to have started on a raid to the left of Cleveland. A mail has been captured at the front with many letters for men in Cumming's Georgia brigade, from deserters and citizens trying to induce them to desert and offering fair promises from the enemy. The bearers of the letters are in jail at Dalton.[4]

April 14, Thursday. Weather cloudy and damp. Our examining board adjourned this morning. We had division drill this evening. We received *The Rebel* today but the Atlanta papers have not yet resumed publication. There are rumors that Forrest routed Grierson at Somerville, west Tennessee. Many recruits are said to be joining him. The tone of the Northern newspapers indicates that a desperate and final attempt will be made to overwhelm us this year but if that fails hostilities must cease. They can bear no more. In the meantime they are making every exertion to abolish slavery in the border states, and the leaders of the abolition party in the Senate say they cannot even wait for an amendment to the Constitution but it must be done by the "war power." They are hopeless of our subjugation and determined to do all possible harm while in their power.

April 15, Friday. Cold and windy. In this region of mountains the reign of winter seems to last a long time. Mr. Brownlow has just arrived from Giles County. He placed in my hands $2,250 from Burwell Abernathy, to be funded. It is nearly all in one-hundred-dollar bills and is taxed one third its value.[5] The newspaper strike in Atlanta still continues. *The Rebel* confirms the rumor of Forrest's movements in west Tennessee. . . .

April 16, Saturday. Still cold and windy and more like autumn than spring. Today is our holiday in camp. The soldiers are supposed to do their washing today by general order, but I doubt whether many of them will comply very strictly with the order. I went to town this morning to see the funding quartermaster but could do nothing as this office has ceased funding since the first of April. . . .

April 17, Sunday. Warm and springlike. Our usual brigade inspection took place but only two regiments were present. The Twenty-Sixth is on post duty at Calhoun, and the Forty-Fifth and

Thirty-Second are at work on fortifications on the Cleveland road. . . . Colonel Walker leaves on furlough for ten days to see his wife at Cassville.

April 18, Monday. We were to have had a review of the army today but the weather was so bad it was deferred. This evening is more like January than April. Spring seems very late this year. We have quite an Alpine climate. . . .

April 19, Tuesday. Weather very cold and windy. Our long-expected review took place. The whole army was drawn up in two lines, the battalions being closed in mass on each other. All the infantry and artillery passed in review before General Johnston. The infantry was variously estimated from thirty thousand to forty thousand men and the pieces of artillery from 103 to 118. The army presented a very fine appearance. . . .

April 20, Wednesday. Weather very fine. The Atlanta newspapers have been again revived and show us daily their welcome faces. . . .

April 21, Thursday. Cloudy and damp. Every day we expect orders to move to the position chosen for us at the front. Colonel Walker started home yesterday and Dr. Thompson will also go in the same direction in a few days. I write and send plenty of letters and receive but few answers. . . . Our board today examined Captain Morrill of the Twenty-Sixth Tennessee, an applicant for the position of major, but we could not recommend him. He seemed rather deficient in good sense.

April 22, Friday. Weather warm but quite windy. Eyes, nose, and mouth and ears full of dust whenever we ventured out. We had an abortive attempt at drill this evening by General Reynolds. . . .

April 23, Saturday. Weather mild but very windy. The whole atmosphere was filled with dust. At 9:00 A.M. we had brigade drill, rather an unusual thing for Saturday, which is our day for washing and cleaning up. . . . Lieutenant Jones arrived in camp from Kingston, bringing with him Littleton, a deserter from Company K, who was found in Biffle's cavalry. Lieutenant Lewis Ames also returned from the Eleventh Tennessee Cavalry, bringing Bill with him. I hired him out to Colonel Clack.

April 24, Sunday. Weather quite variable. It rained very hard this morning, but cleared up later in the day. We had no divine service in camp on account of the weather. The newspapers still bring favorable news. . . . General Brown thinks we will fight here in the next twenty days and also that the battle will be brought on by our advance upon the enemy. I still think, however, that we will not advance until the Virginia campaign opens, and perhaps not then, as all our surplus strength may be employed in reinforcing General Lee. I do not believe at present that the enemy will advance on us, as they rather exaggerate our strength. We have forty thousand; they put us down at sixty thousand.[6]

April 25, Monday. Weather very pleasant. We had brigade inspection and review this morning. Our brigade is in very fine fighting trim now. Desertions have entirely ceased and officers and men alike seem satisfied, in excellent spirits, and entirely confident of success. Everyone relies entirely on Old Joe's genius and experience. We have no newspapers today, but rather more grapevine than usual. . . . Everything now looks as though Old Joe is about to move upon the enemy in our front. We poor Tennesseans are beginning to have some hopes of recovering our state. Everyone is in fine spirits at the prospect and is looking eagerly for the advance.

April 26, Tuesday. Weather quite warm. This morning at sunrise we were drawn up in line, all our baggage packed up, and ordered to march. We took up our new position about five miles from our old camp between the Ringgold and Cleveland roads, at the breastworks which are now rapidly being constructed. The left of our division rests at the foot of Rocky Face Ridge and the right on a small creek. The enemy are reported to be in strong force at Cleveland and are making demonstrations towards Spring Place and our extreme right. Hood's corps is now all in the front and perhaps our lazy camp life is over for the season. . . .

April 27, Wednesday. Weather still warm. We have spent the day in arranging and improving our camp. The streets are laid off regularly at right angles to the fortifications and immediately behind them our headquarters are in front of the breastworks in a grove of small trees. We made an enclosure around our tent with poles and intend to preserve our little trees for the sake of the shade which they may furnish. The leaves are just beginning to put out. We have our quarters quite tastefully arranged. By good luck Dave Martin and I were alone when they were arranging or we would have been shoved into some mudhole or rocky point as usual. . . . We expect Colonel Walker back in camp this evening. Rumors are afloat of an advance of the enemy upon our position.

April 28, Thursday. Weather quite warm. We lay in camp, still cleaning up our grounds. This morning I rode round our picket lines in front of our position. In case of an attack we will occupy the range of hills in front of our breastworks. So far as we can see the latter will be of little service to us, as our reserves will be posted in them. Our brigade will occupy the front line. We hear cannonading all day in the direction of Ringgold but don't know what it means. . . . I received a letter today from my brother Robert. He is still as firm as ever in the cause and has written as strong a letter as could be allowed to pass the examiners. I am much distressed at not hearing from home.

April 29, Friday. Warm but threatening rain. This morning our regiment was again on fatigue duty. I was placed in charge, but on reaching the point indicated we could not find the engineer. While waiting for him we were ordered to the front to meet the enemy who were said to be pressing our cavalry. Our line was posted on the northwestern declivity of a chain of hills. I was placed in command of the skirmishers of the brigade and drew them up in a line half a mile in front of our line of battle. After remaining there some time we were ordered back to camp, the enemy having retired toward Ringgold. I still do not think it probable that we will soon be attacked in our front. No news of any importance in the papers. Loring's division is said to be here and other reinforcements to be on the road. General Brown thinks we shall have fifty thousand men in our army when we fight.

April 30, Saturday. It rained last night and this morning, but the weather cleared up before noon. Still warm and pleasant. We have spring now in earnest. The trees are putting out very fast and the wild honeysuckle is in full bloom. These rough Georgia hills are looking quite beautiful. I rode around with Clack to view our position in front. Very little new in the papers. We are still undecided whether Grant is in our front or not, and whether the grand movement will be made here or in Virginia. I still remain of the same opinion as formerly and do not intend to change it without good reason. The Yankees seem to be in heavy force at Ringgold and Cleveland and perhaps at LaFayette. It is uncertain whether they will move on our right or left flank or more probably whether they will move at all. If they do not soon move upon us I hope Old Joe will move upon them.

May 1, Sunday. Rained last night but cleared up during the day. No news nor noise from the front. The newspapers furnish but little news of importance. Everything remains in suspense. One year ago we received orders to leave Port Hudson for Mississippi. Two years ago we were snugly ensconced at Johnson's Island military prison. Three years ago we were preparing to leave our homes for the tented field. I hope before another year rolls by we shall return to those same homes, though desolated and the mere wrecks of their former selves, yet containing all those whom we hold dearest on earth. Last year I felt very sanguine that the war would terminate before the close of the year, but my opinion was entirely predicated on the contingency that Vicksburg would hold out and that we would hold possession of the Mississippi River. Now my hope is based upon no contingency but it is absolute.

May 2, Monday. Rained a little this morning and then turned [illegible]. We had brigade inspection appointment at 9:00 A.M. All morning we heard a continued firing of small arms across Rocky Ridge and at length artillery opened. While on the field for inspection we received orders to go up to the front as the enemy were advancing. We took our position on the northwestern slope of the ridge in our front and worked hard until evening putting up breastworks. By the time these were completed we were ordered to return to camp as the enemy had retired. We have, I think, quite a strong position, or rather will have when all our works are completed. On our right and a little in front is a very high point called Potato Hill commanding the whole country around and on its top is earthwork with a battery. The left of our line is more liable to attack.

May 3, Tuesday. Weather pleasant and springlike. Everything quiet in camp. We are still engaged in working on the fortifications. We have drawn three days' rations of hard bread and crackers and are required to have them in the haversacks ready to march at a moment's warning. We hear nothing from the enemy but they are evidently trying to create the impression that they are about to advance upon us. I still believe they will make their grand effort in Virginia and not here. . . .

May 4, Wednesday. Weather quite warm. This morning our regiment was ordered on fatigue duty but was relieved to witness the execution of some deserters. Fourteen men from Cumming's and Polk's brigades were shot at one time. They were tied to stakes in a row and the special [illegible] were drawn up in front. The volley was badly delivered and it required several extra shots to finish some of the unfortunate persons. Our whole division was drawn up in line to witness the execution. Nearly all the men were very ignorant and from North Carolina.[7] No further news in the paper. I believe nearly everybody here looks for a fight in this quarter except me.[8]

May 5, Thursday. Still quite warm. Today at 8:00 A.M. my tour of brigade officer of the day commenced. I visited our pickets in the morning. They were all from our regiment. Captain Jones commanded them. Late in the evening first rumors and then orders began to flow in thick and fast. After dark I received an order from General Stevenson to remain during the night with the picket and before I left camp the brigade was ordered to pack all their baggage in the wagons and be ready to move at daylight next morning. I visited the picket and about midnight lay down by the fire at the reserve and slept till three o'clock. The enemy were reported advancing on the Ringgold and Cleveland roads with a heavy force of infantry, our cavalry retiring before them. I still do not believe they are going to make anything other than a feint or demonstration against us at present.

May 6, Friday. Very warm. I visited the videttes at daylight. Everything quiet and in good order. Neither sound nor murmur in our front. Last night General Hindman's division moved inside the fortifications, having previously been encamped across the railroad.[9] When I returned to camp shortly after sunrise I found everything packed up, the wagons loaded, and everyone expecting an order to move. But the morning and the evening passed off quietly, the enemy supposed to be retiring. . . .

May 7, Saturday. Weather still warm. This morning we were ordered out on fatigue duty on the breastworks in our front. We heard skirmishing all morning nearly all around our lines. About 11:00 A.M., I was ordered to take charge of our brigade pickets. After I reached our lines I found our cavalry had run in and was immediately in front of our videttes. About 1:00 P.M. they discovered that they had come in without cause and returned to their position one and a half miles in our front. Colonel Cook came out and told us the Yankees had taken Tunnel Hill. They also occupied Varnell's Station on the Cleveland railroad. I then went up with Lieutenant Wells of the Fifty-Third Alabama Cavalry and visited the cavalry outposts, but saw no Yankees directly in our front. They are still skirmishing at Varnell's Station. Sundown while I write all is quiet.

May 8, Sunday. Very warm. I had a quiet time on picket last night and rode back to the breastworks for half an hour. I took Bob with me when I returned to the picket but rather against his will. Sent off a Union citizen who lived at our picket lines to Colonel Hill, the provost marshal in Dalton.[10] His whole family accompanied him to town after hiding and burying their household effects. We were told that we would probably be attacked at daylight but I did not believe it, though every precaution was taken against surprise. No signs of the enemy in our front today, though they made quite a vigorous attack upon General Pettus' pickets at Rocky Face Ridge. I hear of no new movements today up to 4:00 P.M. I was relieved this morning by Major McGuire and returned to our bivouac at the breastworks.[11]

May 9, Monday. Very warm. Late last evening we were put in motion and before dark reached the top of Rocky Face Mountain. Here we found a stone wall built for a breastwork on the crest, which was very narrow, varying from ten to twenty feet when a precipitous descent commenced on both sides. On the west side near the top there arose a perpendicular wall of rock with a few paths leading down. On this ledge we had our picket line. When it was dark we could see the fires of the Yankee camps all over the valley. Soon in the morning their pickets attacked ours and skirmished all day, but were easily repulsed. They have made a

The battlefield at Resaca, Georgia, in May 1864. Courtesy of the U.S. Army Military History Research Collection.

lodgement on the top of the mountain to our right and have shelled us a little occasionally. They drove our pickets in the valley at our eastern foot, to a point near the works, and at sundown while I write a brisk artillery and musketry fight is going on at the foot of the mountain.

May 10, Tuesday. Weather pleasant, a few slight showers of rain. At daylight the Third moved down the eastern slope of the mountain and took position in the trenches on the slope. After sharpshooting a while we were sent back to the reserve and placed in a ravine behind the breastworks and held there all day. Last evening a vigorous assault was made at two points on the line of Rocky Face, one at the extreme right was repulsed by Pettus' brigade, the other on our left by Maney's.[12] Our loss is very small. So far as heard the enemy have done but little today. Those in front of our right in Crow's Valley have returned, but their pickets skirmished all day with ours. They are reported massing heavy forces on our left wing. . . .

May 11, Wednesday. It rained last night and Dave Martin and myself had to sit up in my little dog tent half the night. This morning we remained without moving until 12:00 noon, when we were posted a little lower down the ravine, still as a reserve for Reynolds' brigade. Nothing of interest occurred to us during the day. The enemy have a battery on a high point of Rocky Face commanding much of our line on the slope and in Crow's Valley. They seem to be massing their forces on the left of our line and only keep up a skirmish and a little cannonading. They attempted to cut the railroad at Resaca but failed, as they did at Mill Creek and Dug gaps. French's and Loring's divisions are said to be at Resaca. Our army is in the highest possible spirits, and as yet there is no straggling. I think our numbers are almost equal to those of the enemy and when the tug comes we are very confident.

May 12, Thursday. Weather cool and at night quite chilly. Sharpshooting and cannonading going on all day as usual, but no assault. In the evening we heard firing in rear of the enemy's left, but knew not the cause. They appear to be massing all their forces on our left beyond Mill Creek Gap, it is supposed with the intention of turning our left. They threw shells quite over Rocky Face Ridge into Crow's Valley. Only one line seems to remain on the western side of that mountain and they are said to be entrenching Tunnel Hill. Late in the evening the Third received orders to move and rejoin our brigade at the foot of the mountain which it did at dark. We then marched through Dalton, a mile and a half on the Spring Place road, where we turned to the right on the Tilton road. We continued our wearisome and harassing march throughout the night. We were perfectly worn out by fatigue and loss of sleep.

Epilogue

IN THE EBB and flow of the battle, the Army of Tennessee had fallen back toward Resaca, with Sherman's army pushing hard. From the Confederate side the constant engagements were frantic affairs, as evidenced in the diary of Taylor Beatty:

> *May 12:* About 11 $^1/_2$ a.m. got a message from Genl. Hood requesting Capt. Sale and myself to join him. Went up to the front and rode all along the lines and could not find him. Rode back and found the Genl. at Genl. J's hd Qts. Indications of a move—all packed up. About 8 p.m. started. Our destination is Tilton about 6 miles below here. Got there about 9 p.m.
>
> *May 13:* Staid at Tilton till 3 p.m. when we left for Resaca. Enemy slowly advancing, nearly up with us before we left. Backwards—Just before we got to Resaca sent back by Genl. H. to fix Stevenson's line, and then Stewart's. Heavy skirmishing on the left where Genl. Polk is. Hardee is in center.
>
> *May 14:* Line changed closer in—we are in form of a triangle our lines forming two sides—river in our rear on which both of our flanks rest—first firing about 9 a.m.—heavy skirmishing all along line. My horse shot about 2 p.m.—slightly—a very long shot. Saw 1st Div.—no one hurt. Insuring [illegible] at G. Stevenson and charged enemy—only small force . . . [1]

On the suggestion of Johnston, Confederate cavalry probed the Federal extreme left and discovered it in the air. Late in the afternoon of May 14, the Confederates attacked with two divisions, one of them Stevenson's, which contained the Third Tennessee.

186

For the Federals the engagement was brief but dangerous. A brigade of Maj. Gen. David S. Stanley's division in the Fourth Corps, containing the Thirty-first and Eighty-first Indiana and 101st Ohio, fell back in disorder, and for a short while the Fifth Indiana Battery under Capt. Peter Simonson was the sole Union defense. Maj. Gen. Joseph Hooker then appeared on the field with James S. Robinson's brigade of the division commanded by Brig. Gen. Alphaeus S. Williams and routed the Confederates.[2]

Such was the larger scene. As for the smaller, at the tops of the few remaining pages of his diary book Barber had filled in the subsequent days of the month in anticipation of entries—one for each page. He dated the pages through Saturday, May 21. He did not write them. In his own diary Chaplain Deavenport explained why:

> . . . three regiments of Brown's brigade (Third, Eighteenth, and Forty-Fifth Tennessee) did all the fighting, the Third leading in the charge. We passed out through an old field a half mile and charged up a hill through a thick woods. It was a grand charge and the enemy were driven hastily back from their entrenched position, leaving knapsacks, haversacks, guns, and it seemed as if all their rammers, for the ditches were lined with them. We gained the second hill and were halted. Our loss was light but we mourned some noble officers and men. In this charge we lost our gallant Major F. C. Barber.[3]

Severely wounded during the charge of May 14, Barber died the next morning. On an empty page of the Bible taken from the major's jacket, his friend Colonel Clack wrote that Barber's last words spoken after being shot were that he knew the Third would do its duty. The pages of the Bible, stitched tightly, open easiest to Ecclesiastes, the third chapter: "To everything there is a season . . . A time to be born, and a time to die . . . "

The Third fought on, as Barber hoped it would. The cost was high. In the summer of 1861 it had mustered 885 men. By February 8, 1862, just before Donelson, troop strength was 750; at reorganization in Jackson it was down to 607. At Raymond it suffered 187 casualties out of 548 engaged. Jackson saw regimental strength reduced to 366, Chickamauga to 274, Missionary Ridge to 195. By December 1863 the ranks rose a little, to 271. But before Atlanta the Third's numbers dwindled rapidly. Colonel Walker was killed near Marietta on June 22, 1864; Lieutenant Colonel Clack took his place and, later, died at Jonesboro. By December 1864, the Third combined with the Eighteenth Tennessee and numbered 17 plus three black servants. The remnant eventually became part of the Fourth Consolidated Tennessee Infantry Regiment, with Colonel Searcy commanding. As part of General Johnston's army, the Third surrendered on April 26, 1865, and was paroled May 1 at Greensboro, North Carolina.[4]

Barber's widow, the former Mary Paine Abernathy, similarly came upon difficult times. When she learned of the death of her husband, she made inquiries and found that the Federals had recovered his body. She journeyed to Nashville to obtain it from the provost marshal and returned to Pulaski where she arranged for his burial in Maplewood Cemetery. After the war she was in straits; her husband left her nothing, and members of her own family, the Abernathys, were destitute, evident when in 1866 her half-brother Burwell wrote a nephew that "We had the armies on us all the time."[5] Perhaps for financial security, she married Hilton A. Carter. She died in 1870 and was interred in Maplewood Cemetery not far from her first husband, the gallant major of the Third Tennessee.

Appendix

Roster of the Third Tennesee Infantry

WHEN THE REGIMENT'S officers returned from imprisonment at Fort Warren and Johnson's Island, and the men came back from Camps Butler, Douglas, and Morton, everyone being exchanged, they reorganized at Jackson, Mississippi, on September 26, 1862. The new colonel, Walker, ordered Captain Barber to write up the histories of the companies and draw up rolls. Barber drew up everything in detail, in several dozen pages, and the rolls accounted not merely for officers and men present but related service to date and listed individuals not present, those absent with or without leave or because of illness or death. As it turned out, September 1862 was perhaps the most advantageous time Walker could have chosen for a roster. At Raymond the next year the regiment suffered heavy casualties, and despite efforts at recruiting the companies never came up to strength. Attrition thereafter bore down until at war's end in 1865 the regiment's survivors numbered a mere handful. The regiment long since had consolidated with other weakened regiments.

Early in 1864, Barber did another detailed roster. It included recruits, accounted for losses, and corrected any errors of the earlier rolls.

At the end of the war, Confederate record keeping turned into chaos as units demobilized in haphazard fashion. Some central records were saved to be incorporated into the massive series *War of the Rebellion: A Compilation of the Official Records of the Union and Confederate Armies.* A few unit records passed into private hands, and such seems to have been the case with the Third Tennessee's records drawn by Barber. An unknown individual sold Barber's rolls to the Duke University Library in 1939.

Material from the following roster does not appear in the Tennessee Civil War Centennial Commission's two-volume *Tennesseans in the Civil War: A Military History of Confederate and Union Units with Available Rosters of Personnel* (Nashville, 1964–65).

Some explanation is necessary concerning this roster, which is combined, alphabetical, and keyed. Barber's two rosters repeated names,

This young soldier, Pvt. W. J. Coker, holds a converted flintlock musket and wears a recycled U.S. belt plate. Captured at Fort Donelson and imprisoned at Camp Douglas in Chicago, he was exchanged on September 23, 1862. He was absent without leave at Springdale, present at the battle of Chickasaw Bayou, present at the bombardment of Port Hudson, present at Raymond, present at the siege of Jackson, and wounded at Chickamauga. Absent without leave from Missionary Ridge, he thereafter disappeared from the roster of the Third Tennessee. As was often the case with Confederate soldiers who, after absences, could not easily find their old units, he may have joined another regiment—or gone home to Tennessee, then within Federal lines, and taken an oath of loyalty to the Union. Courtesy of Herb Peck, Jr.

were not alphabetized, and separated officers from enlisted men, listing the latter by companies. Moreover, as his description of each man's service led to constant repetition, it seemed advisable to give numbers to similar experiences, which then appear after names of members of the regiment:

1. Present at battle of Donelson; captured and imprisoned at Camp Douglas, Illinois; exchanged September 23, 1862
2. Present at battle of Donelson; captured and imprisoned at Camp Chase, Ohio, and Johnson's Island, Ohio; exchanged September 16, 1862
3. Present at battle of Donelson; captured and imprisoned at Camp Butler, Illinois; exchanged September 23, 1862
4. Present at battle of Donelson; captured and imprisoned at Camp Morton, Indiana
5. Sick in quarters at battle of Donelson; captured and imprisoned at Camp Douglas; exchanged September 23, 1862
6. Present at battle of Donelson; escaped after the surrender
7. Present at battle of Donelson; captured and imprisoned at Camp Douglas, escaped from prison
8. Present at battle of Donelson; captured and imprisoned at Camp Douglas; died in prison
9. Absent from company without leave from Donelson; captured and imprisoned at Camp Douglas
10. Present at battle of Donelson; captured; took oath of allegiance to the United States at St. Louis and released
11. Present at battle of Donelson; captured and imprisoned at Camp Douglas; took oath of allegiance to the United States and released
12. Wounded at battle of Donelson; captured and imprisoned at Camp Douglas; exchanged September 23, 1862
13. Wounded at battle of Donelson and sent home
14. Killed at battle of Donelson, February 15, 1862
15. Absent from Donelson, sick
16. Absent from Donelson, sick at home
17. Absent from Donelson, sick at Russellville, Kentucky
18. Discharged or disability
19. Absent from Donelson on detached duty
20. Absent from Donelson on detached teamster detail
21. Joined (or rejoined) regiment at Abbeville, Mississippi, November 1862

22. Joined regiment at Port Hudson, Louisiana
23. Joined (or rejoined) regiment at Grenada, Mississippi
24. Joined (or rejoined) regiment at Grenada, December 7, 1862
25. Present at battle of Springdale
26. Absent from Springdale
27. Absent from Springdale, sick
28. Absent from Springdale on detached duty
29. Absent from Springdale without leave
30. Absent from Springdale with leave
31. Absent from Springdale on recruiting service
32. Wounded at Springdale
33. Captured at Springdale
34. Present at battle of Chickasaw Bayou
35. Absent from battle of Chickasaw Bayou
36. Absent from Chickasaw Bayou, sick
37. Absent from Chickasaw Bayou on detached duty
38. Absent from Chickasaw Bayou without leave
39. Wounded at Chickasaw Bayou
40. Killed at Chickasaw Bayou
41. Present at bombardment of Port Hudson
42. Absent from bombardment of Port Hudson
43. Discharged from Port Hudson as a nonconscript
44. Discharged from Port Hudson as a nonconscript, March 5, 1863
45. Present at battle of Raymond
46. Absent from Raymond, Mississippi
47. Absent from Raymond, sick
48. Absent from Raymond on detached duty
49. Captured at Raymond
50. Captured at Raymond, May 12, 1863
51. Wounded at Raymond
52. Killed at Raymond, May 12, 1863
53. Present at siege of Jackson, Mississippi
54. Absent from siege of Jackson
55. Absent from Jackson, sick
56. Absent from Jackson on detached duty
57. Absent from Jackson, wounded
58. Captured at Jackson
59. Wounded at Jackson
60. Killed at Jackson
61. Present at battle of Chickamauga

62. Absent from battle of Chickamauga
63. Absent from Chickamauga sick
64. Absent from Chickamauga on detached duty
65. Absent from Chickamauga without leave
66. Absent from Chickamauga, wounded
67. Captured at Chickamauga
68. Wounded at Chickamauga
69. Wounded at Chickamauga, September 19, 1863
70. Wounded at Chickamauga, September 20, 1863
71. Killed at Chickamauga, September 19, 1863
72. Killed at Chickamauga, September 20, 1863
73. Present at battle of Missionary Ridge
74. Absent from battle of Missionary Ridge
75. Absent from Missionary Ridge, sick
76. Absent from Missionary Ridge on detached duty
77. Absent from Missionary Ridge without leave
78. Absent from Missionary Ridge, wounded
79. Imprisoned at Alton penitentiary, Illinois
80. Imprisoned at Fort Delaware
81. Imprisoned at Fort Delaware and Port Lookout
82. Furloughed home

ROSTER
*(Information following the period
is from Barber's second roster.)*

Abernathy, C. C.   Surgeon, assigned duty in regt., Feb. 1864
Abernathy, J. L.   Pvt. Co. K.; note 1.   4th corp. Co. A; notes 25, 34, 41, 45, 53, 61, 73
Abernathy, J. M.   Pvt. Co. A; note 1.   Co. G; notes 25, 35 (inebriated), 41, 47, 55, 61 (Sept. 19), 65 (Sept. 20), 77
Abernathy, J. P.   Pvt. Co. K; note 1.   Co. A; notes 25, 34, 41, 51 (in arm), 53, 68 (in arm), 73
Abernathy, James   Pvt. Co. D; died Camp Cheatham, Ky., June 1861
Abernathy, L.   Pvt. Co. I; note 1.   Co. K; notes 29, 38, 41, 45, 53, 63, 75
Abernathy, L. D.   Pvt. Co. A; note 1; died Jackson, Miss., Oct. 8, 1862
Abernathy, Liles E.   Pvt. Co. A; note 1.   Co. G; notes 25, 34, 43 (Mar. 10, 1863)
Abernathy, M. C.   2d sgt. Co. I; note 1.   Pvt. Co. K; note 29; deserted from Jackson, Dec. 25, 1862

Abernathy, M. T. (or M. L.) Pvt. Co. K; note 1. Co. A; notes 25, 34, 44, 46, 54; reenlisted Enterprise, Miss., Aug. 5, 1863; notes 61, 73

Abernathy, Samuel H. 2d corp. Co. K; note 15, Dover hospital; captured and imprisoned Camp Douglas, Ill., exchanged Sept. 23, 1862. 3d sgt. Co. A; promoted 2d sgt. Apr. 12, 1863; notes 25, 38, 41, 52

Abernathy, T. O. Pvt. Co. A; note 5. Co. G; notes 25, 34, 41, 47, 55, 61, 73

Abernathy, William J. Pvt. Co. A; note 1. Co. G; notes 25, 34, 41, 49, 81

Adams, J. Thomas Pvt. Co. A; note 1. 5th sgt. Co. G; notes 25, 34, 41, 51, 57, 66, 78

Adams, Lewis L. Pvt. Co. A; note 4; exchanged Sept. 15, 1862. Co. G; notes 25, 36, 41; transferred First Tenn. Cavalry about Apr. 1, 1863

Agnew, J. F. Pvt. Co. B; note 10; rejoined regt. after exchange. Co. B; note 24; accidentally wounded in hand; notes 35 (on account of wound), 42 (from post), 46, 54 (without leave); deserted from hospital Newton, Miss., Aug. 14, 1863

Alderson, M. L. Pvt. Co. B; died Bowling Green, Ky., Oct. 13, 1861

Alexander, D. G. 2d lt. Co. D; note 2. Elected capt. Co. I at reorganization, Sept. 1862; note 82, Tippah Ford, Miss., Nov. 31, 1862; rejoined command Port Hudson, La., Feb. 1863; notes 41, 45 (both in command of co.), 49; imprisoned Johnson's Island, Ohio, and Point Lookout; exchanged City Point, Va., killed Resaca, Ga.

Alexander, J. F. Pvt. Co. E; made 3d sgt., promoted quartermaster sgt. with depot quartermaster Bowling Green; absent Donelson and remained in quartermaster depot detached from co.

Alexander, J. W. Pvt. Co. E; note 1. 4th sgt. Co. F; notes 25, 34, 41, 45; note 59, July 13, 1863; 66, 73

Alexander, R. F. Pvt. Co. D; note 1. 4th sgt. Co. I; notes 27, 36, 41, 47, 55; died Columbus, Miss., Aug. 1863

Alford, R. N. Pvt. Co. I; absent Donelson on furlough; joined cavalry

Alley, T. J. Pvt. Co. D; note 1. Co. I; notes 25, 34, 41, 45, 53, 61, 73

Alley, W. B. Pvt. Co. D; note 18, Dec. 1861

Alley, William A. (or William R.) Pvt. Co. C; note 1. Co. D; notes 25, 34, 41, 50, 81

Ames, Lewis Pvt. Co. A; absent Donelson detailed to accompany corpse of Sgt. Simpson home; served cavalry until regt. exchanged, when rejoined. Appointed quartermaster sgt. Dec. 15, 1862

Ames, M. C. Pvt. Co. F; note 16; never rejoined

Anderson, D. G. Pvt. Co. G; enlisted Oct. 26, 1862; notes 24, 36 41, 45, 53, 61, 73

Anderson, E. Musician Co. G; note 6; served in Fifth Tenn.; rejoined regt. after exchange; remained in band during every engagement

Anderson, J. P. Pvt. Co. G; enlisted Oct. 26, 1862; notes 24, 34, 41, 45, 53, 63, 73

Anderson, Joel Pvt. Co. G; note 17; joined Col. Hill's Fifth Tenn.; never rejoined

Anderson, S. H. Pvt. Co. D; deserted Bowling Green

Angel, J. M. Pvt. Co. I; note 20; joined cavalry

Anthony, W. W. Pvt. Co. I; note 11, Aug. 1862; never rejoined

Arthurs, William H. Pvt. Co. K; note 1. Co. A; notes 32, 35 (on account of wound), 41, 45, 53, 71

Atkins, William J. Pvt. Co. K; note 1. Co. A; notes 25, 34, 41, 45, 53, 62 (barefooted), 73

Aydelotte, G. P. Pvt. Co. H; note 8, Mar. 3, 1862

Aydelotte, J. P. Pvt. Co. F; note 20; rejoined regt. after exchange. Co. E; notes 24, 36, 43, Mar. 1863

Ayrnett, A. S. 4th corp. Co. A., Oct. 1861; note 9; exchanged Sept. 23, 1862

Ayrnett, John M. Pvt. Co. A; note 17

Bailey, A. M. Pvt. Co. E; note 15, Dover, Tenn.; captured and imprisoned Camp Douglas; escaped June 7, 1862; rejoined regt. after exchange. Co. F; notes 24, 34, 41, 51; note 82 from Canton, Miss., June 1863; rejoined regt. at Rome, Ga., Feb. 11, 1864; detached secret service, Mar. 1, 1864

Bailey, B. W. Pvt. Co. D; note 1. Co. I; notes 25, 34, 41, 50, 81

Bailey, J. E. Pvt. Co. I; note 82 from Jackson at reorganization Sept. 1862 ; never rejoined; deserted to cavalry

Bailey, J. M. Pvt. Co. I; enlisted Dec. 1862; notes 24, 34, 41, 45, 53; deserted Enterprise, Sept. 1863

Barber, Flavel C. Capt. Co. K; note 2, in command of his co. Reelected capt. Co. A at reorganization Sept. 1862; note 31; note 34 (in command of co.); promoted maj. at death of T. M. Tucker, Dec. 29, 1862; notes 41, 45, 53, 62 (home on furlough), 73; killed Resaca

Barber, Robert J. Pvt. Co. A; note 12. Co. G; captured Oxford, Miss., Nov. 1862; exchanged and rejoined regt. Mar. 25, 1863; notes 50, 81

Barnes, C. Fletcher 3d sgt. Co. C; note 7, June 1, 1862; entered cavalry

Barnes, J. H. Pvt. Co. G; enlisted Dec. 17, 1862; note 23, Dec. 20, 1862, as substitute for J. L. Barnes; note 34; died Port Hudson, Feb. 1863

Barnes, J. Luke Pvt. Co. A; note 5. Co. G; note 28; discharged by reason of having furnished a substitute at Camp Lovell, Miss., Dec. 20, 1862

Barnes, L. L. Pvt. Co. C; note 1. Co. D; notes 25, 34, 41, 45, 53, 61, 73

Barnes, M. H. Pvt. Co. C; note 1. 5th sgt. Co. D; notes 25, 34, 41, 45, 53, 61, 73

Barr, Isaac Pvt. Co. H; note 1. Co. C; notes 25, 34, 41, 45; died hospital Lauderdale Springs, June 1863

Bass, James P. Pvt. Co. K; note 7, June 18, 1862; rejoined regt. after exchange. Elected jr. 2d lt. Co. A at reorganization. Sept. 1862; note 25; note 39, mortally Dec. 29, 1862, died Vicksburg, Dec. 30, 1862

Bass, John B. Pvt. Co. K; note 1. Co. A; notes 25, 34, 41, 51, 57, 66, 78

Bass, John M. Pvt. Co. K; note 8, Mar. 11, 1862

Bass, Nathan H. Pvt. Co. A; died home July 1861

Batson, J. J. Pvt. Co. B; note 1. Co. B; notes 28, 37, 42, 45, all as teamster; deserted Canton, June 1863

Batte, G. Pvt. Co. B; note 12. Co. B; notes 25, 34, 41, 45, 53, 68, 73

Batte, Henry Pvt. Co. B; note 1. Co. B; notes 25, 36; died Port Hudson, Jan. 26, 1863

Beal, John M. Pvt. Co. B; note 6; served in partisan rangers; rejoined regt. after exchange. Co. B; notes 24, 34, 41, 45, 53; notes 64, 76, as teamster

Bearden, Henry Pvt. Co. B; note 1. Co. B; notes 29, 34, 41, 45, 53, 71

Bearden, W. C. Pvt. Co. B; note 9; exchanged Sept. 23, 1862. Co. B; notes 25, 36, 41; 51, 57, 66; deserted near Chattanooga, Nov. 2, 1863

Bearden, W. V. S. Pvt. Co. G; note 1. Co. H; notes 25, 34, 41, 52

Beasley, W. T. Pvt. Co. E; note 1. 2d corp. Co. F; notes 25, 36, 41, 45, 55, 63, 73

Beaty, Henry M. 1st sgt. Co. K; note 1. 1st sgt. Co. A; notes 31, 34, 41; note 51, May 12, 1862; note 57; promoted jr. 2d lt. Aug. 7, 1863, at promotion of W. J. Ridgeway; note 61, in command of co. after capt. wounded; note 73

Beaty, J. J. 3d corp. Co. F; note 13; joined Seventeenth Tenn.

Beaty, Thomas B. Pvt. Co. K; note 1. Co. A; notes 25, 37, 41, 45, 53, 69, 73

Beaver, J. S. M. Pvt. Co. H; enlisted Nov. 10, 1862; notes 24, 34; deserted Vicksburg, Jan. 5, 1863

Beaver, W. A. 4th corp. Co. G; note 1; detached as brigade carpenter Abbeville, Miss., Nov. 1862

Beckham, Green B. Pvt. Co. A; note 15, Bowling Green

Bell, Valentine Pvt. Co. C; died Lewis County, Tenn., July 15, 1861

Bell, William Pvt. Co. C; note 1. Co. D; notes 25, 34, 41, 46 (foot sore), 53, 61, 75

Benderman, John W. Pvt. Co. C; note 1. Co. D; notes 25, 34, 41, 51 (mortally, May 12, 1863); died Raymond, Miss., May 13, 1863

Bennett, J. M. Pvt. Co. A; died home Sept. 1861

Bennett, S. B. Pvt. Co. I; note 1. Co. K; notes 29, 34, 41, 45, 55, 63; deserted Lookout Mountain, Nov. 24, 1863

Bentley, A. W. 4th sgt. Co. I; note 18, Camp Trousdale, Ky., Aug. 1861

Bentley, M. V. 1st sgt. Co. I; note 11, Aug. 1862; never rejoined

Bevits, B. G. Pvt. Co. H; enlisted Nov. 10, 1862; notes 24, 34, 41, 50; died prison Fort Delaware

Biles, S. J. Pvt. Co. K; note 1. Co. A; notes 25, 34, 41, 48, 53, 61, 73

Birdwell, Blooming Pvt. Co. K; note 8, Sept. 27, 1862

Birdwell, J. F. Pvt. Co. K; note 1. Co. A; notes 25, 34, 41, 51 (in arm), 53, 68, 73

Birdwell, S. C. Pvt. Co. A; enlisted Oct. 10, 1861; transferred Thirty-second Tenn., Nov. 1, 1863; note 73

Bishop, L. L. Pvt. Co. D; note 1. Co. I; notes 24, 34; note 43, Feb. 24, 1863

Bishop, W. Pvt. Co. D; died Bowling Green, Jan. 1862

Bittick, Jerome 4th sgt. Co. D; note 1. Pvt. Co. I; notes 25, 34; note 43, Feb. 24, 1862

Black, Isaac N. Pvt. Co. D; note 1. Co. I; notes 25, 34, 41, 45; elected jr. 2d lt. Mound Bluff, Miss., June 1863, at death of N. B. Rittenbury; notes 53, 69, 78

Black, Leonidas 2d lt. Co. A; sick at Donelson and unable to take part in charge made by regt., but on duty in breastworks; captured and imprisoned Camp Chase, Ohio; died prison Apr. 21, 1862

Blair, T. W. Pvt. Co. E; note 7, June 5, 1862; joined Bartow's cavalry

Blanton, J. O. Pvt. Co. E; made 1st corp.; note 1. Pvt. Co. F; notes 25, 34, 41, 45, 53, 69, 78

Boatwright, James M. Pvt. Co. B; note 1. Co. B; notes 25, 34, 41, 47, 53, 61, 73

Boatwright, Thomas R. E. Pvt. Co. B; note 3. Co. B; notes 25, 34, 41, 45, 53, 61, 75

Boggus, R. B. Pvt. Co. C; note 1. Co. D; notes 27, 34, 41, 45, 53, left field Chickamauga Sept. 19; note 75

Bogus, Alexander Pvt. Co. H; note 18, Bowling Green, Oct. 1861

Bond, B. W. Pvt. Co. C; note 14

Bond, John H. Pvt. Co. D; enlisted Nov. 1, 1862; note 23, Dec. 24, 1862; notes 38, 41; discharged Port Hudson, Apr. 1863, having furnished a substitute

Bond, T. J. 5th sgt. Co. E; note 1. Pvt. Do. F; notes 25, 34, 41, 52

Boswell, D. B. Pvt. Co. K; sick quarters during Donelson; captured and imprisoned Camp Douglas; died prison Mar. 7, 1862

Bowers, E. D. Pvt. Co. A; enlisted Nov. 8, 1862; notes 25, 34, 41, 47

Bowers, James A. 1st lt. Co. K; apptd. surgeon Third Tenn., Nov. 11, 1861; captured Donelson and escaped Feb. 28, 1862; rejoined regt. Dec. 15, 1862. Made chief surgeon Gregg's brigade 1863; left with wounded Raymond, May 12, 1863, and fell into hands of enemy; rejoined June 1863; made chief surgeon Walker's div. June 1863

Boyett, Robert Pvt. Co. G; note 15, Bowling Green; joined Fifth Tenn.; mortally wounded Perryville, Ky.

Brachine, G. S. Pvt. Co. A; enlisted Nov. 3, 1862; note 23, Dec. 11, 1862; notes 34, 41, 45, 53, 61, 76

Brachine, J. G. Pvt. Co. K; note 1. Co. A; notes 25, 34, 41, 47, 55, 61, 73

Brachine, James Pvt. Co. K; note 20; joined Alabama regt.; wounded near Richmond, Ky.; died

Braden, J. W. Pvt. Co. B; note 1. Co. B; notes 25, 34, 41, 51, 57, 66, 78

Braden, Joseph Pvt. Co. D; deserted Camp Cheatham, May 1861

Branch, John T. Pvt. Co. F; note 7, June 1, 1862; joined cavalry

Branch, M. P. Pvt. Co. B; note 8, Apr. 1862

Brashears, Robert Pvt. Co. I; note 11, Aug. 1862; rejoined regt. after exchange. Co. K; notes 24, 34, 41, 49, 51; paroled and never rejoined

Brennan, D. Pvt. Co. C; note 11, Aug. 1862; remained out of service

Brewer, R. W. Pvt. Co. H; note 1. Co. C; notes 25, 36, 41, 45, 53, 65, 73

Brickeen, A. J. Pvt. Co. B; note 1. Co. B; notes 25, 34, 41, 49; died prison

Brickeen, M. J. Pvt. Co. B; note 9; exchanged Sept. 23, 1862. Co. B; notes 29, 38, 41, 55, 65, 75

Brickeen, William M. 2d lt. Co. D; absent without leave during Donelson; captured and imprisoned Camp Chase and Johnson's Island, exchanged Sept. 16, 1862; not reelected in reorganization and dropped from rolls

Bridgeforth, David J. Pvt. Co. K; note 18, Camp Trousdale; joined Ninth Ala.; killed Richmond, June 1862

Bridges, E. C. L. 1st lt. Co. G; note 2; not reelected at reorganization and dropped from rolls

Briggs, W. W. Pvt. Co. B; died Nashville, Nov. 5, 1861

Brister, W. T. Pvt. Co. A; note 1. Co. G; notes 27, 36, 41, 51, 53, 61, 73 (wounded)

Britton, James Pvt. Co. D; note 20, deserted to enemy

Brown, Campbell 1st lt. Co. E; transferred Army of Northern Virginia, June 1861

Brown, Leon Pvt. Co. A; note 1. Co. G; notes 25, 34, 41; transferred First Texas Cavalry, Port Hudson, Apr. 26, 1863

Brown, Robert M. Pvt. Co. B, note 1. Co. B; notes 25, 36, 41, 47, 55, 61, 73

Brown, Thomas A. Pvt. Co. B; note 1. Co. B; notes 25, 34, 41, 51, 57, 61, 73

Brown, W. H. Pvt. Co. E; note 18, Bowling Green, Dec. 1, 1861

Brownlow, G. F. Pvt. Co. I; enlisted Dec. 1862; notes 24, 36; died Clinton, Miss., Mar. 8, 1863

Brownlow, J. P. Pvt. Co. D; note 13; joined cavalry

Brownlow, R. S. Pvt. Co. D; note 1. 3d corp. Co. I; notes 25, 34, 41, 45, 53, 63, 75

Bruce, George B. Pvt. Co. K; note 1. Co. A; notes 25, 34, 41, 45, 49, 81

Bruce, O. P. Jr. 2d lt. Co. K; resigned Bowling Green, Nov. 1861

Bruce, S. W. Pvt. Co. A; enlisted Oct. 31, 1862; transferred from Thirty-second Tenn., Jan. 1, 1864

Bruce, Thomas J. Pvt. Co. K; note 7, June 18, 1862; joined First Tenn. Cavalry; absent without leave from reorganization; reported to his capt. in Tenn., Nov. 1862; remained in cavalry

Bryant, T. H. Pvt. Co. F; note 1. Co. E; notes 25, 34, 41, 51, 57; note 82 at Enterprise, Aug. 1863; never rejoined

Bryson, J. H. Pvt. Co. C; note 13, rejoined regt. after exchange at Port Hudson, Mar. 14, 1863. Co. D; notes 45, 55, 63, 75

Bryson, John J. Pvt. Co. C; note 1. Co. D; notes 25, 34, 41, 45, 53, 61, 73

Buchanan, Chesley M. Pvt. Co. A; note 13; rejoined Ark. regt. and promoted lt.

Buchanan, Cicero Pvt. Co. D; note 1. Co. I; notes 25, 34, 41, 45, 53, 63, 75

Buchanan, D. Pvt. Co. D; note 13; joined Forty-eighth Tenn.

Buchanan, J. P Pvt. Co. I; enlisted Dec. 1862; notes 24, 34, 41, 45, 53, 61, 73; elected corp. Nov. 8, 1863

Buchanan, R. Pvt. Co. E; discharged Camp Cheatham, July 8, 1861

Buchanan, W. C. Pvt. Co. K; note 1. Co. A; detached as teamster Nov. 1, 1862; in Vicksburg at surrender July 4, 1863; captured and paroled; never reported to his co.

Buford, Charles Pvt. Co. A; note 1. Co. G.; notes 27, 38, 41, 45, 53, 61, 73

Buford, Ebenezer G. Pvt. Co. A; wounded Donelson and sent home permanently disabled; rejoined regt. after exchange; note 18, Holly Springs, Miss., Oct. 1862

Buford, Edward C. (or Edward L.) Pvt. Co. C; note 1. Co. D; notes 25, 34, 41, 45, 53, 62 (sprained ankle), 73

Buford, Gilbert T. Pvt. Co. A; note 1. Co. G; notes 25, 38, 41, 45, 56 (cook); present Chickamauga at beginning of fight but went to rear Sept. 19 and did not return; note 75

Buford, J. W. 2d corp. Co. E; note 17; entered cavalry

Buford, Richard B. 4th sgt. Co. A; note 19, sappers and miners Oct. 1861; permanently detached

Bugg, George B. Pvt. Co. B; enlisted Oct. 19, 1862; joined regt. Holly Springs, Oct. 19, 1862; notes 25, 34; died Port Hudson, Feb. 25, 1863

Bull, John W. Pvt. Co. K; note 1. Co. A; notes 25, 34, 41, 45, 53, 71

Bunch, Alexander Pvt. Co. A; note 1. Co. G; notes 25, 34, 41, 45; captured Canton, July 1863; paroled and rejoined Mar. 1, 1864

Bunch, D. B. Pvt. Co. D; note 1. Co. I; notes 25, 34, 41, 50; paroled and rejoined at Missionary Ridge, Sept. 26, 1863; note 77

Bunch, Enoch H. Pvt. Co. A; note 5. 2d corp. Co. G; notes 25, 34, 41, 45, 53, 65 (during part of both days' fight), 75

Bunch, Francis M. Pvt. Co. A; note 1. 1st sgt. Co. G; notes 25, 34, 41, 51, 53, 65 (during part of both days' fight), 73; present Resaca, New Hope Church, Atlanta, Jonesboro, Murfreesboro

Bunch, J. Pvt. Co. E; note 1; transferred Forty-eighth Tenn. at reorganization at Jackson, Sept. 1862

Bunch, James W. Pvt. Co. A; note 14

Bunch, T. J. Pvt. Co. G; enlisted Nov. 14, 1862; notes 24, 34, 41, 49; paroled and rejoined co. Oct. 1, 1863, note 73

Bunch, W. A. Pvt. Co. D; note 1; note 18, Jackson, Oct. 1862

Burgess, G. B. Pvt. Co. G; died Bowling Green, Nov. 26, 1861

Burgess, H. L. Pvt. Co. H; transferred from Thirty-Second Tenn. at Missionary Ridge, Oct. 1863, note 73

Burgess, J. C. J. Pvt. Co. G; note 1; note 18, Jackson, Oct. 1862

Burgess, J. H. Pvt. Co. G; note 1. 4th corp. Co. H; notes 25, 34, 41, 45, 53, 62 (barefooted), 74; deserted near Dalton, Ga., Dec. 1, 1863

Burkett, Caleb Pvt. Co. C; died home, Aug. 27, 1861

Burkett, W. Edward Pvt. Co. C; note 3. Co. D; notes 25, 34, 41, 45, 53, 71

Burton, William P. Pvt. Co. A; note 8, May 1, 1862

Busby, J. J. Pvt. Co. I; note 19, provost marshal's office, Bowling Green; joined Nixon's Forty-eighth Tenn.

Bynum, John W. Pvt. Co. C; note 1. Co. D; notes 24, 34, 41, 45, 53, 70 (mortally); died at field hospital Chickamauga, Oct. 8, 1863

Bynum, William M.   4th corp. Co. C; note 1.   Pvt. Co. D; notes 25, 34, 41, 45; note 59, mortally, July 11, 1863; died Point Clear hospital near Mobile, Ala., Sept. 23, 1863

Byrd, William   Pvt. Co. I; note 11; never rejoined

Caldwell, J. B.   Pvt. Co. A; enlisted Dec. 1861; transferred from Fifty-third Tenn., Mar. 2, 1863; note 41; died Port Hudson, Apr. 1863

Caldwell, J. P.   Pvt. Co. F; enlisted Dec. 1, 1862; notes 24, 35 (excused by commander on account of cowardice), 41; left field at Raymond without leave; notes 55, 63, 74 (barefooted)

Caldwell, John G.   Pvt. Co. B; note 1.   2d sgt. Co. B; notes 30, 34, 41, 45, 55, 63, 73

Caldwell, W. A.   Pvt. Co. E; note 13; joined Col. Nixon's Forty-eighth Tenn.; rejoined regt. after exchange at Vicksburg, Dec. 27, 1862; notes 35, 41, 45, 53, 61 (Sept. 19), 65 (Sept. 20), 74 (barefooted)

Caldwell, W. H.   Pvt. Co. B; note 1.   Co. B; notes 25, 34, 41, 45, 53, 61, 75

Callahan, S. V.   Pvt. Co. I; died Camp Trousdale, Aug. 20, 1861

Calvert, L. N.   Pvt. Co. B; enlisted Oct. 31, 1862; notes 24, 34, 41, 45, 53, 68, 78

Calvert, W. H.   Pvt. Co. B; note 10, rejoined regt. after exchange. Co. B; notes 24, 34, 41, 45; note 60, July 11, 1863

Campbell A. J.   Pvt. Co. H; note 1.   Co. C; notes 25, 34, 41, 45, 53, 61, 73

Campbell, J. B.   Pvt. Co. E; note 1.   Co. F; notes 27, 34, 41, 45, 53, 62 (barefooted), 73

Campbell, W. A.   Pvt. Co. K; note 1.   Co. A; notes 25, 34; transferred Fifty-third Tenn., Port Hudson, Mar. 5, 1863

Camper, John   Pvt. Co. D; note 6; joined First Tenn. Cavalry and killed

Cannon, A. R.   Pvt. Co. B; note 1.   1st corp. Co. B; notes 24, 34, 41, 47, 55, 68, 78

Cannon, S. H.   Pvt. Co. B; enlisted Nov. 1, 1862; joined regt. Tippah Ford, Nov. 28, 1862; notes 25, 34, 41, 52

Caperton, F. G.   Pvt. Co. I; note 1.   Co. K; notes 29, 38, 41, 54 (without leave), 65, 73; deserted Nov. 30, 1863

Capps, W. R.   Pvt. Co. G; note 1.   Co. H; notes 27, 36, 41, 45

Cardin, Larkin   Pvt. Co. K; note 1.   2d corp. Co. A; notes 25, 36, 41, 48, 54 (having been captured and paroled by enemy), 61, 73

Cardin, William D.   5th sgt., Co. K; note 1.   Pvt. Co. A; notes 25, 34, 41; promoted 3d sgt. at promotion of Abernathy, Apr. 12, 1863; note 52

Cardwell, A. E.   3d sgt. Co. D; note 8, Sept. 4, 1862

Cardwell, J. J.   Pvt. Co. D; note 1.   1st corp. Co. I; notes 25, 34, 41, 45, 53, 69

Carothers, J. E.   2d corp. Co. I; note 1.   5th sgt. Co. K; notes 25, 34, 41, 45, 53, 65, 73

Carter, J. M.   Pvt. Co. I; enlisted Dec. 1862; notes 24, 34, 41, 47, 53, 61, 73

Carter, Jonas   Pvt. Co. K; note 18, Bowling Green, Nov. 1861

Carter, R. V.   Pvt. Co. A; note 20; entered cavalry

Carter, T. T.   Pvt. Co. D; note 1.   Co. I; notes 24, 34, 41, 51, 53, 61, 73

Carter, W. E.   Pvt. Co. D; note 13; joined Forty-eighth Tenn.

Cartwright, Mark   5th sgt. Co. C; absent Donelson by reason of accidental wound; entered cavalry

Cash, T. W.   Pvt. Co. E; note 19 with quartermaster in Bowling Green; rejoined regt. after exchange at Coldwater, Miss., Nov. 15, 1862. Co. F; notes 25, 34, 41; note 43, Apr. 1863

Causby, Thomas   Pvt. Co. A; note 18, Camp Cheatham, May 25, 1861

Cavin, R. B.   Pvt. Co. E; note 16; rejoined regt. after exchange. Co. F; notes 24, 34, 41; note 82 from Port Hudson, Apr. 1, 1863, and never rejoined

Chaffin, E. C.   Pvt. Co. G; note 1.   2d corp. Co. H; notes 25, 34, 41, 52

Chaffin, J. C.   1st lt. Co. I; wounded at Donelson and captured; escaped after surrender; absent at reorganization and dropped from rolls

Chambers, Edward   Pvt. Co. G; enlisted Nov. 10, 1862; note 22, Apr. 1863; notes 47, 55, 61, 75

Chatman, W. T.   Pvt. Co. E; note 14

Cheairs, Nathaniel F.   Elected maj., May 16, 1861; commanded regt. at Donelson after Lt. Col. Gordon wounded; captured and imprisoned Ft. Warren, Mass.; exchanged Aug. 1862; resigned 1862

Cheatham, A. W.   Pvt. Co. K; note 9; exchanged Sept. 23, 1862. Co. A; notes 25, 34, 44

Cheatham, Polk   Pvt. Co. F; note 8, Mar. 10, 1862

Cheatham, W. H.   Pvt. Co. K; died Bowling Green, Dec. 25, 1861

Cheek, R. N.   Pvt. Co. F; note 20; served in cavalry; rejoined after exchange. Co. E; notes 25, 37, 41, 49, 80

Childers, J. V.   3d corp. Co. E; note 19, asst. surgeon in hospital at Nashville; promoted surgeon

Childers, John   Pvt. Co. C; died Camp Trousdale, Sept. 5, 1861

Childers, John W.   Pvt. Co. K; sick in quarters during Donelson; captured and imprisoned Camp Butler; exchanged Sept. 23, 1862. Co. A; notes 25, 34, 41, 50; imprisoned

Childers, Robert H. Pvt. Co. A; enlisted Nov. 4, 1862; notes 21, 25, 34, 41, 47, 55, 70 (mortally)

Childress, J. W. 4th corp. Co. I; note 1. 2d corp. Co. K; notes 25, 34, 41, 45, 53, 61, 73; elected jr. 2d lt. at death of J. H. Hagan, Mar. 1864

Childress, W. H. Pvt. Co. I; note 1. 2d sgt. Co. K; notes 25, 34, 41, 51, 53, 63, 73

Childrey, R. S. Pvt. Co. F; note 1. Co. E; notes 25, 34, 41, 45, 53, 63, 75

Childs, G. W. Pvt. Co. K; note 6; joined army and present Shiloh; rejoined after exchange. Co. A; rejoined Dec. 7, 1862; notes 34, 44

Chiles, James Pvt. Co. G; note 16; joined Fifth Tenn., wounded Richmond; rejoined after exchange Port Hudson, Apr. 1863. Co. H; notes 47, 53, 61, 73

Chiles, Thomas H. 1st sgt. Co. G; died Camp Trousdale, Aug. 21, 1861

Chiles, W. B. Pvt. Co. G; note 1. 3d corp. Co. H; notes 25, 34, 41, 45, 53; made sgt. Jan. 1863; notes 62 (furlough), 73

Christian, N. J. Pvt. Co. H; note 5; transferred Forty-eighth Tenn., Jackson, Sept. 1862

Clack, Calvin J. Capt. Co. A; note 2, in command of his company. Elected lt. col. at reorganization, Sept. 26, 1862; notes 31, 34 (in command of regt.), 41, 45, 53, 61; note 73 (in command of regt.); present at Resaca and Atlanta; killed Jonesboro

Clack, Spencer D. Pvt. Co. A; note 5. 4th corp. Co. G; note 33, Dec. 4, 1862; note 79; exchanged at City Point, Va., rejoined the regt. May 11, 1863; notes 45, 55, 61, 74 (furlough)

Clanton, A. C. Pvt. Co. C; note 8, July 28, 1862

Clark, J. S. Pvt. Co. E; note 20; rejoined after exchange

Clark, J. T. Pvt. Co. E; note 1. Co. F; notes 26 (blindness), 34, 41, 45; made corp. Cane Creek, Miss., July 3, 1863; note 59 (July 11, 1863); died Lauderdale Springs, about Aug. 1, 1863

Claxton, M. D. Pvt. Co. H; enlisted Nov. 1, 1862; notes 24, 34, 41, 45, 55, 63, 75

Claxton, W. L. Pvt. Co. H; enlisted Nov. 10, 1862; notes 24, 34, 41, 52

Clayton, Francis Pvt. Co. H; died Bowling Green, Dec. 14, 1861

Clayton, George Pvt. Co. H; note 1. Co. C; notes 25, 34, 41, 51, 57, 66, 78

Clayton, Henry Pvt. Co. H; note 1. Co. C; notes 27, 34, 41, 45, 53, 61, 73; made 5th sgt. when J. W. Hensley captured, Oct. 31, 1863

Clayton, S. M. 4th sgt. Co. G; note 12. Pvt. Co. H; notes 25, 34, 41, 45; detached as ambulance driver about June 20, 1863; rejoined Feb. 28, 1864

Clift, Thomas Pvt. Co. G; died Bowling Green, Jan. 1, 1862

Clift, W. P.   Pvt. Co. G; note 16; joined Fifth Tenn., then Thirty-second; rejoined after exchange Missionary Ridge, Sept. 22, 1863.   Co. H; note 77; deserted Dalton, Dec. 1, 1863

Clinton, T. J.   Pvt. Co. C; died Maury County, Tenn., Sept. 4, 1861

Cobb, P. F.   Pvt. Co. I; note 11; joined cavalry

Cobb, William   Pvt. Co. I; note 1.   Co. K; notes 25, 34, 41, 45, 53, 64, 76

Cochran, J. J.   Pvt. Co. B; note 19 as nurse in hospital Russellville, Ky.; never rejoined

Coffee, J. P.   Pvt. Co. D; deserted to enemy from Camp Trousdale, Aug. 1861

Coffey, J. F.   Pvt. Co. F; died Bowling Green, Nov. 20, 1861

Coffey, J. M. G.   Pvt. Co. F; note 1.   Co. E; notes 25, 34, 41; died Clinton, Apr. 1863

Coffey, T. J.   Pvt. Co. F; note 1.   Co. E; notes 24, 34, 41, 45, 53, 63, 76

Coker, W. J.   Pvt. Co. B; note 1.   Co. B; notes 29, 34, 41, 45, 53, 68, 77

Coleburn, T. J.   Pvt. Co. C; present Donelson and carried battle flag; captured; took oath of allegiance to the U.S. at St. Louis and released; rejoined after exchange, Sept. 26, 1863, Missionary Ridge; note 75

Collins, John C.   Pvt. Co. C; note 1; note 18, Jackson, Oct. 10, 1862

Collins, W. G.   Pvt. Co. G; note 1.   Co. H; notes 25, 34; made corp. Port Hudson, Feb. 1, 1863; notes 41, 45, 53, 61 (Sept. 19), 65 (Sept. 20), 77

Combs, Charles   Pvt. Co. H; note 11; joined Federal army; drummed out of service and put back in prison; exchanged Sept. 23, 1862. Co. C; notes 26, 35, under arrest; note 41; transferred Capt. McNally's battery, May 4, 1863

Compton, F. S.   Pvt. Co. D; note 1.   Co. I; notes 25, 34, 41, 47; died hospital Brandon, Miss., July 13, 1863

Compton, J. B.   2d corp. Co. B; present Donelson; killed while bearing colors of regt. Feb. 15, 1862

Compton, J. L.   Pvt. Co. B; enlisted Nov. 3, 1862; notes 24, 34, 41, 52

Compton, J. S.   Pvt. Co. B; note 6; rejoined after exchange.   Co. B; notes 24, 34, 41, 45, 53, 72

Compton, Jeffrey   Pvt. Co. G; note 18, Bowling Green, Oct. 6, 1861

Compton, N. F.   Musician Co. D; note 1.   Co. I; apptd. regimental bugler; deserted Lauderdale Springs, Aug. 10, 1863

Compton, W. C.   Pvt. Co. D; note 1.   Co. I; notes 25, 34, 41, 47; died Jackson, June 1863

Conder, G. H.   Pvt. Co. H; note 1.   Co. C; notes 25, 34, 41, 49; escaped and deserted, June 1863

Conder, J. W.   Pvt. Co. H; note 1.   Co. C; notes 25, 34, 41, 51, 57, 66, 78

Conder, M. L.   Pvt. Co. H; note 1.   Co. C; notes 25, 38, 41, 49; escaped and rejoined July 30, 1863; deserted Sept. 6, 1863

Conder, W. J.   Pvt. Co. H; note 1; note 82, from Jackson, Sept. 30, 1862, and deserted

Cook S. G.   Pvt. Co. I; note 20; joined cavalry

Cook, W. R.   Pvt. Co. G; note 1.   Co. H; notes 25, 36; note 18, Port Hudson, Mar. 12, 1863

Cooper, Alexander D.   Pvt. Co. H; died home, July 10, 1861

Cooper, J. H.   Pvt. Co. H; note 1; note 18, at Jackson, Oct. 1862

Cooper, J. O.   Pvt. Co. E; note 1.   Co. F; notes 29, 34, 41; deserted Port Hudson, Apr. 12, 1863

Cooper, L. B.   Pvt. Co. H; note 1.   Co. C; notes 25, 34, 41, 51, 57, 66, 78

Cooper, Robert T.   2d lt. Co. H; exchanged positions with S. L. Tarrent at Camp Cheatham; capt. May 28, 1861; note 2, in command of co. Reelected capt. Co. C at reorganization Sept. 1862; notes 31, 34 (in command of co.), 42 (furlough), 52

Cooper, Samuel G.   Pvt. Co. H; note 8, Apr. 24, 1862

Cooper, T. M.   Pvt. Co. H; mortally wounded Donelson; died on way to Nashville

Cooper, W. J.   Pvt. Co. F; enlisted Dec. 12, 1862; notes 24, 34, 41, 45, 55, 63, 75

Copeland, Anderson   Pvt. Co. C; died Russellville, Feb. 1862

Cosby, E. H. F.   Pvt. Co. G; enlisted Nov. 10, 1862; note 22, Mar. 1863; note 47; captured June 1863, near Big Black, Miss.

Couch, William   Pvt. Co. B; note 15, joined Eleventh Tenn. Cavalry

Courtney, J. H.   Pvt. Co. F; note 1.   Co. E; notes 25, 34, 41, 50; paroled and deserted July 1, 1863

Cowan, Joseph V.   1st sgt. Co. A at Donelson on detached duty in Capt. Porter's battery; captured and escaped after surrender; discharged at Corinth, Miss., by order of Gen. Johnston, Mar. 1862

Cowsert, I. K.   Pvt. Co. E; note 15; joined Forty-seventh Tenn.; rejoined regt. at Dalton, Jan. 1, 1864; appointed 3d sgt. at desertion of T. B. Terrell

Cowsert J. J.   Pvt. Co. F; transferred from Forty-eighth Tenn., Port Hudson, Feb. 1863; notes 41, 49; paroled and deserted

Cowsert, R. S.   Pvt. Co. F; enlisted Sept. 1862; transferred from cavalry Jan. 1863; notes 41, 45, 53, 61 (Sept. 19), 62 (Sept. 20 excused by surgeon), 74 (barefooted)

Cox, P. J.   Pvt. Co. G; note 1; note 18, Jackson, Oct. 6, 1862

Cox, W. J.   Pvt. Co. C; note 1.   Co. D; notes 25, 34, 41, 50, 79; exchanged at City Point, July 1863; rejoined at Enterprise, Aug. 11, 1863; notes 61, 73

Craig, D. A.   Pvt. Co. F; note 1.   Co. E; notes 25, 34, 41, 51; lost right arm and permanently disabled

Craig, James E. 2d corp. Co. C; note 1. Pvt. Co. D; notes 25, 36, 41, 45, 55; note 61, Sept. 19; note 65, Sept. 20; note 73

Craig, James F. Pvt. Co. E; transferred from Thirty-second Miss., Mar. 1, 1864

Craig, John B. Pvt. Co. C; note 18, Bowling Green, Dec. 1861

Craig, R. F. Pvt. Co. C; note 1. Co. D; notes 25, 34, 41, 45, 53, 61, 75

Craig, S. S. Pvt. Co. F; note 1. Co. E; notes 25, 37 (teamster), 41; notes 48, 56, as teamster; appointed commissary sgt. Sept. 1863

Craig, W. J. Pvt. Co. F; note 1. Co. E; notes 25, 34, 41, 45, 53, 69 (slightly), 78

Crawford, E. E. 3d sgt. Co. E; elected lt. June 1861; note 19, sappers and miners; never rejoined

Crews, A. E. 1st corp. Co. F; note 13, rejoined after exchange. Pvt. Co. E; notes 24, 37, 41, 49; paroled and deserted July 1, 1863

Crews, J. H. 2d corp. Co. F; note 14

Crews, P. L. Pvt. Co. E; enlisted Nov. 10, 1862; notes 24, 34, 41, 45, 53, 71

Crews, R. T. Pvt. Co. E; enlisted Nov. 10, 1862; notes 24, 36, 41, 47, 55, 62 (barefooted); deserted Lookout Mountain, Nov. 24, 1863

Crews, W. J. Pvt. Co. F; note 14

Cross, J. M. Pvt. Co. E; enlisted Nov. 10, 1862; notes 24, 34, 41, 51, 57; deserted hospital Raymond about Sept. 1, 1863

Cross, S. H. Pvt. Co. D; enlisted Nov. 1, 1862; note 23, Dec. 1862; notes 34, 41, 45, 55, 65, 75

Cross, S. S. Pvt. Co. E; enlisted Nov. 10, 1862; notes 24, 34, 41, 45, 55; notes 64, 76 with commissary dept.

Crump, G. K. Pvt. Co. E; note 7, June 5, 1862; rejoined regt. after exchange, Vicksburg, Dec. 27, 1862; note 41; deserted May 3, 1863

Culps, R. L. Pvt. Co. K; note 16; joined Ninth Ala.; wounded Richmond

Curtis, W. W. Pvt. Co. E; note 1. Co. F; notes 25, 34, 41, 45, 53; note 82 from Enterprise, Aug. 1863; deserted Sept. 1863

Dabbs, J. C. Pvt. Co. H; note 1; note 18, at Jackson, Oct. 8, 1862

Dabney, J. H. Pvt. Co. G; note 1. Co. H; notes 25, 34, 41, 45, 53, 63; ran at Missionary Ridge

Dabney, N. I. Pvt. Co. E; note 15; discharged Decatur, Ala., about Apr. 1, 1861

Dabney, W. M. 3d sgt. Co. G; note 5. 5th sgt. Co. H; notes 25, 34, 41, 45; note 58, July 15, 1863; imprisoned Camp Morton, Ind.

Darden, Benjamin G. 2d lt. Co. F; note 2. Reelected 2d lt. Co. E at reorganization, Sept. 1862; notes 31, 34, 41, 51, 57; note 82, July 1, 1863

Daugherty, Maxwell *See* Dougherty, Maxwell

Davis, A. B. Pvt. Co. F; note 14

Davis, A. C. Pvt. Co. F; note 16; deserted to enemy

Davis, A. C. Pvt. Co. G; note 16; joined Col. Hill's Fifth Tenn.; promoted lt.

Davis, Black Pvt. Co. E; enlisted Nov. 10, 1862; notes 24, 34, 41, 45; deserted Cane Creek, July 4, 1863

Davis, Carter 1st corp. Co. B; note 6; rejoined after exchange. Pvt. Co. B; notes 24, 34, 41, 45, 53, 72

Davis, G. F. M. 5th sgt. Co. H; note 1. Pvt. Co. C; notes 25, 34, 41; notes 46, 54, 62, 74, all on account of accidental wound

Davis, H. B. Pvt. Co. F; note 6; joined cavalry

Davis, J. H. Pvt. Co. F; note 7, Apr. 15, 1862; joined cavalry

Davis, J. S. Pvt. Co. H; note 18, Bowling Green, Oct. 1861

Davis, R. C. Pvt. Co. F; died Bowling Green, Dec. 15, 1861

Davis, W. M. Pvt. Co. E; notes 17, 24. Co. F; notes 38, 41, 47, 55; deserted near Ringgold, Ga., Sept. 18, 1863

Davis, W. R. Pvt. Co. K; note 15, Dover hospital; captured and imprisoned Camp Butler; exchanged Sept. 23, 1862. Co. A; notes 25, 34, 44

Davis, W. S. Pvt. Co. H; absent Donelson on furlough, entered cavalry

Davis, William Pvt. Co. E; enlisted Nov. 10, 1862; notes 24, 34, 41, 45; deserted Cane Creek, July 4, 1863

Dawson, Mann Pvt. Co. C; note 1. Co. D; notes 25, 34, 41, 45, 53, 69 (slightly and left field), 73

Deavenport, H. Pvt. Co. G; enlisted Nov. 3, 1862; notes 24, 36, 42 (sick), 47, 55, 62 (barefooted), 75

Deavenport, J. D. Pvt. Co. G; note 1. Co. H; notes 25, 34, 41, 45, 53, 61, 73

Deavenport, Thomas H. Pvt. Co. G; note 1. Co. H; appointed chaplain, Oct. 21, 1862; sent up resignation Apr. 1863; received leave until it could be heard from; no reply received; rejoined Jan. 25, 1864

Deen, J. G. B. Pvt. Co. H; note 1; note 18, Jackson, Oct. 1862

Deen, M. L. Pvt. Co. H; note 9, exchanged Sept. 23, 1862. Co. C; notes 25, 34, 41, 51, 57, 66, 78; discharged Dec. 28, 1863

Deen, M. L., Jr. Pvt. Co. H; note 9, exchanged Sept. 23, 1862. Co. C; notes 25, 34; note 43, Feb. 22, 1863

Deen, N. M. Pvt. Co. H; note 9; exchanged Sept. 23, 1862. Co. C; notes 25, 38, 41, 49; escaped and deserted, June 1863

Deen, W. W. Pvt. Co. H; note 9, exchanged Sept. 23, 1862; note 18, Jackson, Oct. 1862

Defoe, J. C. Pvt. Co. I; note 8, May 1862

DeGraffenreid, T. A. Pvt. Co. K; note 1. Co. A; notes 25, 34, 41, 51, 53, 61, 73

Denton, J. H. Pvt. Co. E; note 1. 3d corp. Co. F; notes 25, 34, 41, 45, 53, 65, 73

Dial, J. D. Pvt. Co. I; note 5. Co. K; notes 28, 37, 44

Dickson, James M. Pvt. Co. A; note 16; served in cavalry until exchanged; rejoined Holly Springs, Oct. 1862. Co. G; notes 25, 34, 41, 45, 55, 63, 75

Dobbins, J. J. Pvt. Co. E; note 15; joined Col. Nixon's Forty-eighth Tenn.

Dodson, John Pvt. Co. H; note 1. Co. C; notes 25, 34, 41, 45, 53; deserted Enterprise, Sept. 6, 1863

Doss, W. B. Pvt. Co. G; note 5. Co. H; notes 25, 34, 41, 51; lost left arm; permanently disabled

Dotson, Alexander Pvt. Co. C; note 1. Co. D; notes 29, 34, 41, 45, 53, 63, 73

Dougherty, M. A. Pvt. Co. K; note 1. Co. A; notes 25, 38, 41, 45, 53, 65 (Sept. 20), 73

Dougherty, Maxwell Pvt. Co. B; note 1. 4th sgt. Co. B; notes 25, 34, 41, 45, 53, 68, 73 (wounded)

Douglas, H. B. Pvt. Co. C; note 1; transferred Forty-eighth Tenn., Holly Springs, Oct. 1862

Dowell, L. V. Pvt. Co. E; note 1. Co. F; notes 25, 34, 41, 49; exchanged and rejoined Oct. 1863; note 73; appointed corp. Dec. 1, 1863, at promotion of Reams

Downing J. G. Pvt. Co. H; enlisted Oct. 18, 1862; notes 24, 34; transferred Forty-first Tenn., Fort Hudson, Mar. 1863

Doyel, James A. Jr. 2d lt. Co. H; absent from co. without leave during Donelson; captured and imprisoned Camp Chase and Johnson's Island; exchanged Sept. 16, 1862. Reelected jr. 2d lt. Co. C at reorganization Sept. 1862; notes 25, 38, 41; left field at Raymond without leave; promoted 1st lt. May 1863 and capt. June 1863 when R. T. Cooper killed; note 55; note 82 from Enterprise, Aug. 10, 1863, and never returned

Doyel, J. H. Pvt. Co. H; note 18, Bowling Green, Jan. 1862

Duncan, B. F. Pvt. Co. D; present at Donelson; captured; died prison St. Louis, Feb. 28, 1862

Dungy, Abner Pvt. Co. K; note 6; rejoined regt. after exchange, Dec. 7, 1862. Co. A; notes 34, 41, 45, 53; note 62, on furlough; note 73; deserted Rome, Feb. 14, 1864

Dungy, F. M. Pvt. Co. K; note 1. Co. A; notes 25, 34, 41, 45, 53, 61, 73

Dungy, John   Pvt. Co. K; note 18, Camp Trousdale, Aug. 1861

Dunham, W. C.   1st corp. Co. C; promoted 4th sgt. Sept. 14, 1861; note 1. Elected 1st lt. Co. D at reorganization, Sept. 1862; notes 31, 34, 41, 45, 53, 54, 75

Dunlap, T. F.   4th corp. Co. E; note 7, June 7, 1862; rejoined regt. after exchange Tippah Ford, Nov. 1862   Pvt. Co. F; notes 30, 38, 41, 46 (footsore), 53, 61 (Sept. 19), 65 (Sept. 20), 73; transferred Forty-eighth Tenn., Jan. 15, 1864

Dupree, H. M.   Pvt. Co. I; enlisted Dec. 1862; notes 24, 34, 41, 47, 53, 61, 73

Dupree, P. H.   Pvt. Co. D; note 17; entered cavalry

Durbin, J. A.   Pvt. Co. I; note 6; joined Nixon's Forty-eighth Tenn.

Dycus, J. Q. A.   Pvt. Co. C; note 1.   Co. D; notes 25, 34, 41, 45, 53, 61, 77

Dycus, Joseph   Pvt. Co. C; note 1.   Co. D; notes 25, 34, 41, 50, 81

Dyer, John W.   Pvt. Co. A; note 17; served in cavalry until exchanged; rejoined at Holly Springs, Oct. 1862.   Co. G; notes 25, 34, 41, 45, 53, 69; lost left arm, permanently disabled

Dyer, Zachary T.   Pvt. Co. K; note 1.   Co. A; notes 25, 34, 44

Eddington, H. L. W.   Pvt. Co. E; note 11; deserted to enemy

Edmiston, J. N.   Pvt. Co. I; note 1.   Co. K; notes 25, 34, 41, 45, 55; furloughed from hospital about Aug. 1, 1863; never rejoined

Edmiston, W. S.   Pvt. Co. I; died Russellville, Feb. 11, 1862

Edwards, J. J.   Pvt. Co. C; note 19, quartermaster's depot; joined cavalry

Edwards, P. H.   Pvt. Co. C; note 1. Elected 1st corp. Co. D at reorganization, Sept. 1862; notes 25, 34, 41, 45, 53, 61, 73

Edwards, W. T.   Pvt. Co. E; note 7, June 20, 1862; rejoined regt. after exchange Tippah Ford, Nov. 20, 1862.   Co. F; notes 25, 34, 41, 45, 53, 61, 73; made corp. Dec. 1, 1863

Elder, G. W.   Pvt. Co. A; enlisted Dec. 6, 1861; transferred from Fifty-third Tenn., Mar. 5, 1863; notes 41, 45, 53, 61, 73

Elder, J. H.   Pvt. Co. K; note 1.   Co. A; notes 25, 34, 41, 45, 53; note 61, Sept. 19; note 65, Sept. 20, note 73

Evans, B. W.   2d lt. Co. I; accidentally killed by musket shot Camp Trousdale, Aug. 1861

Everly, John H.   Pvt. Co. A; note 20; served cavalry until exchanged; rejoined Holly Springs, Oct. 1862.   Co. G; notes 27, 36, 42 (sick), 49

Everly, William D.   Pvt. Co. A; note 1.   Co. G; notes 25, 34, 41; note 43, Mar. 1863

Ewing, J. C. Pvt. Co. A; enlisted Nov. 8, 1862; note 23, Dec. 15, 1862; notes 36, 41, 51; note 49, May 15, 1863; paroled and went home; remained without leave

Ezell, J. P. Pvt. Co. G; note 1. Co. H; notes 25, 34, 41, 45; made corp. Mound Bluff, June 25, 1863; notes 53, 71

Ezell, J. P. Pvt. Co. K; died home in Giles County, July 27, 1861

Farley, A. J. Pvt. Co. B; note 6; transferred First Tenn. Cavalry by order of Lt. Gen. Pemberton, Tippah Ford, Nov. 1862

Farley, J. B. 2d sgt. Co. D; note 1. Elected 2d lt. Co. I at reorganization, Sept. 1862; notes 25, 34, 41, 49; imprisoned Johnson's Island

Farley, W. L. Pvt. Co. B; note 13, served cavalry until exchanged; note 24; transferred First Tenn. Cavalry, Grenada, Dec. 1862

Faught, Levi Pvt. Co. D; note 11, never rejoined

Faught, W. C. Pvt. Co. D; note 1. Co. I; notes 29, 38, 41, 45; deserted Jackson, May 14, 1863

Faulkner, F. Pvt. Co. F; note 19, nurse in hospital Nashville; never rejoined

Faust, J. M. Pvt. Co. I; note 9; exchanged Sept. 23, 1862. Co. K; absent without leave from every engagement; deserted Brandon, July 20, 1863

Faust, Richard Pvt. Co. I; note 1. Co. K; notes 27, 36, 41, 47, 55, 61, 75

Featherstone, A. G. Pvt. Co. D; note 1. Co. I; notes 25, 37 (cook), 41, 46 (without leave), 55

Featherstone, John Pvt. Co. D; note 6; joined ninth battalion of Tenn. cavalry

Ferguson, G. M. Pvt. Co. I; note 1. Co. K; notes 25, 34, 44

Ferguson, J. H. Pvt. Co. F; enlisted Dec. 1, 1862; notes 24, 34; died Port Hudson, Feb. 16, 1863

Ferguson, T. V. Musician, Co. E; note 1. 5th sgt. Co. F; note 33, Dec. 3, 1862; released upon taking oath of allegiance to U.S. at Oxford, Dec. 21, 1862; deserted and joined First Tenn. Cavalry

Ferguson, Thomas Pvt. Co. K; drummed out of service by sentence of court martial, Camp Cheatham, July 1861

Ferguson, W. A. Pvt. Co. I; note 1. Co. K; notes 25, 34, 41, 45, 55, 61, 77

Fisher, George W. Pvt. Co. C; note 8, Mar. 1, 1862

Fisher, J. D. Pvt. Co. I; note 8, Apr. 23, 1862

Fisher, William Pvt. Co. C; note 1. Co. D; note 25, captured Water Valley, Dec. 4, 1862; note 79; exchanged City Point, May 1, 1863; rejoined Jackson, May 10, 1863; notes 45, 53, 62 (barefooted), 73

Fite, Elias   Pvt. Co. H; note 18, Bowling Green, Dec. 1861

Fite, P. F.   Pvt. Co. H; note 1.   4th corp. Co. C; notes 25, 35, 41, 45, 53; note 62, on furlough; note 73

Fite, W. F.   Pvt. Co. H; note 1.   Co. C; notes 25, 34, 41, 45, 53, 61, 75

Fitzpatrick, John   Pvt. Co. B; note 15; rejoined after exchange; transferred First Tenn. Cavalry by order of Lt. Gen. Pemberton, Tippah Ford, Nov. 1862

Fitzpatrick, M. J.   Pvt. Co. F; note 7, Aug. 1862; joined cavalry

Flanigan, J. D.   Pvt. Co. H; note 1.   4th sgt. Co. C; notes 25, 34, 41, 45, 53, 71

Flautt, John D.   3d corp. Co. A; detached in commissary dept. Camp Cheatham, July 25, 1861; detailed in quartermaster dept. Corinth, Apr. 15, 1862; rejoined after exchange Oct. 1, 1862. Appointed quartermaster, Oct. 21, 1862, at resignation of J. L. Herron

Flippin, Joseph   Pvt. Co. A; note 1.   Co. G; notes 25, 34, 41, 45; note 58, July 15, 1863

Flippin, Thomas J.   Pvt. Co. A; note 1.   3d corp. Co. G; notes 25, 34, 41, 45, 53, 63, 73

Ford, A. C.   Pvt. Co. D; died home, Dec. 1861

Forsythe, H.   Pvt. Co. G; enlisted Nov. 16, 1862; notes 24, 36, 42 (sick), 47, 53, 61, 75

Foster, F. S.   Pvt. Co. H; enlisted Nov. 10, 1862; notes 24, 34, 41, 45, 53, 65; deserted Chattanooga Valley, Oct. 27, 1863

Foster, John   Pvt. Co. I; note 18, Camp Cheatham, July 1861

Foster, W. A.   Pvt. Co. G; note 1.   Co. H; notes 25, 34, 41, 45, 53, 63, 75

Foster, W. T.   Pvt. Co. G; note 20; joined First Tenn. Cavalry; never rejoined

Franklin, W. L.   Pvt. Co. K; note 6; rejoined after exchange, Dec. 11, 1862.   Co. A; notes 34, 41, 52

Franks, J. W.   Pvt. Co. B; note 1.   3d sgt. Co. B; notes 29, 34, 41, 45, 55, 64, 76

Franks, W. H.   Pvt. Co. G; note 1.   Co. H; notes 25, 34; transferred Co. B, Vicksburg, Jan. 3, 1863; notes 41, 45, 53, 61, 73

Freeman, Fuller   Pvt. Co. I; accidentally injured and sent home before Donelson; never rejoined

Freeman, H. J.   Pvt. Co. K; enlisted Nov. 12, 1862; notes 24, 36, 41, 50; imprisoned

Freeman, J. F.   3d corp. Co. G; note 1.   Pvt. Co. H; notes 25, 34, 41, 45; note 58, July 15, 1863; imprisoned

Freeman, J. L.   Pvt. Co. I; note 1.   Co. K; notes 25, 34, 41, 52

Freeman, John Pvt. Co. G. note 11, Aug. 1862; joined Thirty-second
  Tenn., Co. H; rejoined at Missionary Ridge, Sept. 22, 1863; deserted
  Chattanooga Valley, Nov. 1, 1863

Fray, W. E. Pvt. Co. B; enlisted Nov. 5, 1862; notes 24, 36, 41 (sick), 47;
  note 58, July 15, 1863, and imprisoned at Camp Morton

Fry, Eber Made hospital steward May 17, 1861; escaped Donelson after
  surrender; never rejoined

Fry, J. M. Pvt. Co. B; note 5; deserted Oxford, Nov. 1862; joined Holman's Tenn. battalion of cavalry

Fry, M. M. Pvt. Co. B; discharged Bowling Green, Dec. 17, 1861; entered
  cavalry

Fry, W. B. Pvt. Co. B; note 1; note 18, Jackson, Miss., Sept. 29, 1862

Fry, W. P. Pvt. Co. B; note 1. Co. B; note 33, Dec. 3, 1862, note 79; exchanged Apr. 1863; rejoined regt. Osyka, Miss., May 6, 1863; notes 45,
  53, 61, 73

Fuller, A. B. Pvt. Co. K; note 1. Co. A; notes 25, 34, 41, 45, 53, 61, 73

Furgerson, M. H. Pvt. Co. K; enlisted Nov. 16, 1862; notes 22 (Jan. 28,
  1863), 41, 45, 55, 61; deserted Chattanooga Valley, Oct. 23, 1863

Furgerson, T. H. Pvt. Co. K; enlisted Oct. 22, 1862; notes 24, 34, 41, 45,
  53, 68, 78

Galloway, E. S. Pvt. Co. F; note 1; detached as butcher for division under command of Brig. Gen. Tilghman, Nov. 20, 1862; wounded and
  captured at Vicksburg; note 82, died Oct. 17, 1863

Galloway, Robert Pvt. Co. E; enlisted Nov. 10, 1862; notes 24, 34, 41,
  47, 53, 61, 73; made corp. Dec. 1, 1863

Gannon, Patrick Pvt. Co. C; note 11, June 4, 1862; joined the enemy

Garner, J. K. P Pvt. Co. A; note 1. Co. G; notes 25, 34, 41, 51, 57,
  66, 78

Garrett, D. B. Pvt. Co. B; note 1. Co. B; notes 25, 34, 41, 45, 53, 61, 75

Garrett, D. P. Pvt. Co. H; note 1. 1st corp. Co. C; notes 25, 34, 41, 45,
  53, 71

Garrett, J. S. Pvt. Co. F; note 6; never rejoined

Garrett, S. Pvt. Co. F; made 3d sgt.; note 13; rejoined regt. after exchange

Garrett, S. L. P. Pvt. Co. G; note 1. Co. H; notes 25, 34; transferred
  Forty-first Tenn., Port Hudson, Mar. 12, 1863

Garrett, W. R. M. Pvt. Co. I; note 1. Co. K; notes 25, 34, 41, 51, 57,
  63, 75

Garrett, W. T. Pvt. Co. G; note 16; joined First Tenn. Cavalry; never
  rejoined

Garrison, William E. Pvt. Co. K; note 1. 1st corp. Co. A; notes 25, 34, 41, 47, 54 (captured and paroled by the enemy), 61; transferred to Thirty-second Tenn., Oct. 1863

Geisler, F. Pvt. Co. B; note 1. Co. B; notes 25, 36, 41, 49, 80; deserted to enemy

Gentry, H. D. Pvt. Co. H; note 1. Co. C; notes 25, 34, 41, 52

George, J. M. A. Pvt. Co. K; note 18, Camp Trousdale, Aug. 1861; joined Forty-first Tenn.

George, John H. Pvt. Co. C; transferred Twenty-sixth Tenn., Dec. 1861

Gibbs, W. H. Pvt. Co. K; note 15, Nashville; joined Forty-fourth Tenn. and promoted lt.

Gibson, G. W. Pvt. Co. D; note 1. Co. I; notes 25, 34, 41, 45, 53, 61, 73

Gibson, J. P. Pvt. Co. I; enlisted Dec. 1862; note 22, Apr. 1863; notes 50, 80; released and joined enemy

Gibson, W. H. Pvt. Co. D; note 1. Co. I; notes 25, 34; died Port Hudson, Feb. 1863

Giddens, James 4th sgt. Co. C; promoted jr. 2d lt. Sept. 14, 1861; note 2; not reelected and dropped from rolls

Gifford, Frank Pvt. Co. F; note 1. Co. E; notes 24, 37, 44

Gilbert, H. C. Pvt. Co. K; died Camp Cheatham, June, 1861

Gillmore, J. M. 3d sgt. Co. H; made 1st sgt. at promotion of W. Harder, Dec. 1861; note 1. Pvt. Co. C; notes 25, 34, 41, 50

Gilmore, J. J. Pvt. Co. D; note 1. 3d sgt. Co. I; notes 25, 34, 41, 45, 53, 70, 78

Gilmore, John Pvt. Co. E; enlisted Nov. 10, 1862; never reported

Glenn, J. B. Pvt. Co. B; died Camp Cheatham, June 17, 1861

Goad, J. R. 3d sgt. Co. F; died Camp Cheatham, Aug. 7, 1861

Golden, T. M. Pvt. Co. E; present Donelson; captured and imprisoned Camp Douglas; killed in prison by a comrade, W. H. Kilpatrick, Apr. 1862

Goldman, Joseph 2d sgt. Co. B; note 7, Mar. 1862; rejoined after exchange. Pvt. Co. B; notes 25, 34, 41, 45, 53, 68, 78

Goode, Patrick Pvt. Co. A; note 3. Co. G; notes 25, 34, 41, 45, 53, 61, 73; killed Resaca

Goodloe, H. G. Pvt. Co. D; notes 24, 34, 41, 45, 53, 62 (barefooted), 77

Goodloe, John P. Pvt. Co. C; note 13; rejoined after exchange. Co. D; notes 24, 38, 41; left field without leave at Raymond and Jackson; accidentally injured Enterprise, Aug. 1863; notes 62, 74 (on account of hurt)

Goodloe, Rufus T. Pvt. Co. C; died Maury County, Tenn., June 11, 1861

Goodman, C. H. Pvt. Co. H; note 8, Mar. 14, 1862

Goodman, W. E. Pvt. Co. H; note 1; note 18, Jackson, Oct. 1862

Goodnight, R. A. Pvt. Co. H; enlisted Nov. 10, 1862; notes 24, 34, 41, 45, 53, 61 (Sept. 19), 65 (Sept. 20), 75

Goodrich, J. T. Pvt. Co. F; note 1. 4th sgt. Co. E at reorganization Sept. 1862; notes 25, 34, 41, 45, 59 (slightly, July 11, 1863), 61, 73

Gordon, E. H. F. Capt. Co. B; in command of co., note 2; not reelected at reorganization and dropped from rolls

Gordon, Edward M. Pvt. Co. A; mortally wounded at Donelson; died on way to Nashville

Gordon, J. F. Pvt. Co. C; note 1. Co. D; notes 25, 34, 41, 51, 57, 62 (on furlough), 75

Gordon, John A. Pvt. Co. A; transferred Col. Biffle's cavalry Bowling Green, Oct. 1861

Gordon, Jonathan Pvt. Co. C; note 18, Sept. 1861

Gordon, Thomas M. L. Elected lt. col. May 16, 1861; command regt. Donelson; wounded in charge on Taylor's battery; sent to Nashville before surrender; resigned 1862

Granberry, John J. Pvt. Co. C; note 13; discharged

Grant, G. F. Pvt. Co. E; deserted Camp Trousdale, Aug. 12, 1861

Grant, George H. Pvt. Co. K; note 15, Bowling Green; never rejoined

Graves, Frank Pvt. Co. E; enlisted Nov. 10, 1862; transferred from Forty-eighth Tenn., Port Hudson, Apr. 1863; note 45; deserted Cane Creek, July 4, 1863

Graves, J. L. Pvt. Co. D; note 15; rejoined after exchange. Co. I; notes 24, 34, 42 (sick), 47, 55; note 18, Enterprise, Aug. 1863

Graves, P. P. Pvt. Co. F; note 1. Co. E; notes 27, 34, 41, 47, 55, 63, 75

Green [no first name] Pvt. Co. D; deserted Camp Trousdale, Aug. 1861

Green, J. L. Pvt. Co. I; note 1. Co. K; notes 25, 34, 41, 45, 53, 63, 75

Green, J. S. Pvt. Co. B; absent Donelson on furlough; discharged as non-conscript

Green, John Pvt. Co. I; note 1. Co. K; notes 29, 34, 41, 45, 56; deserted Brandon, July 20, 1863

Green, V. A. S. Pvt. Co. I; note 1. 1st corp. Co. K; notes 29, 34, 41, 45, 55, 63, 75

Green, W. A. Pvt. Co. I; note 1. Co. K; notes 24, 34, 41, 51, 57, 66, 78

Griffin, O. R. Pvt. Co. B; note 1. Co. B; notes 29, 34, 44

Griffis, Robert V. 5th sgt. Co. B; note 1. 1st sgt. Co. B; notes 25, 34, 41, 51, 57, 70, 78

Griffis, W. W. Pvt. Co. B; enlisted Nov. 5, 1862; notes 24, 36, 41, 47, 53, 61, 73

Griggs, R. P. Pvt. Co. G; note 13; served cavalry and rejoined after exchange. Co. H; notes 25, 34, 41, 45, 53, 61, 74 (barefooted)

Griggs, Y. M. Pvt. Co. G; note 8, Mar. 26, 1862

Grigsby, F. M. Pvt. Co. B; died Camp Trousdale, Sept. 15, 1861

Grigsby, J. N. Pvt. Co. B; note 15; served cavalry until exchanged. Co. B; notes 25, 34, 41, 51, 57, 66, 78

Grigsby, M. G. Pvt. Co. B; enlisted Oct. 19, 1862; joined at Holly Springs; notes 25, 34, 41, 45, 53, 61, 73

Grimes, J. P. Pvt. Co. C; note 18, Aug. 1861

Grimes, John F. Pvt. Co. C; note 13; rejoined after exchange. Co. D; notes 24, 34, 41, 51, 57, 66, 78

Grimes, S. H. Pvt. Co. H; note 1. Co. C; notes 25, 36, 41, 48, 53, 62 (barefooted), 73

Grinder, Henry Pvt. Co. H; note 1. Co. C; notes 25, 34, 41, 45, 53, 72

Grinder, J. C. Pvt. Co. H; note 8, July 6, 1862

Grinder, William Pvt. Co. H; note 1. Co. C; notes 25, 34, 41, 45, 53, 72

Griswell, W. R. Pvt. Co. B; note 1. Co. B; notes 25, 36, 41, 47, 53, 63, 73

Grubbs, W. L. Pvt. Co. A; note 20; never rejoined

Guthrie, Fleming Pvt. Co. C; note 14

Hackney, W. F. Musician Co. B; note 1. Pvt. Co. B; notes 25, 38, 41, 52

Hagan, J. H. 3d sgt. Co. I; note 1. Jr. 2d lt. Co. K; notes 31, 36, 42 (sick), 45, 55, 63, 75; died home, Lawrence County, Tenn., Feb. 9, 1864

Hainey, John L. Pvt. Co. A; note 17; joined First Tenn.

Hale, J. P. Pvt. Co. D; note 13; rejoined after exchange. Co. I; notes 24, 34, 41, 45; detailed teamster in Maj. Gen. Walker's supply train, June, 1863; rejoined at Dalton, Feb. 1864; 2d sgt. Feb. 20, 1864

Hall, G. M. Pvt. Co. D; enlisted Aug. 1, 1862; note 22, by transfer from Ninth Tenn. Cavalry, Mar. 14, 1863; notes 47, 53, 63, 75; captured on retreat to Dalton, Nov. 27, 1863

Hall, James K. P. Pvt. Co. A; note 1. Co. G; notes 27, 36, 41; deserted May 4, 1863, near Clinton

Hall, T. A. M. Pvt. Co. D; enlisted Nov. 1, 1862; notes 24, 36, 41, 45, 53, 69 (slightly and left field), 77

Hall, T. J. Pvt. Co. C; note 1. Elected 3d corp. Co. D at reorganization, Sept. 1862; notes 25, 34, 41, 51, 57, 66, 78

Halley, J. M. Pvt. Co. K; enlisted Nov. 1, 1862; joined Dalton, Dec. 18, 1863; deserted Dalton, Jan. 31, 1864

Hamlett, J. H. Pvt. Co. A; note 1. Co. G; notes 25, 34, 41, 49, 81

Hamlin, W. T. Pvt. Co. G; note 1. Co. H; notes 27, 36, 41, 45, 53, 65, 77

Hamrick, J. H. Pvt. Co. H; note 1. Co. C; notes 25, 34, 41, 45, 53, 68, 78; made 4th corp. Oct. 31, 1863

Hancock, Enoch Pvt. Co. A; note 7, June 19, 1862; served in cavalry until exchanged. Co. G; notes 24, 34, 42 (sick), 45, 53, 61, 73

Hancock, Luke Pvt. Co. A; died home Aug. 16, 1861

Hannah, D. H. 1st Lt. Co. D; note 2; not reelected at reorganization and dropped from rolls

Harder, W. B. Pvt. Co. H; note 1. Co. C; notes 25, 37, 41, 45, 53; sgt. July 1863; notes 61, 73

Harder, William J. 1st sgt. Co. H; elected 1st lt. upon resignation of O. T. Plummer, Dec. 1861; note 2. Reelected 1st lt. Co. C at reorganization Sept. 1862; note 25, in command of co.; notes 34, 41; resigned Port Hudson by reason of disability, Mar. 25, 1863

Hardiman, P. H. Pvt. Co. K; note 20; joined cavalry

Hardin, J. M. Pvt. Co. I; died Bowling Green, Nov. 1861

Hare, F. A. Pvt. Co. I; note 1. Co. K; notes 25, 34, 41, 45, 55, 61; deserted Lookout Mountain, Nov. 24, 1863

Hargrove, J. N. Pvt. Co. E; note 9; exchanged Sept. 23, 1862. Co. F; notes 29, 37 (teamster), 42, 46 (under arrest), 56, 64, 76 (all as teamster)

Hargrove, W. B. Pvt. Co. K; note 1. Co. A; notes 28, 37 as teamster; note 41; notes 48, 56 as teamster; notes 62, 74 on sick leave; died See's hospital near Lauderdale Springs, Apr. 10, 1864

Hargrove, Wade L. 2d sgt. Co. K; note 1. Pvt. Co. A; notes 25, 34, 41, 45, 53, 69, 78

Harmond, E. W. Jr. 2d lt. Co. G; note 2; not reelected at reorganization Sept. 1862; joined Eleventh Tenn. Cavalry

Harris, G. W. Pvt. Co. B; note 6; entered First Tenn. Cavalry

Harris, I. T. Pvt. Co. D; note 1. Co. I; notes 24, 34, 41, 45, 55, 63, 73

Harris, J. A. Pvt. Co. G; note 13; joined Thirty-second Tenn.; rejoined after exchange Missionary Ridge, Sept. 22, 1863. Co. H; note 74, with leave

Harris, W. B. Pvt. Co. C; note 1. Co. D; notes 25, 36, 41, 45; transferred Ninth Tenn. Cavalry, June 23, 1863

Harwell, B. W. Pvt. Co. I; note 18, Camp Trousdale, Aug. 1861

Harwell, J. H. Pvt. Co. D; note 1. Co. I; notes 25, 34, 41, 50, 81

Harwell, J. M. Pvt. Co. I; note 9, exchanged Sept. 23, 1862. Co. K; ran in every engagement; deserted near Dalton, Nov. 30, 1863

Harwell, R. F. Pvt. Co. A; note 8, May 13, 1862

Harwell, W. E. Pvt. Co. D; note 1. Co. I; notes 25, 34, 41, 45, 53, 72

Harwell, W. M. Pvt. Co. B; note 1. Co. B; notes 25, 37, 41, 45, 53, 61, 73; killed Resaca

Harwood, M. P. Pvt. Co. D; note 1. Co. I; notes 25, 34, 41, 51, 57, 61, 73

Hassell, James Pvt. Co. E; note 15; rejoined after exchange. Co. F; notes 24, 34, 41, 45, 55, 71

Haygood, G. W. Pvt. Co. A; note 1. Co. G; notes 25, 34, 41, 52

Hays, J. L. Pvt. Co. E; note 6; entered cavalry

Hays, Jerome Pvt. Co. D; died Bowling Green, Dec. 28, 1861

Hays, W. F. Pvt. Co. G; note 1. Co. H; notes 25, 34, 41; left Port Hudson, May 2, 1863, when regt. marched to Miss.; captured and paroled Port Hudson, July 1863

Hazelwood, H. V. Pvt. Co. K; note 1. Co. A; notes 25, 37, 41, 51 (lost right arm); disabled for active service; captured by enemy in Giles County, Jan. 1864

Helnick, Miram Pvt. Co. B; note 8, Mar. 27, 1862

Helton, T. B. Pvt. C. H; note 1. Co. C; notes 25, 38, 41, 45, 53, 63, 74 (barefooted)

Henderson, J. C. Asst. surgeon, assigned duty 1863; relieved Feb. 5, 1864

Henderson, J. F. Pvt. Co. E; enlisted Nov. 10, 1862; joined Vicksburg, Dec. 26, 1862; notes 36, 41, 45, 55, 63, 73; permanently detached in hospital Jan. 4, 1864

Henderson, J. P. Pvt. Co. A; enlisted Nov. 3, 1862; notes 21, 25, 34, 41, 45, 53, 70; corp. Nov. 1, 1863; note 73

Henderson, J. S. Pvt. Co. B; present at Donelson; died prison St. Louis, Mar. 16, 1862

Henderson, T. B. Pvt. Co. K; note 1. Co. A; notes 25, 34, 41, 45, 53; note 58, July 15, 1863, and imprisoned

Henderson, W. A. 5th sgt. Co. F; note 16; entered cavalry. Pvt. Co. E; note 22, Jan. 25, 1863; notes 41, 45, 53, 61, 75

Henley, J. S. Pvt. Co. H; note 1. Co. C; notes 25, 34, 41, 45, 53, 63, 74 (barefooted)

Henshaw, John F. Pvt. Co. C; note 1. Co. D; notes 25, 34, 41, 45, 53, 56, 64 (both as teamster), 73

Hensley, A. S. Pvt. Co. H; note 11; never rejoined

Hensley, E. B. Pvt. Co. H; died home, Aug. 17, 1861

Hensley, J. W. 2d corp. Co. H; made 3d sgt. upon promotion of J. M. Gillmore, Dec. 1861; note 1. 5th sgt. Co. C; notes 25, 34, 41, 50; imprisoned.

Henson, J. F. See Hinson, J. F.

Henson, W. J. Pvt. Co. D; note 1; note 18, Jackson, Oct. 1862

Herrin, B. F. Pvt. Co. K; enlisted Nov. 22, 1862; notes 24, 34, 41, 51, 57, 66; note 18, Missionary Ridge, Sept. 30, 1863

Herron, C. F., Jr. 2d lt. Co. I; absent Donelson on furlough; never rejoined

Herron, J. L. Appointed quartermaster Jan. 1862; captured Donelson and imprisoned Camp Chase and Ft. Warren; exchanged Aug. 1862. Reappointed quartermaster at reorganization, Sept. 1862; resigned Oct. 20, 1862, Coldwater

Hewitt, Lafayette 2d corp. Co. D; note 14

Hickerson, William Pvt. Co. H; note 1. Co. C; notes 25, 37 (cook), 43, Feb. 22, 1863

Hickey, James Pvt. Co. G; enlisted Sept. 7, 1863; joined Enterprise, Sept. 7 as substitute for George Short; deserted same day

Hickman, J. D. Pvt. Co. D; note 1. Co. I; notes 25, 34, 41, 45, 53; present at beginning of Chickamauga but left field without leave; deserted Chattanooga Valley, Nov. 6, 1863

Hickman, J. G. Pvt. Co. D; note 1. Co. I; notes 25, 34, 41, 45, 53, 69 (mortally); died Atlanta, Sept. 25, 1863

Hickman, John D. Pvt. Col. I; enlisted Dec. 1862; notes 24, 34, 41, 51, 57, 66, 78

Hickman, R. D. Pvt. Co. I; enlisted Dec. 1862; notes 24, 34, 41, 45, 53, 61, 74 (barefooted)

Hickman, W. A. Pvt. Co. D; note 15; discharged at Tupelo, Miss., June 1862

Hickman, W. H. Pvt. Co. I; enlisted Dec. 1862; notes 24, 34, 41, 45, 53, 65, 74 (barefooted)

Higdon, J. C. Pvt. Co. B; note 6; joined Forty-first Miss.

Hildreth, John Pvt. Co. I; note 1. 1st lt. Co. K; note 25, in command of co.; notes 34, 41, 45, 53; note 59, July 11, 1863; notes 66, 73

Hinson, David Pvt. Co. H; note 1; note 18, Jackson, Oct. 1862

Hinson, J. F. Pvt. Co. H; note 1; note 82, from Jackson, Sept. 30, 1862; never rejoined

Hinson, J. P. Pvt. Co. H; note 1. Co. C; notes 25, 34, 41, 45, 53, 67, Sept. 20; imprisoned

Hobbs, Caleb Pvt. Co. B; note 1. Co. B; notes 30, 38, 41, 45, 56, 65, 73

Hobbs, William Pvt. Co. G; died Nashville, Nov. 25, 1861

Hodge, J. M. Pvt. Co. B; enlisted Nov. 1, 1862; notes 24, 37, 41, 45, 53, 63, 73

Hodge, S. W. Pvt. Co. B; note 1. Co. B; notes 25, 34, 41, 45, 55, 63, 73

Hodge, W. A. Pvt. Co. B; died Bowling Green, Jan. 28, 1862

Hodge, William H. 3d corp. Co. K; note 15, Dover hospital; captured and imprisoned Camp Douglas, exchanged Sept. 23, 1862. 4th sgt. Co. A; notes 25, 34; elected jr. 2d lt. Jan., 1863, at death of Bass; promoted 2d lt., Feb. 1, 1863, at promotion of Jones; notes 41, 47, 53; resigned for disability Aug. 7, 1863

Hogan, J. H. Pvt. Co. F; note 1. Co. E; notes 25, 38, 41, 45, 53; made color sgt. Sept. 10, 1863; notes 61, 73

Hoge, G. S. Pvt. Co. D; enlisted Nov. 1, 1862; notes 24, 34, 42 (sick), 45, 53, 65, 75

Holden, David Pvt. Co. C; note 1. Co. D; notes 25, 34, 41, 45, 53, 63, 75

Holding, J. G. 4th corp. Co. F; note 1. Pvt. Co. E; notes 26 (furlough), 34, 41; notes 48, 56, 64, all in ordnance dept.; deserted to enemy at Lookout Mountain, Nov. 24, 1863

Holland, A. C. Pvt. Co. K; note 15; died home

Holland, Jesse A. 1st corp. Co. K; note 1. 2d sgt. Co. A; note 25; transferred First Tenn. Cavalry, Dec. 15, 1862

Holland, John W. Pvt. Co. K; note 1. Co. A; notes 25, 34, 41, 45, 53, 71

Holland, W. J. Pvt. Co. E; note 1; died Jackson, Oct. 1862

Holly, J. P. Pvt. Co. G; note 20; served First Tenn. Cavalry; rejoined after exchange; detached as teamster at Holly Springs, Oct. 1862

Holt, Algernon S. Pvt. Co. A; note 1; detached at Tippah Ford, Nov. 1862; captured at Vicksburg, July 4, 1863; paroled and deserted Aug. 1863

Holt, F. M. Pvt. Co. G; enlisted Nov. 15, 1862; notes 24, 36, 42 (sick), 47; present during part of siege of Jackson; deserted Lauderdale Springs, about Aug. 1, 1863

Holt, I. A. Pvt. Co. F; note 13; rejoined after exchange at Port Hudson about Apr. 1, 1863. Co. E; notes 47, 56; permanently detached from co. on hospital duty Enterprise, Aug. 5, 1863

Holt, John Pvt. Co. F; note 1. 1st corp. Co. E at reorganization Sept. 1862; notes 25, 34, 41, 45, 53, 71

Holt, Thomas H. Pvt. Co. A; note 1. Co. G; notes 25, 34, 41, 45, 53, 61, 73

Holt, V. S. Pvt. Co. I; died Camp Cheatham, July 10, 1861

Holt, Wyatt L. Pvt. Co. A; note 1. Co. G; notes 25, 34, 41, 49; paroled and rejoined Chattanooga Valley, Nov. 1, 1863; note 73

Hopkins, Benjamin F. Pvt. Co. A; note 7, May 31, 1862; rejoined after exchange. Co. G; notes 24, 34, 41, 45; note 58, July 15, 1863; escaped and rejoined co. Nov. 17, 1863; note 73

Hopkins, L. Pvt. Co. D; died Russellville, Feb. 6, 1862

Horne, A. C. Pvt. Co. I; enlisted Dec. 1862; notes 24, 34, 41, 50, 51; paroled and never rejoined

Horne, D. C. Pvt. Co. D; note 15, in hospital; note 24; transferred First Tenn. Cavalry, Grenada, Dec. 24, 1862

Horne, R. S. Pvt. Co. D; note 1

Howard, Aaron Pvt. Co. K; enlisted Nov. 1, 1863; joined Dalton, Dec. 18, 1863

Howard, Joseph C. Pvt. Co. C; died home, Sept. 1861

Howard, William Pvt. Co. C; died home Sept. 1861

Howell, M. Pvt. Co. C; note 20; deserted to enemy Mar. 1862

Howlett, J. S. Pvt. Co. F; note 1; detached from co. at Jackson as asst. surgeon of Twelfth Ark., Oct. 5, 1862; deserted Nov. 1862

Hubbard, J. R. Pvt. Co. I; note 10; rejoined after exchange. Co. K; notes 24, 36, 44

Hubbard, R. M. Pvt. Co. I; note 1. Co. K; notes 24, 34, 41, 45, 53; deserted Brandon, July 1863

Hubbard, W. J. Pvt. Co. I; note 1. Co. K; notes 24, 34, 41, 45, 53; deserted Brandon, July 1863

Hubbell, B. R. Musician, Co. F; note 1. Pvt. Co. E; notes 32 (slightly), 38, 44

Hubbell, C. E. Pvt. Co. D; note 8, Mar. 1862

Hubbell, G. W. 1st corp. Co. D; note 1. Pvt. Co. I; notes 25, 34, 41, 45, 53, 70, 78

Hudson, J. M. Pvt. Co. G; transferred from Co. I, Second Tenn. at Bowling Green; note 18, Bowling Green

Hudson, J. S. Pvt. Co. I; note 1. Co. K; notes 24, 34, 41, 52

Hughes, A. B. Pvt. Co. F; died Bowling Green, Oct. 3, 1861

Hughes, James W. Pvt. Co. K; note 14

Hughes, S. D. Pvt. Co. I; absent from his co. without leave during Donelson; captured; escaped after surrender; never rejoined regt.

Hughes, Thomas M. Pvt. Co. K; note 1. Co. A; notes 25, 35 (with leave), 41, 45, 53, 65 (Sept. 19), 61 (Sept. 20), 73

Hunnicutt, W. E. Pvt. Co. A; notes 21, 25, 36; note 18, Port Hudson, Mar. 5, 1863

Hunter, F. Pvt. Co. K; note 15, Nashville; joined Seventeenth Tenn.; absent without leave from reorganization; reported to his capt. Nov. 1862; joined Forty-fourth Tenn.

Hunter, J. W. Pvt. Co. K; note 10; joined Seventeenth Tenn.; absent without leave from reorganization; reported to his capt. Nov. 1862; joined Forty-fourth Tenn.

Hunter, James B. Pvt. Co. C; note 18, Bowling Green, Nov. 1861

Hunter, John S. 1st sgt. Co. C; note 10, Mar. 1862; discharged as nonconscript Mar. 1863

Hutchcraft, W. B.   Pvt. Co. E; note 1.   Co. F; notes 29, 34, 41, 49; paroled and never rejoined

Ingram, J. Fount   2d sgt. Co. C; note 19, sappers and miners, Oct. 1861; entered First Tenn. Cavalry

Ingram, J. G.   Pvt. Co. C; note 19, sappers and miners Dec. 1861

Ingram, W. C.   Pvt. Co. C; sick at Donelson and sent off with wounded; rejoined after exchange Grenada, Dec. 10, 1862. Co. D; notes 38, 41; left field early Raymond; notes 55, 63, 77

Irwin, G. W.   Pvt. Co. C; note 19 quartermaster's dept. Nov. 1861

Irwin, W. M.   Pvt. Co. E; transferred from Forty-eighth Tenn., Jan. 7, 1864

Jackson, John A.   Pvt. Co. C; note 1.   Elected 1st sgt. Co. D at reorganization, Sept. 1862; notes 25, 35 (inebriated), 41, 51, 57, 66, 78

Jackson, John M.   Pvt. Co. G; note 16; served First Tenn. Cavalry; rejoined after exchange.   Co. H; notes 25, 34, 41, 45, 53, 61, 75

Jackson, R. C.   Pvt. Co. C; absent Donelson on detached duty in commissary dept.; took oath of allegiance to U.S. in Maury County; rejoined after exchange; detached in quartermaster's dept. Dec. 15, 1862; on duty Atlanta

Jackson, S. A.   Pvt. Co. E; note 1.   Co. F; notes 25, 34, 41, 51; furloughed Aug. 1863, and never rejoined

Jackson, Thomas L.   Pvt. Co. A; note 1.   Co. G; notes 25, 35 (inebriated), 41, 52

James, David   Pvt. Co. F; note 1.   Co. E; notes 27, 34, 41; note 18, Port Hudson, Mar. 1863

James, Thomas   Pvt. Co. B; died home, Aug. 1, 1861

James, W. N.   Pvt. Co. B; note 1.   Co. B; notes 30, 34, 41, 49, 81; exchanged Jan. 1, 1864

James, W. F.   Pvt. Co. G; note 1.   Co. H; notes 25, 34, 43, Feb. 20, 1863

Jarrett, Jeffrey   Pvt. Co. F; died Russellville, Feb. 20, 1862

Jarrett, P.   Pvt. Co. F; died Russellville

Jarrett, William   Pvt. Co. F; note 18, Camp Cheatham, July 20, 1861

Jenkins, R. P.   Pvt. Co. E; note 1

Jenkins, Robert P.   Pvt. Co. F; appointed hospital steward Sept. 26, 1862

Jennings, Benjamin E.   Pvt. Co. D; enlisted Nov. 1, 1862; notes 24, 34, 41, 45, 55, 63, 75; died Cassville, Ga., Dec. 5, 1863

Jennings, Walter S.   Jr. 2d lt. Co. C; note 2.   Elected capt. Co. D at reorganization Sept. 1862; notes 25, 34, 41, 45, 53 (all in command of his co.), 63 (on furlough), 73 (in command of co.)

Jewell, W. A. Pvt. Co. C; note 1. Co. D; notes 25, 37, 41, 45, 53, 69 (slightly and left field), 73

Johns, A. J. Pvt. Co. C; note 1. Co. D; notes 25, 34, 41, 48; deserted Cane Creek, July 5, 1863

Johnson, D. T. Pvt. Co. I; note 11; rejoined regt. after exchange. Co. K; notes 24, 34, 41, 51 (slightly), 53; deserted Enterprise, Aug. 12, 1863

Johnson, E. C. Pvt. Co. I; note 8, May 1862

Johnson, H. Pvt. Co. E; note 15; joined cavalry; killed Richmond

Johnson, M. H. 1st corp. Co. H; note 1. 3d sgt. Co. C; notes 25, 34, 41, 45; elected jr. 2d lt. at promotion of S. K. Johnston, June 19, 1863; notes 53, 61, 73; promoted 2d lt. at death of S. K. Johnston, Dec. 1863

Johnson, Thomas F. Pvt. Co. K; sick in quarters Donelson; captured; died prison St. Louis, Feb. 21, 1862

Johnson, V. A. Pvt. Co. I; note 1; bore colors after fall of Compton at Donelson; note 82 from Jackson and never rejoined on account of sickness

Johnson, V. B. Pvt. Co. E; note 18, Camp Trousdale, Aug. 15, 1861

Johnson, W. D. Pvt. Co. E; note 1. Co. F; notes 25, 34, 41, 45, 53, 61 (Sept. 19), 65 (Sept. 20), 73

Johnson, W. J. L. Pvt. Co. E; died Bowling Green, Jan. 1, 1862

Johnston, S. K. Pvt. Co. H; made 4th corp. Feb. 1862; note 1. Pvt. Co. C; notes 27, 34, 41; elected jr. 2d lt. Apr. 1863; notes 45, 53; promoted 2d lt. May 1863; died Sept. 6, 1863

Jones, Alfred 2d lt. Co. G; present Donelson acting as asst. surgeon; captured and imprisoned Camp Chase; escaped Mar. 1862; reentered asst. surgeon Seventeenth Tenn.

Jones, Anderson Pvt. Co. I; note 11, Aug. 1862

Jones, George W. Capt. Co. F; in command of company, note 2. Reelected capt. Co. E at reorganization, Sept. 1862; notes 31, 34, 41, 45 (all in command of co.), 55, 63, 75

Jones, J. S. Pvt. Co. I; note 11, Aug. 1862

Jones, James L. Pvt. Co. B; note 15; joined First Tenn. Cavalry; rejoined Nov. 19, 1863; note 75

Jones, R. R. Pvt. Co. F; note 1. Co. E; notes 27, 34, 41; elected 5th sgt. Apr. 5, 1863; notes 45, 53, 64, 76

Jones, S. B. Pvt. Co. H; enlisted Oct. 28, 1862; notes 24, 34; transferred Co. K, Port Hudson, Feb. 1863; notes 41, 50; imprisoned

Jones, Thomas W. Pvt. Co. A; note 1. Co. G; notes 25, 34, 43, Mar. 10, 1863

Jones, Willis H. 2d lt. Co. K; note 2. Reelected 2d lt. Co. A at reorganization Sept. 1862; notes 31, 34; promoted 1st. lt. at promotion of T. E. McCoy; notes 41, 48, 53; note 61, in command of Co. E; note 76

Kannon, E. D.   Pvt. Co. F; note 10, entered cavalry

Keaton, J. H.   Pvt. Co. I; note 13; rejoined regt. after exchange. Co. K; notes 24, 36, 42 (sick); died Jackson, Apr. 1863

Kelley, T. B.   *See* Kelly, T. B.

Kelly, Charles   Pvt. Co. C; note 1.   Elected 3d sgt. Co. D at reorganization Sept. 1862; notes 25, 34, 41, 45, 55, 61, 75; captured on retreat to Dalton, Nov. 26, 1863

Kelly, T. B.   Pvt. Co. I; note 1.   3d sgt. Co. K; notes 29, 36, 41, 45, 53, 65, 77

Kelso, T. C. S.   Pvt. Co. D; note 15; rejoined regt. after exchange. Co. I; notes 22 (Feb. 1863), 41, 45, 56 (teamster), 61 (Sept. 19), 65 (Sept. 20), 73

Keltner, J. A.   Pvt. Co. I; enlisted Dec. 1862; note 24; furloughed Grenada, Dec. 1862; never rejoined

Keltner, J. C.   Pvt. Co. D; note 1.   Co. I; notes 25, 36, died Graysport, Miss., Feb., 1863

Kendrick, C. W. H.   Pvt. Co. D; note 14

Kennedy, John   Pvt. Co. A; note 1.   1st corp. Co. G; notes 25, 34, 41, 45, 53, 70, 78

Kennedy, Joseph   Pvt. Co. A; note 13; joined Scott's La. Cavalry

Kennedy, W. P.   Pvt. Co. K; note 3.   Co. A; notes 28, 37, 41, 48, 53, 64, 76; transferred Thirty-second Tenn., Feb. 25, 1861

Kennedy, William L.   Pvt. Co. C; died home, July 22, 1861

Kerr, W. G.   Pvt. Co. B; note 7, June 3, 1862; rejoined after exchange

Keutch, J. P.   Pvt. Co. C; transferred from First Tenn. Cavalry, Nov. 1, 1863; note 73

Keyton, Larry   Pvt. Co. C; note 19 with sappers and miners, Oct. 1861

Kilpatrick, W. H.   Musician Co. E; present Donelson; captured and imprisoned Camp Douglas; confined in Illinois Penitentiary one year for killing T. M. Golden in prison; released after serving time; never rejoined

Kimbrough, D. C.   Pvt. Co. G; note 10; joined Morgan's Cavalry; never rejoined

Kincaid, D. W.   Pvt. Co. G; note 1.   Co. H: notes 25, 34; made sgt. at Port Hudson, Jan. 15, 1863; notes 41, 45, 53, 61 (Sept. 19), 65 (Sept. 20); 73

Kincaid, Robert   2d corp. Co. G; died Camp Cheatham, June 15, 1861

King, E. A.   Pvt. Co. C; note 13; made lt.; mortally wounded at Corinth

King, J. W.   Pvt. Co. K; note 1.   Co. A; notes 25, 34, 41, 45, 58 (July 15, 1863); imprisoned

King, Robert   Pvt. Co. C; note 1

King, Thomas B.   Pvt. Co. K; sick in quarters during Donelson; captured; died on board steamboat on Miss. River, Feb. 18, 1862

King, W. S.   1st corp. Co. G; note 17; rejoined regt. after exchange. Pvt. Co. H; notes 25, 34, 41, 51, 57, 66, 78

Kittrell, J. H.   Pvt. Co. C; note 1.   Co. D; notes 25, 36, 41, 45; note 59, July 13, 1863, and lost right arm; discharged Lauderdale Springs, Sept. 10, 1863

Kittrell, J. R.   Pvt. Co. C; note 1.   Co. D; notes 25, 38, 43, Mar. 8, 1863

Kittrell, W. A.   3d corp. Co. C; note 8, Apr. 1, 1862

Knight, G. W.   Pvt. Co. D; note 1; note 18, Jackson, Oct. 1862

Knox, H. M.   Pvt. Co. B; note 1.   Co. B; notes 25, 34, 41, 45, 53, 61, 75

Knox, J. M.   Pvt. Co. B; note 1.   Co. B; notes 25, 34, 41, 53, 61, 73; elected jr. 2d lt. at promotion of W. T. Mitchell, Nov. 29, 1863

Kosier, Daniel   Pvt. Co. B; note 1.   Co. B; note 18, Jackson, Sept. 1862; rejoined regt. as substitute Port Hudson, Feb. 1863; notes 49, 81

Laird, R. M.   Pvt. Co. B; transferred from Co. K, Camp Trousdale; note 1.   Co. B; notes 25, 34, 41, 45, 53, 61, 73

Laird, Robert M.   Pvt. Co. K; transferred to Third Tenn., Co. B, Camp Trousdale, Sept. 1861

Lamar, J. W.   Pvt. Co. F; note 1.   Co. E; notes 25, 34, 41, 51, 57, 66, 78

Lamar, L. S.   Pvt. Co. F; note 1.   Co. E; notes 25, 34, 41, 45, 53, 61, 73

Lamar, W. B.   Pvt. Co. F; note 20; joined Thirty-second Tenn.; rejoined Dalton, Dec. 20, 1863

Lamb, J. T.   Pvt. Co. E; died Nashville, Oct. 1861

Lambert, J. L.   Pvt. Co. B; note 20; rejoined regt. after exchange. Co. B; notes 25, 35, 41; transferred Co. E, Port Hudson, Apr. 1863

Langford, Joseph   Pvt. Co. C; note 1.   Co. D; notes 29, 34, 41, 45; note 58, May 15, 1863; paroled, exchanged and rejoined Missionary Ridge, Oct. 1, 1863; note 73

Langford, N. B.   Pvt. Co. H; sick in quarters Donelson; captured and imprisoned Camp Douglas; took oath of allegiance to U.S. and released; never rejoined

Langford, Samuel   Pvt. Co. H; died Camp Cheatham, July 6, 1861

Langford, William   Pvt. Co. H; note 11; never rejoined

Langley, J. A.   Pvt. Co. C; note 20; rejoined after exchange Tippah Ford, Nov. 1862.   Co. D; notes 25, 34, 41, 48, 53; deserted Enterprise, Sept. 6, 1863

Langley, Thomas H.   Pvt. Co. C; note 20; discharged May 1862

Lanier, R. F. Pvt. Co. D; note 15, Nashville. Co. I; notes 24, 34, 41, 45, 53, 63, 73

Latta, William A. Pvt. Co. A; note 16; joined First Tenn. Cavalry; wounded Corinth; discharged on account of wound

Lauderdale, J. G. Pvt. Co. K; note 1. Co. A; notes 25, 34; transferred Fifty-third Tenn., 1863

Lawhorn, J. L. Pvt. Co. H; note 1. Co. C; notes 25, 34, 41; made sgt. Apr. 1863; notes 45, 53, 61, 73; made 1st sgt. Jan. 1864

Laymaster, W. H. Pvt. Co. I; note 20; never rejoined

Leftwich, T. J. Pvt. Co. E; note 1. Co. F; notes 29, 34, 41, 45, 53, 61, 73; captured on retreat to Ringgold, Nov. 26, 1863

Leneave, T. M. Pvt. Co. F; note 1; note 18, Jackson, Sept. 28, 1862

Lester, John C. Pvt. Co. A; note 1. Promoted 2d lt. Co. G after reorganization, Sept. 1862; notes 25, 34, 42 (sick), 47, 55; notes 61, 73, in command of co.

Lewellyn, J. H. Pvt. Co. I; note 1. Co. K; note 25; sick every other engagement

Liles, John L. Pvt. Co. I; note 1. Co. K; detailed teamster at every engagement except Chickamauga, where sick

Liles, L. L. Pvt. Co. I; note 1. Co. K; notes 25, 34, 41, 51, 57, 66, 78

Lindsay, Alonzo 1st corp. Co. I; elected 2d lt. at death of S. W. Evans, Aug. 1861; note 2. 2d lt. Co. K; notes 27, 36, 41, 45, 53, 61 (Sept. 19), 62 (Sept. 20, sprained ankle), 75

Lindsay, James M. Pvt. Co. C; note 1. Co. D; notes 25, 34; transferred Forty-eighth Tenn., Port Hudson, Mar. 1, 1863

Lindsay, Thomas F. Musician Co. A; note 13 permanently disabled; never rejoined

Lipford, J. L. Asst. surgeon, assigned duty June 1, 1863; relieved July 1, 1863

Littleton, C. F. Pvt. Co. I; note 1. Co. K; notes 24, 34, 41, 52

Littleton, J. M. Pvt. Co. I; note 5; note 82 from Jackson at reorganization; never rejoined but deserted to cavalry

Littleton, J. W. Pvt. Co. I; made quartermaster sgt. Jan. 1862; note 1. Pvt. Co. K; notes 25, 34, 41, 51, 57, 66, 78

Littleton, R. S. Pvt. Co. I; acting asst. surgeon, note 1; transferred Twenty-seventh Ala., Oct. 1862

Lock, J. P. Jr. 2d lt. Co. D; note 2. Elected 1st lt. Co. I at reorganization, Sept. 1862; notes 31, 36, 42 (sick), 47, 55, 63, 75

Lock, W. A. Pvt. Co. D; note 1; note 18, Jackson, Oct. 1862

Lockridge, G. B. Pvt. Co. E; note 10, rejoined after exchange. Co. F; notes 24, 34, 41, 45, 51, 69, 75

Lockridge, J. W. Pvt. Co. E; note 10; rejoined after exchange. Co. E; notes 24, 35 (on account of accidental injury), 41, 45, 53, 69, 75

Logue, Ephraim Pvt. Co. I; notes 22 (Feb. 1863), 41, 51, 57; deserted Lauderdale Springs, Aug. 1863

London, C. C. Pvt. Co. F; note 1. Co. E; notes 25, 34, 41, 50, 80

London, J. M. Pvt. Co. F; note 1. Co. E; notes 25, 34, 41, 48, 58, May 14, 1863; paroled, exchanged and rejoined co. Aug. 20, 1863; died Enterprise, Sept. 15, 1863

Long, Albert Pvt. Co. C; note 18, Sept. 1861

Long, Henry Pvt. Co. C; transferred First Tenn. Cavalry, Bowling Green, Nov. 1861

Long, Johnson 2d lt. Co. C; promoted 1st lt.; note 2; not reelected at reorganization and dropped from rolls

Loveless, B. F. Pvt. Co. K; enlisted Mar. 19, 1863; notes 22 (Mar. 19, 1863), 41, 45, 53, 67; imprisoned

Lowry, J. T. Pvt. Co. B; note 7, June 21, 1862; joined Eleventh Tenn.

Lucy, W. H. Pvt. Co. A; note 20; rejoined regt. after exchange. Co. G; notes 24, 34, 42 (sick), 49, 81

Lytle, Frank Pvt. Co. I; note 20; rejoined regt. after exchange. Co. K; notes 24, 34, 41, 45; died Canton, June 21, 1863

McAllister, F. L. Pvt. Co. I; note 1. Co. K; notes 29, 34, 41; ran at Raymond; note 53; ran at Chickamauga and Missionary Ridge; deserted Dalton, Nov. 30, 1863

McAllister, N. A. Pvt. Co. K; enlisted Nov. 12, 1862; notes 24, 34, 41, 52

McAllister, O. H. P. Pvt. Co. I; note 1. Co. K; notes 25, 34, 41, 45, 53, 65, 73

McAllister, W. A. Pvt. Co. I; died Camp Trousdale, Aug. 17, 1861

McCain, H. M. Pvt. Co. F; note 18, Camp Cheatham, July 1, 1861. Pvt. Co. E; notes 24, 34; note 18, Port Hudson, Mar. 1863

McCallum, J. D. Pvt. Co. K; note 17; joined First Tenn. Cavalry

McCallum, James J. Pvt. Co. A; note 18, Bowling Green, Oct. 1861

McCallum, William 1st corp. Co. A; note 18, Camp Trousdale, Sept. 1861

McCanless, J. B. Pvt. Co. G; made 1st sgt. upon death of T. H. Chiles; note 1. 1st Co. H; notes 28 (in commissary dept.), 34 (in command of co.), 41, 45, 53, 63, 73

McCanless, S. H. Pvt. Co. G; note 13, lost right arm; rejoined after exchange; note 18, Grenada, Dec. 23, 1862

McCarroll, James   Pvt. Co. E; note 19 as apothecary; rejoined after exchange Vicksburg, Dec. 17, 1862.   Absent Chickasaw Bayou, being without arms; note 18 at Port Hudson, Feb. 1863

McCarter, Thomas   Pvt. Co. B; note 1.   Co. B; note 32, Dec. 3, 1862; died near Springdale, Miss., Dec. 20, 1862

McClain, Martin   Pvt. Co. C; note 13; joined Col. Nixon's Forty-eighth Tenn.

McClelland, F. S.   Pvt. Co. G; note 19, ordnance dept. in Bowling Green; never rejoined

McCloud, C. C.   Pvt. Co. D; note 1; note 18, Jackson, Oct. 1862

McClure, L. S.   Pvt. Co. G; note 1.   Co. H; notes 25, 34, 41, 45, 53, 61, 75

McCormick, R. B.   Pvt. Co. E; 3rd corp.; note 1.   Elected 1st lt. Co. F at reorganization, Sept. 1862; capt. upon resignation of H. P. Pointer; notes 27, 36, 41, 45, 53, 63, 73

McCoy, J. W.   Pvt. Co. A; enlisted Nov. 21, 1862; notes 23 (Dec. 11, 1862), 34, 41, 50, 81

McCoy, Samuel H.   Pvt. Co. K; note 12, lost arm; note 18, Jackson, Sept. 19, 1862

McCoy, Thomas E.   Jr. 2d lt. Co. K; elected Nov. 26, 1861, at resignation of O. P. Bruce; note 2.   Elected 1st lt. Co. A at reorganization Sept. 1862; notes 25, 34; capt. at promotion of F. C. Barber; notes 41 (in command of co.), 47, 69, 73 (both in command of co.)

McCracken, J. F.   Pvt. Co. A; note 17; served in cavalry until exchanged; note 22, Feb. 1863.   Co. G; notes 41, 45, 53, 65, 75

McCracken, John W.   Pvt. Co. A; note 1.   Co. G; notes 25, 34, 41, 50, 80; died prison

McDonald, R. F.   Pvt. Co. A; note 1.   Co. G; notes 25, 34, 41, 45, 55, 67 (Sept. 20)

McGaugh, B. F.   Pvt. Co. G; note 13, lost right arm; rejoined after exchange; note 18, Grenada, Dec. 23, 1862

McGaugh, N. C.   Pvt. Co. G; note 1.   Co. H; note 25, 34, 41, 45, 53, 72

Mack, John B.   Pvt. Co. C; note 16; rejoined after exchange at Holly Springs, Oct. 1862.   Co. D; note 32, Dec. 3, 1862; captured and paroled Jackson; rejoined Port Hudson, Apr. 1, 1863; transferred Ninth Tenn. Cavalry, Apr. 9, 1863

Mack, W. R. C.   Pvt. Co. F; note 1.   Co. E; notes 25, 36, 41, 48, 55, 64, 76

McKissack, Alan   Pvt. Co. E; note 1.   1st sgt. Co. F; notes 25, 34, 41, 50, imprisoned

McKissack, J. T.   Pvt. Co. F; enlisted Dec. 5, 1862; notes 24, 34, 41, 45, 55, 63, 75.   Detached on hospital service Feb. 12, 1864

Macklin, M. M.   Pvt. Co. A; note 1.   Transferred Fifty-third Tenn., Jackson, Oct. 1862

McKnight, D. A.   Pvt. Co. C; note 1.   Co. D; notes 25, 34, 41, 49, 81

McKnight, G. W.   Pvt. Co. E; enlisted Nov. 10, 1862; notes 24, 34, 42 (sick); died Clinton, La., Mar. 24, 1863

McKnight, J. S.   Pvt. Co. F; note 1.   Co. E; notes 25, 34, 41, 48, 53, 62 (barefooted); deserted Lookout Mountain, Nov. 24, 1863

McKnight, J. W.   Pvt. Co. B; note 20; joined Fifty-third Tenn.

McLaurine, G. T.   3rd corp. Co. B; note 19 to commissary dept; rejoined regt. after exchange. Pvt. Co. B; notes 25, 34, 41, 50, 81

McLaurine, W. J.   Pvt. Co. A; note 18, Bowling Green, Dec., 1861

McLean, J. L.   Pvt. Co. I; note 1.   3d corp. Co. K; notes 25, 34, 41, 51, 57, 66, 78

McMahon, J. A.   Pvt. Co. G; note 1.   4th sgt. Co. H; sent home on recruiting service from Jackson, Oct. 1862; died at home, Oct. 19, 1862

McMahon, T. G.   Pvt. Co. G; note 1.   1st sgt. Co. H; notes 25, 34, 41, 51, 57, 66, 78

McMillan, A. H.   Pvt. Co. I; note 1.   Co. K; notes 27, 36, 42 (sick), 47, 55, 61, 74 (barefooted)

McMillion, J. P.   Pvt. Co. G; present Donelson; captured; died in prison St. Louis, Mar. 1862

McMillion, J. P.   Pvt. Co. H; enlisted Nov. 10, 1862; notes 24, 34, 41, 53, 65; deserted Chattanooga Valley, Oct. 27, 1863

McMillion, S. B.   Pvt. Co. H; enlisted Nov. 10, 1862; notes 24, 34, 41, 45, 53, 65, 77; deserted Dalton, Dec. 1, 1863

McMullin, James   Pvt. Co. G; died at home, Aug. 5, 1861

McNeece, Joseph   Pvt. Co. D; note 5.   Co. I; notes 29, 36, 41, 46 (without leave), 55, 63, 75

McRobert, John A.   Musician Co. A; note 18, Camp Cheatham, July 20, 1861

Madigan, Dennis   Pvt. Co. K; note 1; transferred Tenth Tenn., Oct. 1862

Madison, William J.   Pvt. Co. A; 1st corp. Sept. 1861; note 15, Bowling Green; jr. 2d lt., Thirty-fifth Tenn.

Mahoney, Thomas   Pvt. Co. F; note 1.   Co. E; notes 25, 34, 41, 45; notes 56, 64, 76 (all as teamster)

Mantlo, J. J.   Pvt. Co. G; note Co. H; notes 25, 34, 42 (sick), 47, 53, 70, 78

Mantlo, W.   Pvt. Co. B; note 20; joined cavalry

Marks, L. F.   Pvt. Co. D; note 1.   1st sgt. Co. I; notes 25, 34, 41, 45, 53, 61, 73

Marks, L. H.   Pvt. Co. D; note 1. Co. I; note 25; transferred First Tenn. Cavalry, Grenada, Dec. 24, 1862

Marsh, R. J.   Pvt. Co. G; note 13, rejoined regt. after exchange. Co. H; notes 24, 34, 41, 45, 53, 72

Martin, C. W.   Pvt. Co. B; note 12. Co. B; notes 28, 37, 42, 48 (all as teamster); deserted Canton, June, 1863

Martin, David S.   Jr. 2d lt. Co. A; note 2. Promoted 1st lt. Co. G at re-organization Sept. 1862; notes 25, 34, 41, 45, 53 (in command of Co. G), 62 (home on furlough), 73

Martin, Felix G.   Pvt. Co. B; note 7, Apr. 6, 1862; rejoined regt. after exchange. Co. B; notes 30, 34, 41, 52

Martin, G.   Pvt. Co. F; died Camp Cheatham, July 7, 1861

Martin, H. A.   Pvt. Co. F; note 1. 5th sgt. Co. E at reorganization Sept. 1862; notes 25, 34, 41, 49; paroled and deserted July 1, 1863

Martin, James   Pvt. Co. F; died Camp Cheatham, Aug. 1, 1861

Martin, John   Pvt. Co. G; enlisted Dec. 13, 1862; on detached duty until Mar. 8, 1864, when rejoined co. at Dalton

Martin, N. E.   Pvt. Co. B; note 5

Martin, William, M.   Pvt. Co. G; note 1. 1st corp. Co. H; notes 25, 34, 41, 51, 53, 61, 73

Mash, L. J.   1st sgt. Co. F; resigned and returned to ranks Aug. 5, 1861; note 1. Pvt. Co. E; notes 26 (furlough), 34, 44

Mash, W. R.   Pvt. Co. F; note 1. Co. E; notes 25, 34, 41, 52

Massey, William J.   Pvt. Co. A; note 1. Co. G; notes 25, 34, 42 (furlough), 45, 53, 69 (but did not leave field), 73

Matthews, Benjamin F.   Capt. Co. I; in command of his co., note 2. Capt. Co. K; note 28; notes 34, 41, 45, 53 (all in command of co.); note 62 (with leave); note 73 (in command of co.)

Matthews, Edward H.   Pvt. Co. K; died Bowling Green, Oct. 1861

Matthews, G. D.   Pvt. Co. F; note 13; rejoined regt. after exchange. 4th corp. Co. E at reorganization Sept. 1862, notes 25, 34, 41, 50; exchanged and rejoined regt. Sept. 10, 1863; note 67, Sept. 19; escaped and rejoined regt. Oct. 1, 1863

Matthews, J. C.   Pvt. Co. D; enlisted Nov. 1, 1862; notes 24, 34, 41, 47, 55, 69 (slightly), 75; captured Maury County, Tenn.

Matthews, J. F.   Pvt. Co. F; note 1. Elected 2d lt. Co. E at reorganization, Sept. 1862; notes 25, 34, 41, 45, 53, 63, 75

Matthews, John T.   Pvt. Co. C; note 1. Co. D; notes 25, 34, 41, 47; died Lauderdale Springs, July 4, 1863

Matthews, N. J.   Pvt. Co. C; note 1, Co. D; notes 25, 34, 41, 45, 53, 61, 73

Matthews, R. H. Pvt. Co. C; note 13; rejoined regt. after exchange. Co. D; notes 24, 34, 41, 45, 53, 69, 78

Matthews, S. E. S. Pvt. Co. C; note 1. Co. D; notes 25, 34, 41, 46 (guard duty), 53, 69, 78

Matthews, W. H. Pvt. Co. H; note 1. Co. C; notes 25, 34, 41, 45, 53, 65, 74 (barefooted)

Maxey, C. Pvt. Co. I; note 18, Camp Cheatham, June 1861

Maxey, S. H. Pvt. Co. B; note 1. Co. B; notes 32, 35 (on account of wound), 82 (Port Hudson, Feb. 25, 1863); never rejoined co.

Maxwell, J. L. Pvt. Co. C; note 3. Co. D; notes 27, 34, 41, 46 (guard duty), 53, 61, 73

May, T. B. Pvt. Co. I; note 1. Co. K; notes 25, 34, 41, 52

Mayfield, J. G. Pvt. Co. H; note 20; served in cavalry; rejoined regt. after exchange. Co. C; notes 25, 35, 41, 50

Mayfield, William 3d corp. Co. H; note 1. Pvt. Co. C; notes 25, 34, 41, 48, 53, 61; made sgt. Oct. 31, 1863; note 73

Meese, O. Pvt. Co. E; note 1; died hospital Jackson, Oct. 1862

Merrill, George W. Pvt. Co. K; died Camp Trousdale, Sept. 1861

Miles, F. M. Pvt. Co. I; note 1. Co. K; notes 25, 34, 41, 45, 53, 61, 77

Miles, N. F. Pvt. Co. K; enlisted Nov. 12, 1862; joined Holly Springs, Oct. 1862; notes 25, 34, 41, 45, 53, 72

Millican, J. M. Pvt. Co. B; note 12. Co. B; notes 25, 34, 41, 45, 53, 61, 73

Misenheimer, M. A. Pvt. Co. A; wounded Donelson and lost leg; sent home; discharged by order of Gen. Johnston

Mitchell, J. O. Pvt. Co. B; enlisted Oct. 31, 1862; notes 24, 34, 41, 45, 53, 65, 73

Mitchell, J. W. Pvt. Co. B; note 1. Co. B; notes 25, 34, 41, 51, 57, 66, 78

Mitchell, M. M. Pvt. Co. B; enlisted Nov. 9, 1862; joined regt. Port Hudson as conscript, Mar. 1863; notes 47, 55, 63; captured Missionary Ridge

Mitchell, Philip B. Pvt. Co. A; note 13; joined cavalry

Mitchell, Robert A. 1st lt. Co. B; note 2. Elected capt. at reorganization Sept. 1862; notes 27, 37 (member of court martial), 42 (sick leave), 45, 53 (both in command of co.), 63, 73 (in command of co.)

Mitchell, Samuel C. Pvt. Co. A; note 1. Co. G; notes 25, 37, 42 (detached duty), 48, 53; present at Chickamauga until evening of 20th when retired without leave; note 74

Mitchell, Thomas E. Pvt. Co. K; note 20; rejoined regt. after exchange. Co. A; notes 28, 37 (both as teamster), 41, notes 48, 56, 64 (all as teamster), 73

Mitchell, William T. Jr. 2d lt. Co. B; sick in quarters during Donelson; captured and imprisoned Camp Chase and Johnson's Island; exchanged Sept. 16, 1862. Reelected jr. 2d lt. after reorganization Sept. 1862; notes 25, 34, 41, 45, 53, 61, 73; promoted 2d lt. at promotion of M. T. West, Sept. 8, 1863

Moore, F. A. L. Pvt. Co. D; absent from Donelson on furlough; joined First Tenn.

Moore, J. T. 4th sgt. Co. B; note 1. Pvt. Co. B; notes 30, 34, 41, 45, 53, 61, 73

Moore, John W. Pvt. Co. K; note 1. Co. A; notes 25, 34, 41, 51, 57, 63, 73

Moore, T. J. Pvt. Co. E; note 7, June 7, 1862; never rejoined regt.

Morris, E. T. Pvt. Co. H; note 9; took oath of allegiance to U.S. and released; rejoined regt. after exchange. Co. C; notes 24, 34, 43 (Feb. 22, 1863)

Morris, J. L. Pvt. Co. I; note 7, Mar. 31, 1862; entered cavalry

Morris, J. P. Pvt. Co. E; note 1. Co. F; notes 25, 34, 41, 45, 53, 65; deserted Lookout Mountain, Nov. 24, 1863

Moss, J. A. Pvt. Co. C; note 1. Co. D; notes 25, 34, 41, 46 (guarding baggage), 53, 61, 73

Moss, James D. 1st lt. Co. C; died home, Sept. 4, 1861

Moss, Thomas G. Pvt. Co. C; note 18, Camp Trousdale, Aug. 1, 1861

Moss, Thomas H. Asst. surgeon, assigned to duty in regt. Feb. 5, 1864

Murphy, E. Y. Pvt. Co. F; note 1. Co. E; notes 25, 34, 41, 51, 53; appointed 1st sgt. July 1, 1863; notes 61, 73

Murphy, James B. 1st lt. Co. F; note 2. Reelected 1st lt. Co. E at reorganization, Sept. 1862; notes 25, 34, 41, 50; imprisoned Johnson's Island

Murphy, Patrick Pvt. Co. E; note 1; detached Jackson, Sept. 26, 1862, as blacksmith in govt. works

Murry, H. L. Pvt. Co. G; note 13, joined cavalry; never rejoined regt.

Nance, J. R. Pvt. Co. H; enlisted Nov. 4, 1862; notes 24, 36, 42 (sick), 47, 53; ran at Chickamauga; deserted Lookout Mountain, Nov. 20, 1863

Napier, R. R. Pvt. Co. H; note 12. Co. C; notes 25, 35 (on account of wound received at Donelson), 41; notes 46, 54, 62, 74 all excused by surgeon

Nave, A. H. Pvt. Co. I; transferred from Fifty-third Tenn., Port Hudson, May 3, 1863; notes 45, 53, 64 (teamster), 76 (teamster)

Neal, W. W. Pvt. Co. I; note 18, Camp Cheatham, June 1861

Neely, R. B.   Pvt. Co. F; note 1.   Co. E; notes 25, 34, 41, 45; note 59, July 11, 1863; notes 63, 75

Neill, James B.   Pvt. Co. A; note 1; note 18, Jackson, Oct. 12, 1862

Nelson, B. H.   Pvt. Co. C; note 1.   Co. D; notes 24, 34, 41, 52

Nelson, C.   Pvt. Co. K; joined Dalton, Jan. 18, 1864

Nelson, C. H.   Pvt. Co. K; note 15, Nashville; entered cavalry

Nelson, J. H.   Pvt. Co. K; note 19, nurse in Nashville hospital; entered cavalry

Nelson, J. L.   Pvt. Co. A; enlisted Apr. 15, 1862; transferred from Thirty-second Tenn., Nov. 1, 1863; note 73

Nelson, William D.   Pvt. Co. C; note 13; discharged

Nelums, D. A.   Pvt. Co. E; note 1; note 18, Jackson, Sept. 1862

Nevills, John   Pvt. Co. G; died Nashville, June 1861

Nevils, Robert F.   Pvt. Co. A; note 13; entered cavalry

Newcomb, James W.   Pvt. Co. E; note 1.   4th corp. Co. F; notes 32, 35, (on account of wound), 41; deserted Port Hudson, Mar. 30, 1863; arrested and rejoined regt. Apr. 28, 1863; notes 46 (under arrest), 55, 65; deserted Chattanooga, Nov. 7, 1863

Newlin, W. J.   Pvt. Co. B; note 1.   Co. B; notes 25, 37, 41, 50, 80

Newton, William J.   Pvt. Co. H; enlisted Nov. 10, 1862; notes 24, 34, 41, 45; deserted Canton, May 29, 1863

Newton, Willis J.   Pvt. Co. H; enlisted Nov. 10, 1862; notes 24, 34, 41, 45; deserted Canton, May 29, 1863

Nichol, N. M.   Pvt. Co. E; note M; rejoined regt. after exchange. Co. F; notes 24, 34, 43, Feb. 1863

Nipp, Andrew J.   Pvt. Co. A; note 1.   Co. G; notes 25, 34, 41, 48, 56, 70, 76 (teamster)

Norman, W. F.   Pvt. Co. I; note 1.   4th corp. Co. K; notes 25, 34, 41, 51, 57, 62 (sore eyes), 74 (sore eyes)

Norwood, N. A.   Pvt. Co. C; note 13; rejoined regt. after exchange.   Co. D; notes 24, 35 (inebriated), 41, 45, 53; died Lauderdale Springs, Sept. 11, 1863

Nowlin, D. L.   Pvt. Co. I; note 1.   Co. K; notes 24, 34, 41, 45, 53, 72

Orman, R. L.   Pvt. Co. E; note 1.   Co. F; notes 25, 34, 41, 45, 53, 65; deserted Missionary Ridge, Nov. 25, 1863

Orman, W. E.   Pvt. Co. E; note 18, Camp Cheatham, June 1861; rejoined regt. Vicksburg, Dec. 27, 1862; note 37 with surgeon; note 18, Port Hudson, Mar. 1863

Orr, C. R.   Pvt. Co. G; note 16; served in Fifth Tenn.; rejoined regt. after exchange.   Co. H; notes 24, 34, 41, 45, 53, 61, 73

Orr, Calvin J. Pvt. Co. G; note 1.   Jr. 2d lt. Co. H; notes 25, 34, 41, 45, 53, 62 (on furlough), 73

Orr, J. B. Pvt. Co. G; note 1.   2d sgt. Co. H; notes 25, 34, 41, 51 (mortally); died Raymond, May 14, 1863

Orr, W. W. Pvt. Co. H; enlisted Oct. 18, 1862; notes 24, 34, 41, 45, 53, 70, 78

Osborne, J. W. Pvt. Co. A; enlisted Dec. 17, 1861; transferred from Thirty-second Tenn., Oct. 29, 1863; note 73.

Osborn, James Pvt. Co. I; died Camp Cheatham, June 6, 1861

Osborn, James A. Pvt. Co. K; note 1.   Co. A; notes 25, 34, 41, 45, 55, 65 (evening Sept. 19), 61 (Sept. 20), 73

Owen, A. T. Pvt. Co. E; note 1.   Co. F; notes 25, 34, 41, 47, 55, 69; died Atlanta, Oct. 9, 1863

Owen, R. W. Pvt. Co. E; note 1; furloughed Jackson, Oct. 1862; rejoined regt. at Vicksburg, Dec. 27, 1862.   Co. F; notes 35 (unarmed), 41, 45, 53, 62 (barefooted), 76

Owen, W. J. Pvt. Co. E; note 1.   Co. F; notes 29, 34, 41, 49, paroled and rejoined co. May 1863; notes 53, 61 (Sept. 19), 62 (Sept. 20), 73

Pack, James F. Pvt. Co. A; note 1.   Co. G; notes 25, 34, 41, 45, 56, 64 (both as teamster), 73

Page, D. G. Pvt. Co. B; note 1.   Co. B; notes 30, 37, 44

Page, G. W. Pvt. Co. D; note 15 at Nashville; rejoined regt. after exchange.   Co. I; notes 24, 36, 43 (Feb. 24, 1863)

Paine, J. A. Pvt. Co. I; died home, Aug. 1861

Parham, E. J. *See* Parham, T. J.

Parham, E. T. Pvt. Co. E; note 15; rejoined regt. after exchange. Co. F; notes 24, 34, 41, 45, 53, 63; died Marion, Ala., Oct. 16, 1863

Parham, T. J. Pvt. Co. E; note 15; rejoined regt. after exchange. Co. F; notes 24, 34, 41, 49, 81; died prison

Park, I. M. Pvt. Co. G; absent from co. during Donelson until evening of Feb. 15; captured and imprisoned Camp Douglas; exchanged Sept. 23, 1862.   Co. H; notes 29, 35 (drunk), 41, 46 (drunk), 56, 62 (barefooted); captured while drunk on Lookout Mountain, Nov. 24, 1863; imprisoned Rock Island, Ill.

Park, J. L. Pvt. Co. G; note 1.   Co. H; notes 25, 34, 41, 45, 53, 61, 77

Parker, John W. Pvt. Co. A; note 7, May 18, 1862; never rejoined regt.

Parker, W. R. Pvt. Co. I; note 1.   Co. K; notes 25, 34, 41, 52

Parsons, J. B. Pvt. Co. G; note 1.   Co. H; notes 25, 34; notes 42, 46, 54 (all on furlough); 61 (Sept. 19), 65 (Sept. 20), 77

Pate, B. C. Pvt. Co. D; note 1.   Co. I; notes 25, 34, 41, 51, 81

Pate, J. M.   Pvt. Co. B; note 1.   Co. B; notes 25, 37, 42 (detached duty); notes 46, 54, 62, 74 (all excused by surgeon on account of defective vision)

Patterson, B. F.   Pvt. Co. I; enlisted Dec. 1862; notes 24, 34, 41, 48, 53, 65, 73

Patterson, W. A.   Pvt. Co. D; note 1.   Co. I; notes 25, 34, 41, 48, 53, 69 (mortally); died Cassville, Oct. 1863

Paul, Uriah   Pvt. Co. F; note 6; rejoined regt. after exchange. Co. E; notes 24, 38, 41, 59, 57; deserted about Aug. 1, 1863

Paxton, J. A.   Pvt. Co. H; transferred from Forty-first Tenn. at Port Hudson, Mar. 1863; notes 41, 45; deserted near Yazoo City, Miss., about June 12, 1863

Paxton, L.   Musician Co. H; transferred from Forty-first Tenn. at Port Hudson, Mar. 1863; present in ranks Raymond; in band in every other engagement

Peaton, William   Capt. Co. D; present at Donelson; captured and took oath of allegiance to U.S. at Columbus, Ohio, and released; never reported to command

Peavyhouse, F. M.   Pvt. Co. H; note 1.   Co. C; notes 25, 34, 41, 52

Peavyhouse, J. N.   Pvt. Co. H; note 1.   Co. C; notes 25, 34, 41, 52

Peavyhouse, W. P.   Pvt. Co. H; absent from co. during Donelson detailed as nurse to sick in quarters; captured and imprisoned Camp Douglas, exchanged Sept. 23, 1862; died Jackson, Nov. 14, 1862

Pennington, Isaac   Pvt. Co. K; note 18, Camp Trousdale, Aug. 1861

Perkins, Spencer   Pvt. Co. G; enlisted Oct. 17, 1863; joined Missionary Ridge, Oct. 28, 1863; note 75

Perkinson, B. E.   Pvt. Co. C; note 1. 2d corp. Co. D; notes 25, 34, 41, 45, 53; note 82, from Enterprise, Aug. 11, 1863; captured home, Sept. 1863

Perry, Wiley S.   Appointed asst. surgeon May 17, 1861; absent Donelson in charge of sick at Russellville; resigned

Petty, R. O.   Pvt. Co. K; note 16; never rejoined regt.

Phelps, R. R.   2d sgt. Co. I; notes 25, 34, 41, 45, 53, 65; deserted Lookout Mountain, Nov. 24, 1863

Phillips, D. B.   Pvt. Co. G; note 1.   Co. H; notes 24, 34, 41, 45, 53, 64, 77

Phillips, John   2d sgt. Co. A; note 5

Phillips, John   Sgt. maj.; notes 29, 34, 41, 45, 53, 61, 74 (sick leave)

Pickard, Y. S.   Pvt. Co. C; note 8, Apr. 8, 1862

Pillow, R. A.   Pvt. Co. I; note 11

Pittard, A. G.   Pvt. Co. G; enlisted Nov. 3, 1862; notes 24, 34, 42 (sick), 47, 55, 63, 75

Pittard, John W. Pvt. Co. A; note 13; served in cavalry until regt. exchanged; rejoined Holly Springs, Oct. 1862. Co. G; notes 26, 35 excused by surgeon; note 18, Port Hudson, Feb. 1863

Pittard, T. S. Pvt. Co. G; enlisted Nov. 3, 1862; note 23, Dec. 1862; notes 34, 42 (sick), 47, 55, 63, 75

Pitts, Andrew J. Pvt. Co. A; note 5. Co. G; notes 25, 34, 41, 45, 53, 70, 73

Pitts, S. Houston Pvt. Co. A; note 17; served in cavalry until regt. exchanged; rejoined regt. Port Hudson, Feb. 1863. Co. G; notes 51, 57, 66, 78

Plummer, C. B. Pvt. Co. A; wounded Donelson; sent Clarksville, Tenn.; captured and paroled; never rejoined regt.

Plummer, Oliver T. 1st lt. Co. H; resigned Bowling Green, Nov. 1861

Plummer, P. Bruce 2d corp. Co. A; detailed as clerk to Col. Brown commanding brigade Sept. 1861; left Donelson with wounded Feb. 15, 1862; never rejoined regt.

Plummer, R. M. 4th sgt. Co. H; elected 2d lt. upon promotion of R. T. Cooper, Dec. 1861; note 2. Elected 2d lt. Co. C at reorganization Sept. 1862; notes 25, 34; resigned Port Hudson for disability, Feb. 19, 1863

Pointer, Henry F. Capt. Co. E; in command of co., note 2. Reelected capt. of co. at reorganization Sept. 1862; resigned immediately Sept. 26, 1862

Polk, William Appointed sgt. maj. May 17, 1861; note 13; appointed adj. Forty-eighth Tenn. in reorganization, Sept. 1862

Pope, Alexander Pvt. Co. H; note 8, July 30, 1862

Pope, B. L. Pvt. Co. H; note 1. Co. C; notes 25, 34, 41, 45, 55; died Yazoo City, Aug. 1863

Pope, D. R. Pvt. Co. H; died Bowling Green, Dec. 4, 1861

Pope, J. T. Pvt. Co. H; note 18, Camp Trousdale, Aug. 1861. Co. C; notes 25, 34, 41, 51, 57, 66, 73

Pope, W. A. Pvt. Co. E; note 15; joined another command; killed Shiloh

Porch, J. F. Pvt. Co. G; note 1. Co. H; notes 25, 34, 41, 45, 53, 70, 78

Porter, John Pvt. Co. C; note 18, Camp Trousdale, Aug. 1861

Poteet, E. J. Pvt. Co. D; note 8, June 1862

Powers, B. F. Pvt. Co. G; died Camp Cheatham, June 1, 1861

Pryor, W. J. Pvt. Co. I; note 4; took oath of allegiance to U.S. and released

Pullen, E. T. Pvt. Co. F; note 1. Co. E; notes 25, 34, 41, 45, 60, July 11, 1863

Pullen, G. W. Pvt. Co. E; enlisted Nov. 10, 1862; notes 24, 34, 41, 46 (footsore), 54 (footsore), 65; deserted Lookout Mountain, Nov. 24, 1863

Pullen, J. T. Pvt. Co. F; note 18, Bowling Green

Pully, Isaac V. Pvt. Co. K; note 1. Co. A; notes 25, 34, 41, 45, 55, 69, 73

Putnam, Thomas 2d sgt. Co. F; note 18, Bowling Green, Jan. 25, 1862

Quillen, Willis Pvt. Co. H; note 1. Co. C; notes 25, 34, 41, 45, 53, 61, 73

Rainey, G. W. Pvt. Co. G; note 17; never rejoined regt.

Rainey, T. J. Pvt. Co. G; note 17; joined Fifth Tenn.; never rejoined regt.

Ralls, J. H. Pvt. Co. A; enlisted Nov. 4, 1862; notes 24, 41, 45, 55, 61, 73

Ralston, J. A. Pvt. Co. G; note 1. 2d lt. Co. H; notes 31, 34, 41, 45, 53, 64, 76

Ramsey, G. E. Pvt. Co. F; died Russellville, Feb. 14, 1862

Ray, F. M See Rhea, F. M.

Ray, Thomas Pvt. Co. K; transferred from Forty-eighth Tenn. Port Hudson, May 2, 1863; notes 46 (barefooted), 53; deserted Enterprise, Aug. 12, 1863

Reams, J. H. Pvt. Co. E; note 7 June 5, 1862; rejoined regt. after exchange. Co. F; notes 24, 34, 41, 46 (footsore), 53, 61; elected jr. 2d lt. at promotion of Straley; note 73

Reed, A. J. Pvt. Co. A; enlisted Oct. 30, 1862; notes 24, 34, 41, 45, 59 (July 11, 1863), 66, 78

Reed, Jesse B. Pvt. Co. A; note 16; served in cavalry until regt. exchanged. Co. G; notes 25, 34, 41, 45, 53, 69, 73

Reed, Richard R. Pvt. Co. A; note 18, Bowling Green, Oct. 1861

Reed, Thomas 4th corp. Co. K; note 15, Dover hospital; captured and imprisoned Camp Douglas, exchanged Oct. 1862. Pvt. Co. A; notes 21, 27, 34, 41, 49, 81

Renfrow, B. W. Pvt. Co. F; note 1. Co. E; notes 25, 34, 44

Renfrow, Barclay Pvt. Co. F; died Russellville, Feb. 6, 1862

Renfrow, R. T. Pvt. Co. F; absent from Donelson detailed to carry home brother's corpse; entered cavalry

Renfrow, W. P. Pvt. Co. F; note 7, June 1, 1862; rejoined regt. after exchange. Co. E; notes 24, 34, 41; left field without leave Raymond; notes 53, 61, 75

Reynolds, B. F. Pvt. Co. D; note 1. 2d corp. Co. I; notes 25, 34, 45, 53, 65, 73

Reynolds, David O. Pvt. Co. A; note 16; rejoined regt. after exchange. Co. G; notes 24, 36, 41, 49; paroled and deserted July 1863

Reynolds, E. L.   Pvt. Co. G; enlisted Nov. 1, 1862; notes 24, 34, 42 (sick), 47, 55, 61 (except a part of Sept. 19), 73; killed New Hope Church

Reynolds, G. I.   Pvt. Co. B; died home, Aug. 1861

Reynolds, J. H.   Pvt. Co. B; note 1.   3d corp. Co. B; notes 25, 34, 41, 51, 57, 66, 77

Reynolds, J. H.   Pvt. Co. E; note 1.   Co. F; notes 24, 34, 41, 45, 53, 65; deserted Lookout Mountain, Nov. 24, 1863

Reynolds, James L.   Pvt. Co. A; note 1.   Co. G; notes 25, 34, 41, 45, 53, 71

Reynolds, John D.   Pvt. Co. A; note 5.   4th sgt. Co. G; notes 25, 34, 41, 45, 55, 63, 75

Reynolds, Leroy W.   Pvt. Co. A; note 16; rejoined regt. after exchange Holly Springs, Oct. 1862.   Co. G; notes 25, 34, 41, 51, 57, 66, 78

Rhea, David   1st lt. Co. A Donelson; captured and imprisoned Camp Chase; escaped Mar. 1862.   Promoted capt. Co. G at reorganization Sept. 1862; notes 25, 34, in command of co.; notes 42 (sick) 47, 55, 53, 75

Rhea, F. M.   Pvt. Co. G; note 1.   Co. H; absent without leave during every engagement; deserted near Yazoo City, June 5, 1863

Rhodes, G. F.   Pvt. Co. G; note 12, did not leave field.   Co. H; notes 32, 38, 41, 45, 53, 69, 73

Rhodes, John A.   Pvt. Co. G; note 1.   Co. H; notes 25, 34, 43, (Mar. 7, 1863)

Richardson, A. J.   Pvt. Co. I; note 1.   Co. K; notes 25, 34; died Port Hudson, Feb. 11, 1863

Richardson, J. A.   Pvt. Co. F; note 1.   2d corp. at reorganization Sept. 1862; notes 25, 34, 41, 45, 53, 67 (Sept. 19)

Richardson, J. D.   Pvt. Co. F; note 1.   Co. E; notes 25, 34, 41, 45, 53, 68 (slightly), 73; transferred to Forty-eighth Tenn., Jan. 1, 1864

Richardson, W. J.   Pvt. Co. B; note 1.   Co. B; notes 25, 34, 41, 45, 53, 63, 73

Riddle, J. A.   Pvt. Co. I; note 1.   Co. K; notes 25, 34, 41, 45, 53, 61, 73

Ridgeway, William J.   Pvt. Co. K; made 3d sgt. when J. Simms reduced; note 1.   Pvt. Co. A; notes 28, 34; elected jr. 2d lt. Feb. 12, 1863, at promotion of Hodge; notes 41, 51, 57; promoted 2d lt. Aug. 7, 1863, at resignation of Hodge; notes 66, 78

Rittenbury, D. M.   3d corp. Co. D; note 1.   Pvt. Co. I; notes 28, 34, 41, 49; paroled and deserted May 28, 1863

Rittenbury, N. B.   Pvt. Co. D; note 1.   Elected jr. 2d lt. Co. I at reorganization, Sept. 1862; notes 25, 34, 41, 51 (mortally, May 12, 1863); died Raymond, June 13, 1863

Robards, J. G. 3d corp. Co. I; died Camp Cheatham, July 1861

Roberts, Monroe Pvt. Co. G; note 16; joined Anderson's cavalry; rejoined regt. after exchange. Co. H; absent sick from every engagement

Roberts, Noah Pvt. Co. H; enlisted Nov. 5, 1862; notes 24, 34, 41; ran from field at Raymond; notes 53, 65, 77

Roberts, Thomas Pvt. Co. G; note 1. Co. H; notes 25, 34, 41, 51; died Raymond

Robinson, William R. Pvt. Co. C; note 1. Co. D; note 27; died Jackson, Dec. 21, 1862

Rodgers, Henry Pvt. Co. A; note 12. Co. G; notes 25, 34, 41, 45, 53, 70, 77

Rodgers, J. T. Pvt. Co. H; enlisted Oct. 25, 1862; notes 24, 34, 41, 52

Rodgers, John B. Pvt. Co. G; note 1. Co. H; notes 25, 34, 41, 45; made sgt. June 25, 1863; notes 53, 61, 73

Rothrock, G. M. Pvt. Co. G; note 7, June 5, 1862; joined First Tenn. Cavalry; never rejoined regt.

Rountree, B. F. Pvt. Co. F; transferred from Forty-eighth Tenn. at Dalton, Jan. 7, 1864

Rountree, J. A. Pvt. Co. E; note 19, as harness maker; remained on detached service

Rountree, T. J. Pvt. Co. E; note 16; rejoined regt. after exchange at Coldwater, Nov. 1862. Co. F; notes 25, 34, 41, 49, 81

Rountree, W. D. 1st sgt. Co. E; note 1; discharged as nonconscript Jackson, Sept. 1862

Rowe, James H. Pvt. Co. K; note 16; joined First Tenn. Cavalry

Roy, Benjamin P. Made depot quartermaster at Bowling Green, Nov. 19, 1861; transferred from regt. and made transportation agent at Corinth, Apr. 1, 1862; promoted brigade quartermaster in Brown's brigade, Sept. 30, 1862

Rumage, A. J. Pvt. Co. E; note 15 at Bowling Green; joined an Arkansas regt.

Russell, G. W. Pvt. Co. F; note 1. Co. E; notes 25, 36, 41, 45; died at Canton, June 23, 1863

Russell, H. W. Pvt. Co. F; note 9; exchanged Sept. 23, 1862; note 18, Jackson, Sept. 28, 1862

Russell, William A. Pvt. Co. A; note 1. Co. G; notes 25, 34, 41, 45, 55; died Lauderdale Springs, Sept. 2, 1863

Rutledge, J. D. Pvt. Co. B; note 8, Apr. 6, 1862

Rutledge, Wallace W. Made ordnance sgt. Aug. 1861; returned to duty in his co. Sept. 17, 1861; 3d sgt. Co. A; note 1. Promoted jr. 2d lt. Co. G. after reorganization, Sept. 1862; notes 29, 38; notes 41, 45 (in command of his co.); note 50; imprisoned Johnson's Island.

Sands, J. E.   Pvt. Co. B; enlisted Oct. 30, 1862; notes 24, 34, 41, 45, 53, 61; deserted near Chattanooga, Nov. 5, 1863

Sands, S. F.   Pvt. Co. B; note 1. 2d corp. Co. B; notes 25, 34, 41, 45, 53, 71

Sands, W. P.   Pvt. Co. B; enlisted Oct. 30, 1862; notes 24, 34, 41, 45, 53, 61, 73

Scott, A. L.   Pvt. Co. F; died Camp Cheatham, Aug. 12, 1861

Scott, C. S.   Pvt. Co. F; note 1.   Co. E; notes 26 (furlough), 34, 41, 45, 53, 61, 75

Scott, D. C.   Pvt. Co. E; enlisted Nov. 10, 1862; joined regt. at Vicksburg, Dec. 26, 1862; notes 36, 41, 51, 57, 66, 78

Scott, F. P.   Pvt. Co. I; note 1; furloughed Jackson at reorganization and never rejoined command; deserted to cavalry

Scott, H. E.   Pvt. Co. E; enlisted Nov. 10, 1862; notes 24, 34, 41, 47, 55, 63, 73

Scott, Henry   Pvt. Co. E; enlisted Nov. 10, 1862; notes 22 (Feb. 15, 1863), 41, 45, 53, 70, 78

Scott, J. K. P.   Pvt. Co. F; note 15; joined Col. Nixon's Forty-eighth Tenn.; killed Richmond, Ky.

Scott, W. A.   Pvt. Co. D; note 8, June, 1862

Scruggs, L. S.   Pvt. Co. B; note 19, as blacksmith; not present at reorganization, Sept. 1862; deserted Atlanta

Scruggs, William F.   Pvt. Co. K; note 1.   Co. A; notes 33, 79; exchanged Apr. 1863; rejoined regt. May 10, 1863; notes 45, 53, 70, 78

Seagraves, M. L.   Pvt. Co. B; note 1. 4th corp. Co. B; notes 25, 34, 41, 49, 81

Seagraves, W.   Pvt. Co. D; died at home, Sept. 1861

Shannon, A. J.   Pvt. Co. I; note 9; exchanged Sept. 23, 1862. Co. K; notes 29, 36, 41, 49; paroled and went home; captured at home and imprisoned

Shannon, M. J.   Pvt. Co. B; note 10; rejoined regt. after exchange. Co. B; notes 30, 34, 41, 45, 53, 61, 73

Shapard, James B.   Pvt. Co. K; note 1.   Co. A; notes 25, 38, 41, 45, 53, 62 (furlough), 73

Sharp, J. F.   Pvt. Co. H; note 8, Mar. 22, 1862

Sharp, J. G.   Pvt. Co. H; note 1.   Co. C; notes 25, 34, 41, 52

Sharp, J. H.   Pvt. Co. H; absent from Donelson home on furlough; joined cavalry

Sharp, J. J.   Pvt. Co. E; note 16, rejoined regt. after exchange. Co. F; notes 24, 34, 41, 47, 55, 65; deserted Lookout Mountain, Nov. 24, 1863

Sharp, M. V.   Pvt. Co. E; died Camp Trousdale

Shields, J. T.   Pvt. Co. I; note 1.   Co. K; notes 25, 34, 41, 50, 80

Shook, J. C. Pvt. Co. D; discharged Bowling Green; joined Thirty-eighth Tenn.

Shook, W. A. Pvt. Co. D; note 1. Co. I; notes 25, 34, 41, 48, 53, 61, 75

Short, George E. Pvt. Co. G; enlisted Nov. 15, 1862; notes 24, 34, 41, 45, 53; discharged Enterprise, Sept. 1863, by reason of having found a substitute

Short, James B. Pvt. Co. A; note 13; discharged on account of wound at Jackson, Oct. 1862

Shuler, W. H. Pvt. Co. D; note 14

Silas, John Pvt. Co. G; note 7, Mar. 1862; never rejoined regt.

Simmons, Jesse Pvt. Co. D; died Bowling Green, Nov. 1861

Simmons, M. M. Pvt. Co. B; died Camp Cheatham, June 29, 1861

Simmons, W. W. Pvt. Co. B; note 1. Co. B; notes 25, 34, 41, 45, 55, 68, 78

Simpson, John F. Pvt. Co. K; note 1. Co. A; notes 21, 25, 34, 41, 45, 53, 61, 75; made sgt. Dec. 1862, at promotion of Hodge

Simpson, William F. Made 5th sgt. from 4th corp. Co. A, Oct. 1861; transferred to Thirty-second Tenn., Dec. 1861; died soon after at Bowling Green

Sims, George Pvt. Co. H; died home, Jan. 21, 1862

Sims, J. W. Pvt. Co. H; note 1. Co. C; notes 25, 34, 41, 51, 57, 66, 78

Sims, James H. Pvt. Co. K; made 3d sgt. when Wren reduced; reduced to ranks; note 15, Bowling Green; rejoined regt. after exchange, Dec. 12, 1862. Co. A; notes 34, 43 (Mar. 1863)

Sims, W. F. Pvt. Co. H; died home, Sept. 20, 1861

Sisco, William Pvt. Co. H; note 1. 3d corp. Co. C; notes 25, 35, 41, 51, 57, 66, 76

Smith, B. F. Pvt. Co. I; note 20

Smith, D. J. 4th corp. Co. B; note 1. 5th sgt. Co. B; notes 31, 34, 41, 49, 81

Smith, E. H. Pvt. Co. G; note 1; appointed bugler for regt.

Smith, G. B. Pvt. Co. I; note 1. Co. K; present at start of every engagement but always missing at end; deserted from Lookout Mountain, Nov. 18, 1863

Smith, J. E. Pvt. Co. D; enlisted Nov. 1, 1862; joined regt. Vicksburg, Dec. 31, 1862; notes 41, 47, 55, 61, 73

Smith, J. S. Pvt. Co. B; note 16; served in Col. Hill's regt. until regt. exchanged. Co. B; rejoined regt. Vicksburg, Dec. 27, 1862; notes 36, 41, 51, 57, 66, 78

Smith, Jacob Pvt. Co. I; note 11

Smith, James   Pvt. Co. H; note 1.   Co. C; notes 25, 34, 41, 45, 53, 61, 73 (mortally wounded); died Jan. 20, 1864

Smith, Martin   Pvt. Co. C; transferred from Forty-eighth Tenn., Apr. 1863; notes 45, 53, 61, 73

Smith, Munford   Pvt. Co. C; made corp. Sept. 14, 1861; note 1.   Elected 2d sgt. Co. D at reorganization, Sept. 1862; notes 31, 34, 41, 50; paroled and exchanged Aug. 15, 1863; notes 63, 73

Smith, Thomas   Pvt. Co. A; enlisted Nov. 5, 1862; note 23, Dec. 11, 1862; notes 36, 41, 47, 55, 63, 75

Smith, W. R.   Pvt. Co. I; note 1.   4th sgt. Co. K; notes 25, 34, 41, 53, 63, 75

Smith, William R.   Pvt. Co. A; made 3d corp.; note 1.   Pvt. Co. G; notes 25, 34, 41, 45, 56, 64, 76

Smith, William W. Pvt. Co. A; made 5th sgt. Dec. 1861; note 1.   Pvt. Co. G; notes 25, 34, 41, 45, 53, 61, 73

Smoot, Richard   Pvt. Co. G; note 7, July 4, 1862; rejoined regt. after exchange.   Co. H; notes 25, 34; note 18, Port Hudson, Jan. 12, 1863

Spivey, W. H.   Pvt. Co. B; note 16; served in First Tenn. Cavalry until regt. exchanged; present Farmington, Iuka, Corinth.   Co. B; notes 24, 36, 41, 45, 53, 63, 74 (barefooted)

Spratt, A. J.   Pvt. Co. E; note 1.   Co. F; notes 25, 34, 41, 45, 55, 63, 75

Spratt, C. B.   Pvt. Co. E; note 15; discharged from service

Springer, Aaron   Pvt. Co. I; note 1; note 82 from Jackson at reorganization and never rejoined command

Springer, Ananias   Pvt. Co. I; died Camp Cheatham

Stanfield, W. R.   Pvt. Co. E; note 1.   Co. F; notes 24, 34, 41, 49; imprisoned

Stanley, Henry M.   Pvt. Co. A; enlisted Oct. 28, 1862; notes 24, 34, 41, 45, 53, 61, 76

Steele, Nathanial G.   Pvt. Co. A; note 12.   Co. G; notes 25, 34, 41, 45, 60, July 11, 1863

Steele, S. W.   Made 1st lt. of engineers

Stepp, Logan   Pvt. Co. K; note 1.   Co. A; notes 25, 34, 41, 45, 53, 71

Stevens, R. S.   Pvt. Co. D; note 1; note 18, Jackson, Oct. 1862

Stevens, T. J.   Pvt. Co. D; note 13; rejoined regt. after exchange. Co. I; notes 24, 34, 41, 50, 81

Stevenson, D. G.   2d sgt. Co. E; note 1.   Elected 2d lt. Co. F at reorganization Sept. 1862; immediately promoted to 1st lt.; notes 25, 34 (in command of his co.); notes 41, 45, 53, 70 (mortally); died Marietta, Ga., Sept. 1863

Stevenson, Thomas L. Pvt. Co. A; note 6; served in Forty-fourth Tenn. until regt. exchanged; rejoined regt. at Port Hudson, Feb. 1863. Co. G; notes 41, 45, 53, 65 (Sept. 20), 77

Stevenson, W. E. F. Pvt. Co. K; note 1. Co. A; notes 25, 37, 41, 53, 61, 73

Steward, Charles 2d sgt. Co. H; note 18, Camp Trousdale, Aug. 1861

Stewart, Joseph P. Pvt. Co. C; note 1. Co. D; notes 25, 35, 41, 45, 53, 63, 73

Stewart, William Pvt. Co. I; died Camp Cheatham, Nov. 9, 1861

Stockard, D. F. Pvt. Co. C; note 1. Co. D; notes 25, 34, 41, 51, 57, 66, 78

Stockard, Hiram A. Pvt. Co. Co; note 1. Elected 4th corp. Co. D at re-organization, Sept. 1862; notes 25, 34, 41, 45, 53, 61, 73

Stone, William H. Pvt. Co. K; note 1. Co. A; notes 25, 38, 41, 45, 59 (July 11, 1863), 66, 78

Story, A. T. Pvt. Co. D; note 1. Co. I; notes 25, 34, 41, 51, 57, 63, 75

Story, David Pvt. Co. D; died at home, Sept. 1861

Stout, C. C. Pvt. Co. K; note 18, Bowling Green, Jan. 1862

Stout, Samuel H. Appointed surgeon May 17, 1861; transferred to Gordon Hospital, Nashville, Nov. 11, 1861; made post surgeon Chattanooga, 1862; made medical director of hospitals, Army of Tennessee

Straley, G. P. Pvt. Co. E; note 1. Elected jr. 2d lt. Sept. 30, 1862; notes 25, 34, 41; sent to hospital sick from Port Hudson about Apr. 15, 1863, and never rejoined his co.

Street, Alexander Pvt. Forty-eighth Tenn.; enlisted Sept. 9, 1861; transferred to Third Tenn., Co. B about March 1, 1863; transferred to Co. E at Port Hudson, Apr. 1863; notes 47, 53, 61, 75; died at Marietta, Apr. 25, 1864

Stribling, J. B. Pvt. Co. I; note 1. Co. K; notes 25, 34, 41, 45, 53, 65 (most of battle), 73

Strickland, A. J. Pvt. Co. H; note 1. 2d corp. Co. C; notes 25, 34, 41, 45, 53, 61, 75

Strickland, B. J. Pvt. Co. H; note 1. Co. C; notes 25, 34, 43 (Feb. 22, 1863)

Strickland, Samuel D. Pvt. Co. H; made 2d sgt. Aug. 1861; note 1. 2d sgt. Co. C; notes 25, 34, 41; elected 2d lt. at promotion of J. A. Doyel, May 1863; notes 45, 53 (in command of his co.), 64, 76

Strong, J. P. Pvt. Co. G; enlisted Feb. 1863; note 22, Apr. 1863; notes 45, 53; deserted near Meridian, Miss., July 30, 1863

Stroud, G. W. Pvt. Co. B; note 1. Co. B; notes 25, 34; note 82, from Port Hudson, Feb. 25, 1863, for thirty days; rejoined regt. Nov. 1863; note 73

Sullivan, Ambrose Pvt. Co. K; note 15, Nashville; died home

Sumner, G. W. Pvt. Co. K; note 18, Camp Cheatham, June 1861

Suttle, Leroy W. Pvt. Co. A; note 16, served with cavalry until regt. exchanged; rejoined regt. Holly Springs, Oct. 1862. Co. G; absent from every engagement in which regt. participated either sick, on detail, or in hospital

Suttle, William D. Pvt. Co. A; note 4. Co. G; notes 25, 36, 41, 49; paroled and rejoined regt. Jan. 20, 1864, having been absent six months without leave; killed in North Carolina

Swinea, Bryant Pvt. Co. G; note 16; never rejoined regt.

Swinea, Henry S. Pvt. Co. K; note 1. Co. A; notes 25, 34, 41, 45, 53, 61, 75

Swinea, S. W. Pvt. Co. A; enlisted Nov. 8, 1862; notes 21, 25, 34, 41, 45, 53, 69; went home without leave

Swinea, W. F. Pvt. Co. A; enlisted Nov. 8, 1862; notes 21, 25, 34, 41, 45, 65, 73

Sylvester, Thomas M. Pvt. Co. K; note 1. Co. A; notes 27, 36, 42 (sick), 47, 55, 61 (sent to rear due to exhaustion), 75

Tanner, H. J. Pvt. Co. I; note 20; rejoined regt. after exchange. Co. K; notes 25, 34, 41, 45, 53, 61, 73

Tarrent, Samuel L. Capt. Co. H; exchanged positions with Lt. R. T. Cooper, Camp Cheatham; resigned Bowling Green, Nov. 1861; served as pvt. in ranks at Donelson; notes 1, 18

Tayes, J. P. Pvt. Co. I; notes 1. Co. K; notes 25, 34, 44

Taylor, G. W. 2d sgt. Co. G; note 9; exchanged Sept. 23, 1862. Pvt. Co. H; never was in a fight, always absent without leave except at Missionary Ridge where detailed as a teamster

Taylor, J. B. Pvt. Co. H; enlisted Oct. 30, 1862; notes 24, 34, 41, 51, 57, 66, 78

Taylor, J. C. H. Pvt. Co. H; enlisted Oct. 30, 1862; notes 24, 34, 41, 45, 53, 70, 78

Taylor, J. R. Pvt. Co. F; note 1. 3d corp. Co. E at reorganization Sept. 1862; notes 25, 34, 41, 52

Taylor, J. W. Pvt. Co. A; enlisted Oct. 29, 1862; notes 24, 34, 41, 45, 53, 70, 78; note 82, from hospital Dec. 1863; gave himself up to the enemy

Taylor, John Pvt. Co. G; note 16; joined the service and rejoined regt. after exchange. Co. H; notes 25, 34, 41, 45, 53, 64, 73; killed at Resaca, May 14, 1864

Taylor, M. P. Pvt. Co. F; appt. 1st sgt. at resignation of L. J. Mash; note 1

Taylor, Rory   Pvt. Co. A; note 18, Camp Trousdale, Aug. 1861

Taylor, Theodore   Pvt. Co. D; note 1.   Co. I; notes 25, 34, 41, 45, 55, 63; deserted Lookout Mountain, Nov. 24, 1863

Taylor, William   Pvt. Co. F; note 1.   Co. E; notes 27, 36, 42 (sick), 47, 55; died at Lauderdale Springs about July 1, 1863

Tennery, E. K. P.   Pvt. Co. A; note 5.   Co. G; notes 25, 34, 41, 45, 53, 67 (Sept. 20)

Tennery, Pleasant H.   Pvt. Co. A; note 5.   Co. G; notes 25, 34, 41, 51, 53, 72

Terrell, J. B.   See Terrell, T. B.

Terrell, T. B.   Pvt. Co. E; note 1.   3d sgt. Co. F; notes 31, 34, 41, 45, 53, 63; deserted Missionary Ridge, Nov. 25, 1863

Thom, Edward C.   Pvt. Co. E; note 1.   Co. F; notes 25, 34, 41, 45, 53, 64, 76

Thomas, Benjamin S.   Pvt. Co. F; note 1; 3d sgt. Co. E at reorganization, Sept. 1862; appointed ordnance sgt. Sept. 26, 1862

Thomas, J. E.   Pvt. Co. F; present at Donelson; captured and died in prison St. Louis, Mar. 10, 1862

Thompson, A. C.   Pvt. Co. B; enlisted Nov. 4, 1862; notes 24, 34, 41, 45, 55; deserted from hospital Sept. 1863

Thompson, A. F.   Pvt. Co. F; note 1.   2d sgt. Co. E at reorganization Sept. 1862; notes 25, 37, 41, 45, 53, 63, 75

Thompson, A. H.   Pvt. Co. F; note 1.   Co. E; notes 25, 34, 41, 45, 53, 63, 75

Thompson, H. L.   Pvt. Co. B; note 1.   Co. B; notes 27, 36, 41; deserted Apr. 1863

Thompson, H. S.   Pvt. Co. B; enlisted Jan. 28, 1863; joined regt. Port Hudson as conscript; notes 41, 45, 55; deserted hospital Sept. 1863

Thompson, J. A.   Pvt. Co. E; note 1.   Co. F; notes 25, 34, 41, 45, 53, 65, 73

Thompson, J. L.   Pvt. Co. B; note 1.   Co. B; notes 25, 34, 41, 51, 57, 82 (Sept. 3, 1863); captured at home

Thompson, J. M.   3d sgt. Co. B; note 1.   Elected 1st lt. at reorganization Sept. 1862; notes 25, 34 (in command of his co.), 45, 55; died at Enterprise, Sept. 8, 1863

Thompson, J. T.   Pvt. Co. E; note 8, Mar. 18, 1862

Thompson, J. T. S.   Jr. 2d lt. Co. E; note 6, Feb. 18, 1862; rejoined regt. after exchange. Asst. surgeon assigned to duty in regt. Sept. 26, 1862; detailed on secret service, Feb. 22, 1864

Thompson, J. W.   Pvt. Co. E; enlisted Nov. 10, 1862; notes 24, 34, 41, 48, 55, 61, 73

Thompson, N. A.   Pvt. Co. C; deserted to enemy Camp Cheatham, June 1861

Thompson, Peter   Pvt. Co. G; enlisted Mar. 1, 1863; notes 22 (Mar. 1), 41, 45, 58; imprisoned

Thompson, Thomas   Pvt. Co. E; note 19 with quartermaster's dept.; rejoined regt. after exchange.   Elected jr. 2d lt. Co. F in reorganization, Sept. 1862; promotion 2d lt. immediately; notes 31, 34, 41, 45, 55, 61, 73

Thorp, C. F. M.   Pvt. Co. B; note 5.   Co. B; notes 25, 34, 41, 45, 53, 61, 73

Thorp, J. P.   Pvt. Co. B; enlisted Nov. 3, 1862; notes 24, 36, 41, 53, 57, 61, 75

Thurman, E. S.   Pvt. Co. D; note 1.   Co. I; notes 25, 34, 41, 45, 55, 61, 73

Thurman, J. P.   Pvt. Co. I; enlisted Dec. 1862; notes 24, 34, 41, 45, 53, 62 (barefooted); deserted Lookout Mountain, Nov. 16, 1863

Thurman, W. W.   Pvt. Co. I; enlisted Dec. 1862; notes 35 (surgeon's order), 41, 45, 53, 65; deserted Lookout Mountain, Nov. 24, 1863

Tidwell, B. M.   Pvt. Co. D; died Camp Cheatham, June 1861

Tidwell, C. W.   Pvt. Co. I; note 1.   1st sgt. Co. K; notes 31, 34, 41, 48; notes 54, 62, 74 (all on account of sore eyes)

Tillery, W. H.   Pvt. Co. A; enlisted Nov. 18, 1862; notes 21, 25, 34, 42 (sick); died at Clinton, Mar. 27, 1863

Tinnon, Robert M.   Pvt. Co. A; note 5.   Co. G; notes 27, 37, 41, 45, 53, 69, 78

Tomlinson, M. B.   4th sgt. Co. F; note 1; transferred Forty-eighth Tenn. at Jackson, Sept. 28, 1862; elected lt.

Tracy, N. F.   Pvt. Co. I; note 1.   Co. K; notes 29, 34; transferred Forty-eighth Tenn. at Port Hudson, Apr. 1862

True, N. P.   Pvt. Co. I; note 15, Bowling Green; died at home, Mar. 1862

Tucker, D. H.   Pvt. Co. A; enlisted Oct. 27, 1862; notes 24, 34, 41, 45, 53, 67 (mortally); died Marietta, Nov. 13, 1863

Tucker, J. D.   Pvt. Co. E; note 1.   Co. F; notes 25, 35, 42, 46 (without leave), 53, 61, 73

Tucker, J. N.   Pvt. Co. A; enlisted Oct. 27, 1862; never reported to regt.

Tucker, Matthew   Pvt. Co. G; note 13; never rejoined regt.

Tucker, T. B.   Pvt. Co. E; note 1.   2d sgt. Co. F; notes 25, 34, 41, 53, 67 (Sept. 20, 1863); escaped and rejoined his co. about Oct. 1, 1863; note 73

Tucker, Thomas M.   2d lt. Co. E; apptd. adj. of regt. May 1861; wounded Donelson; captured and imprisoned Camp Chase and Ft. Warren; exchanged Aug. 1862.   Elected major at reorganization Sept. 26, 1862; notes 25, 40 (Dec. 29, 1862)

Tucker, W. F. Pvt. Co. K; note 1. 5th sgt. Co. A; notes 25, 34, 41, 50, 81

Tune, Thomas M. Pvt. Co. C; note 1. Elected 4th sgt. Co. D at reorganization, Sept. 1862; notes 25, 37, 42 (sick), 48, 53, 63, 73

Tune, William H. Pvt. Co. C; died Bowling Green, Nov. 1861

Tune, William T. Pvt. Co. C; sick in hospital at Dover during Donelson; imprisoned Camp Butler; exchanged Sept. 23, 1862. Co. D; notes 27, 34, 41, 48, 53, 69, 78

Turnbow, Calvin Pvt. Co. H; note 1. Co. C; notes 25, 36, 41, 45, 53, 68, 78

Turnbow, George Pvt. Co. H; note 1. Co. C; notes 25, 34; died Terry Hospital, Miss., Mar. 14, 1863

Turner, Jesse Pvt. Co. H; made 4th sgt. upon promotion of R. M. Plummer, Feb. 1862; note 1. 1st sgt. Co. C; notes 31, 34, 41, 45, 53, 61; elected jr. 2d lt. when M. H. Johnston promoted; note 73

Turner, Samuel Pvt. Co. H; note 8, May 5, 1862

Ussery, E. P. Pvt. Co. D; died Camp Cheatham, June 1861

Ussery, G. H. Pvt. Co. G; note 1. Co. H; notes 25, 34, 41, 47, 55, 63, 76 (teamster)

Vance, James M. Pvt. Co. K; note 1, exchanged Oct. 1862. Co. A; note 21; notes 27, 34; made sgt. Feb. 1863 at promotion of Hodge; note 41; died Port Hudson, Apr. 1863

Vancleave, T. Y. Pvt. Co. G; note 16; served Fifth Tenn.; rejoined regt. after exchange. Co. H; notes 24, 34; transferred to Forty-first Tenn. at Port Hudson, Mar. 6, 1863

Vaughn, D. Pvt. Co. I; enlisted Dec. 1862; notes 24, 34, 41, 50, 81; died in prison

Vaughn, T. D. Pvt. Co. I; note 1. Co. K; notes 29, 34, 41, 45, 53, 63, 75

Vincent, George Pvt. Co. H; note 1. Co. C; notes 25, 34, 41, 45, 53, 72

Vincent, J. A. Pvt. Co. F; note 6; rejoined regt. after exchange. Co. E; notes 24, 38, 41, 47, 55; deserted from hospital at Lauderdale Springs, Aug. 1, 1863

Vincent, John Pvt. Co. C; transferred from First Tenn. Cavalry, Dec. 1862; notes 25, 34, 41, 45, 53, 61, 73

Wade, Daniel F. Capt. Co. C; in command of his co.; note 13; not re-elected at reorganization and dropped from rolls

Wade, T. B. 4th sgt. Co. E; note 7, May 1, 1862; transferred to Holman's batt. of cavalry

Wade, W. R. B.   Pvt. Co. G; made 2d corp. upon death of R. Kincaid; note 1; appointed wagon master Sept. 26, 1862; detached as brigade wagon master June 1863; rejoined his co. Feb. 24, 1864

Waldrup, A. J.   Pvt. Co. B; enlisted Oct. 30, 1862; notes 24, 34, 41, 45, 53, 61, 76 (as teamster)

Waldrup, D. W.   Pvt. Co. B; enlisted Nov. 1, 1862; notes 24, 38; notes 42, 46, 54 (all without leave); notes 65, 77

Waldrup, G. M.   Pvt. Co. B; note 1.   Co. B; notes 30, 34, 41, 45, 53, 61, 73

Waldrup, J. M.   Pvt. Co. B; note 8, Mar. 26, 1862

Waldrup, T. J.   Pvt. Co. B; enlisted Oct. 30, 1862; notes 24, 34, 41, 45, 61, 75

Walker, Calvin H.   Capt. Co. G; note 2 (in command of his co.). Elected col. at reorganization, Sept. 26, 1862; notes 25 (in command of regt.), 36 (sick leave at home), 41, 45, 53, 61, 75 (sick leave); present at Resaca; killed New Hope Church

Walker, J. C.   4th corp. Co. D; note 1.   Pvt. Co. I; notes 25, 36, 41; transferred to Fifty-third Tenn. at Port Hudson, May 2, 1863

Walker, J. F.   Pvt. Co. C; note 1.   Co. D; notes 25, 34, 41, 45, 53, 61, 75

Walker, J. T.   Pvt. Co. I; note 1.   Co. K; captured on retreat from Holly Springs, Nov. 1862; exchanged and rejoined May 9, 1863; notes 46 (without leave), 53; deserted from Enterprise, Aug. 12, 1863

Walker, James S.   5th sgt. Co. G; made ordnance sgt. Dec. 1861; note 1. Capt. Co. H; notes 31, 36, 41 (in command of his co.), 51, 53, 69, 75

Walker, N. G.   Pvt. Co. F; note 1.   1st sgt. Co. E at reorganization Sept. 1862; notes 31, 34, 41, 52

Walker, T. B.   Pvt. Co. B; note 1.   Co. B; notes 29, 34, 41, 47, 53, 63, 75

Walker, W. R.   Pvt. Co. E; enlisted Nov. 10, 1862; notes 24, 36, 41; note 18 at Port Hudson, Mar. 20, 1863

Walls, W. A.   Pvt. Co. D; note 1.   Co. I; notes 25, 34, 41, 45, 53; died Lauderdale Springs, July 24, 1863

Walters, George   Pvt. Co. I; note 18, Camp Trousdale, Aug. 1862

Warren, Walter M. (or Walter W.)   Pvt. Co. C; note 1.   Co. D; notes 25, 34, 41, 45; elected jr. 2d lt. June 15, 1863, at death of Y. R. Watkins; notes 53, 61, 73

Watkins, Samuel   Pvt. Co. C; transferred to First Tenn., May 1861

Watkins, T. J.   Pvt. Co. C; note 1.   Co. D; notes 25, 34, 41, 47, 53, 70, 78

Watkins, W. W.   Pvt. Co. D; enlisted Nov. 1, 1862; notes 24, 34, 41, 45, 55, 61, 75

Watkins, Y. R.   Pvt. Co. C; note 1.   Elected jr. 2d lt. Co. D at reorganization Sept. 1862; notes 25, 34, 41, 82 (Apr. 14, 1863); died at home May 16, 1863

Watson, Daniel J. Pvt. Co. A; enlisted Nov. 18, 1862; notes 21, 25, 38, 41, 45, 58 (July 15, 1863); escaped and rejoined regt.; note 65, shot himself through the hand and deserted shortly after battle

Watson, Henry W. Pvt. Co. K; note 1. 3d corp. Co. A; notes 25, 34, 41, 45; promoted 3d sgt. at death of Larkin, June 3, 1863; notes 53, 65, 73

Watson, James Pvt. Co. E; note 1. Co. F; note 33, Dec. 3, 1862; released by taking oath of allegiance to U.S., Dec. 20, 1862; deserted

Watson, S. Pvt. Co. E; note 1. Co. F; notes 27, 36, 41, 49; imprisoned

Weatherford, M. Pvt. Co. I; note 1. Co. K; notes 25, 34, 41, 50; paroled and rejoined at Yazoo City, June 1863; notes 53, 69, 73

Weaver, William Pvt. Co. C; note 14

Webb, E. Pvt. Co. G; transferred from First Tenn. by order of Gen. Bragg at Lookout Mountain, Nov. 1863; deserted immediately

Webb, Frank M. Pvt. Co. A; note 13; joined cavalry

Webb, Jesse Pvt. Co. H; enlisted Nov. 10, 1862; notes 24, 34, 41, 53, 58 (July 15, 1863)

Webster, William Pvt. Co. H; enlisted Nov. 3, 1862; notes 24, 34, 41, 51, 57; ran from field at Chickamauga; deserted in Chattanooga Valley, Oct. 27, 1863

Welch, J. W. Pvt. Co. I; note 1; Died Jackson, Oct. 1862

Wells, J. F. Pvt. Co. F; note 1. Co. E; notes 25, 34, 41, 49, 80

Wells, Jeff Pvt. Co. E; enlisted Nov. 10, 1862; note 24; deserted from Grenada, Dec. 18, 1862; notes 22 (Mar. 22, 1863), 45; deserted during siege of Jackson, July 15, 1863

Wells, R. L. Pvt. Co. B; absent without leave from Donelson; captured; took oath of allegiance to U.S. and released; rejoined regt. after exchange. Co. B; notes 30, 34, 41, 45, 53, 61, 73

Wells, Thomas J. Pvt. Co. A; note 1. 3d sgt. Co. G; notes 31, 34, 41, 45 (infirmary corps), 53, 64, 76

Wells, W. T. Pvt. Co. E; enlisted Nov. 10, 1862; notes 24, 34, 41, 47, 55, 63, 75

West, J. P. Pvt. Co. I; enlisted Dec. 1862; notes 24, 34, 41, 45, 55; deserted from Lauderdale Springs, Aug. 1863

West, M. T. Pvt. Co. B; note 1. Elected 2d lt. at reorganization Sept. 1862; notes 31, 34, 41, 45, 53, 61 (in command of his co.), 70, 73; promoted to 1st lt. at death of J. M. Thompson

West, M. V. Pvt. Co. I; enlisted Dec. 1862; notes 24, 36, 41, 47, 55

Westbrook, A. C. 4th corp. Co. H; notes 9, 82 (from Jackson, Sept. 30, 1862); died at home, Oct. 1862

Westbrook, A. C. 4th corp. Co. H; notes 9, 82 (from Jackson, Sept. 30, 1862); died at home, Oct. 1862

Westbrook, J. N. Pvt. Co. H; note 9, exchanged Sept. 23, 1862. Co. C; notes 25, 36, 41, 45, 53, 63, 74 (barefooted)

Westmoreland, R. H. 1st sgt. Co. B; note 5. Pvt. Co. B; notes 25, 38, 41, 45, 53, 61, 73

White, Thomas W. Pvt. Co. K; note 4, exchanged Sept. 15, 1862. Co. A; notes 25, 36, 41, 45, 53, 65 (part of the battle); transferred to Thirty-second Tenn., Oct. 1, 1863

White, W. W. Pvt. Co. E; note 1.

White, W. W. Pvt. Co. G; note 18, Camp Trousdale, Aug. 1, 1861

White, Wiley P. Pvt. Co. A; enlisted Oct. 30, 1862; notes 24, 34, 41, 49; imprisoned

Whitfield, J. W. Pvt. Co. K; note 1. Co. A; notes 25, 34, 41, 45, 53; made 1st sgt. Aug. 7, 1863, at promotion of Beaty; notes 61, 73

Whitfield, W. S. Pvt. Co. K; note 1. Co. A; notes 25, 34, 41, 50, 81

White, James Pvt. Co. D; note 20; rejoined regt. after exchange. Co. I; notes 22 (Feb. 1863), 41, 45, 53, 65, 73

Whittaker, C. M. Pvt. Co. G; note 5. Co. H; note 26 (accidental wound); furloughed Dec. 1862; never rejoined his regt.

Whittaker, W. A. Pvt. Co. G; note 5; furloughed at Jackson, Sept. 26, 1862; never rejoined his regt.

Wilcox, M. Pvt. Co. D; note 1; died in hospital Jackson, Sept. 1862

Wilcoxon, Thomas Pvt. Co. I; enlisted Dec. 1862; never joined the regt.

Wilkes, B. L. Appointed Commissary May 17, 1861; captured at Donelson; imprisoned Camp Chase; died in prison Mar. 1862

Wilkes, James Pvt. Co. B; notes 12, 18 (Jackson, Sept. 1862)

Wilkes, John S. Made commissary sgt. May 17, 1861; note 1. Appointed commissary at reorganization Sept. 1862; absent on furlough from Sept. 26, 1862, to Dec. 15, 1862; office abolished by Act of Congress, Sept. 1, 1863

Wilkes, R. S. Pvt. Co. E; enlisted Nov. 10, 1862; note 24; apptd. commissary sgt. Dec. 15, 1862; left command on sick leave June 23, 1863; died at Aberdeen, Miss., Sept. 1863

Wilkinson, Tyree R. Pvt. Co. A; note 4; exchanged Sept. 15, 1862 Co. G; notes 25, 37, 41, 45, 53, 61 (Sept. 19), 65 (Sept. 20), 77

Willeford, H. C. Pvt. Co. B; enlisted Oct. 30, 1862; notes 24, 34, 41, 45, 55; furloughed from Lauderdale Springs, Sept. 1863; did not rejoin his command

Williams, A. J. Pvt. Co. H; transferred from Forty-first Tenn. at Port Hudson, Mar. 5, 1863; notes 41, 45; captured July 1863; paroled and never rejoined his co.

Williams, B. F.   Pvt. Co. A; note 16; served with Col. Hill's Fifth Tenn.; killed at Farmington, Miss.

Williams, C. L.   Pvt. Co. H; transferred from Forty-first Tenn. at Port Hudson, Mar. 5, 1863; notes 41, 45, 58 (July 15, 1863)

Williams, Gatewood   Pvt. Co. A; note 18, Camp Cheatham, June 1, 1861

Williams, Grogan   Pvt. Co. G; note 1.   Co. H; notes 27, 36, 41, 45, 53, 61, 75

Williams, Horace   Pvt. Co. E; note 1.   1st corp. Co. F; notes 25, 34, 45, 51; died Raymond, June 20, 1863

Williams, J. H.   Pvt. Co. D; note 1.   Co. I; notes 25, 34, 41, 45, 53, 61, 73; made 3d sgt. Dec. 2, 1863

Williams, M. P.   Pvt. Co. G; note 17; joined Fifth Tenn.; wounded Perryville, Ky.; rejoined regt. after exchange Enterprise, Aug. 1863; notes 64, 76

Williams, Marcus   Pvt. Co. A; promoted chaplain of regt. Camp Cheatham, May 17, 1861; left Donelson with wounded Feb. 14, 1862

Williams, O. W.   Pvt. Co. C; note 1.   Co. D; notes 24, 35, 41; left field without leave at Raymond; notes 55, 63, 75

Williams, R. H.   Pvt. Co. I; present at Donelson; captured; died in prison St. Louis, Feb. 25, 1862

Williams, R. R.   Pvt. Co. C; note 1.   Elected 2d lt. Co. D at reorganization Sept. 1862; notes 25, 34, 41, 45, 53, 61 (in command of his co.), 73

Williams, T. J.   Pvt. Co. C; note 20; never rejoined regt.

Williams, Thomas   Pvt. Co. B; note 19 as blacksmith; never rejoined regt.

Williams, W. A.   Pvt. Co. G; note 17; never rejoined regt.

Williams, W. J.   Pvt. Co. F; enlisted Dec. 12, 1862; notes 24, 36, 42 (sick), 47; detached on hospital duty about June 1, 1863

Williamson, J. T.   Jr. 2d lt. Co. F; note 13; entered cavalry

Williamson, James   Pvt. Co. F; note 16; joined another command and appt. lt.

Willis, J. H.   Pvt. Co. I; note 15; died at home, Apr. 1862

Wilsford, G.   Pvt. Co. D; note 1.   5th sgt. Co. I; notes 25, 34, 41, 45, 53, 61; died in Atlanta hospital, Nov. 1863

Wilsford, W. J.   Pvt. Co. D; note 1; detached as teamster at Tippah Ford, Nov. 1862; captured at Port Hudson, July 1863; paroled and deserted soon after

Wilson, Felix G.   4th sgt. Co. K; note 15, Nashville, detached in medical dept.; never rejoined regt.

Wilson, R. L.   1st corp. Co. E; note 19, as harness maker; never rejoined regt.

Wilson, S. J.   Pvt. Co. I; note 20; joined cavalry

Wilson, Vincent W.   Pvt. Co. K; note 19, hospital at Bowling Green; re-joined regt. after exchange; on detached duty in hospital from shortly after reorganization

Wilson, W. B.   Pvt. Co. B; note 1; note 18, Holly Springs, Oct. 1862

Wisdom, J. L.   Pvt. Co. I; note 1.   Co. K; notes 25, 34, 41, 45, 53, 82 (from Enterprise, Aug. 10, 1863); never rejoined command

Wisdom, J. M.   Pvt. Co. K; enlisted Apr. 5, 1863; notes 22 (Apr. 5, 1863), 45, 53; deserted from Enterprise, Aug. 12, 1863

Wisdom, J. W. F.   Pvt. Co. I; note 7, Mar. 31, 1862; rejoined regt. after ex-change.   Co. K; notes 22 (Feb. 1863), 41; notes 45, 53, (but left field without leave during both); deserted from Enterprise, Aug. 12, 1863

Wood, J. H.   Pvt. Co. G; note 15; joined First Tenn. Cavalry; never re-joined regt.

Woodward, John   Pvt. Co. G; note 16; rejoined regt. after exchange at Port Hudson, Mar. 1863; notes 42 (nurse in hospital), 48; deserted near Yazoo City, June 5, 1863

Woodward, T. L.   Pvt. Co. D; note 15, Nashville; rejoined regt. after ex-change.   Co. I; note 24; absent sick from every engagement

Wooten, A. W.   Pvt. Co. C; note 1; rejoined regt. at Tippah Ford, Nov. 1862.   Co. D; notes 29, 34, 41, 45, 58 (May 15, 1863); paroled; deserted June 1, 1863, from Demopolis, Ala.

Worsham, J. H.   Pvt. Co. G; enlisted Nov. 1862; notes 24, 34, 42 (sick), 47, 55, 63, 75; substitute for W. J. Lewis

Wren, Thomas W.   3d sgt. Co. K; reduced to ranks June 1861; at Bowling Green, Sept. 18, 1861, tore down Federal flag on roundhouse and was accidentally hurt; absent from Donelson on this account; captured in Nashville and imprisoned Camp Chase; exchanged Sept. 15, 1862; note 18, Jackson, Sept. 29, 1862

Wright, Daniel F.   Surgeon, assigned to duty in regt. July 3, 1863; re-signed Dec. 1, 1863

Wright, J. R.   Pvt. Co. A; note 1; note 18, Jackson, Oct. 12, 1862

Wright, John D.   Pvt. Co. A; note 1.   2d sgt. Co. G; notes 25, 41, 45, 53, 61, 73

Yokely, Isaac   1st sgt. Co. D; note 1.   Pvt. Co. I; notes 25, 34, 41, 50; paroled and deserted Raymond, May 28, 1863

Yokely, S. L.   Pvt. Co. D; note 1.   Co. I; notes 25, 34, 41, 52

Young, A. A.   Pvt. Co. G; note 1; note 18, Jackson, Sept. 26, 1862

Young, Thomas   Pvt. Co. G; died at home, Aug. 25, 1861

Notes

INTRODUCTION

1. Edwin A. Barber, *Genealogy of the Barber Family: The Descendants of Robert Barber of Lancaster, Pennsylvania.* Material for the introduction is chiefly from an account by Barber written in August 1862 while awaiting release from prison on Johnson's Island off Sandusky, Ohio, in Lake Erie, together with short histories of the regiment's companies, also by Barber, now in the Duke University Library in Durham, North Carolina. After capture, imprisonment, and exchange, the regiment's officers and men reorganized at Jackson, Mississippi, where the then–new colonel, Calvin H. Walker, ordered a drawing up of the histories. A careful checking of the compiled service records of Barber, Walker, and Walker's successor as regimental commander, Colonel Calvin J. Clack, now in the National Archives, revealed nothing beyond the above-mentioned materials and information otherwise available.

2. *1860 Census—Tennessee*, vol. 1 A–Crag.

3. M. T. Newman, "Bethany Presbyterian Church: Historic Sketch of Famous Old Institution," typescript, courtesy of Margaret Butler, Pulaski, Tennessee.

4. Margaret Butler, "The Life of John C. Brown," 2–3, 13–16, 108–119; Ezra J. Warner, *Generals in Gray: Lives of the Confederate Commanders*, 35–36. Brown's autograph album, compiled while a prisoner at Fort Warren, is in folder 1, box 5, Brown Papers, Civil War Collection, Tennessee State Library and Archives, Nashville (hereafter cited as TSLA).

5. For Martin see Margaret Butler, *Legacy: Early Families of Giles County*, 114. Cheairs memoir, p. 2, folder 7, box 12, Civil War Collection, TSLA; see also Robert M. McBride, "The 'Confederate Sins' of Major Cheairs," 121–35. Cheairs's letters from Fort Warren to his daughter and sister are in folder 6, box 1, Cheairs Papers, Sherrell Figuers Papers, TSLA.

6. Barber was taking part in the Confederate invasion of Kentucky, which Thomas L. Connelly has described as "probably one of the greatest mistakes of the war." Kentucky people were Kentuckians first, Unionists or Confederates second. The invasion divided the state and lost a buffer the Confederacy desperately needed, for Tennesseans had not yet organized for defense. Responsible department commanders were Maj. Gen. Leonidas Polk, followed by Albert Sidney Johnston; Polk sent a force to occupy Columbus, Kentucky, and Johnston arranged occupation of Bowling Green (Connelly, *Army of the Heartland: The Army of Tennessee, 1861–1862*, pp. 51–55, 65). Buckner, a Kentuckian who chose the Confederate side, graduated from the United States Military Academy at West Point in 1844, and after service in the Mexican War, in which he received two brevets to

the rank of captain, he resigned in 1855 to enter business. During the Civil War he traversed the ranks from brigadier to lieutenant general. Afterward, for a short time, he edited the *Louisville Courier*, just before its merger with the *Journal*, and busied himself in an effort, eventually successful, to recover valuable property in the heart of Chicago inherited by his wife. Governor of Kentucky in 1887–91, he died in 1914, the last of the lieutenant generals of the Confederacy. See Arndt M. Stickles, *Simon Bolivar Buckner: Borderland Knight*.

7. A native of Kentucky and a graduate of West Point in 1851, Helm became a lawyer and married Emily Todd, half sister of Mary Todd Lincoln. In 1861 he recruited the First Kentucky Cavalry and was appointed brigadier general the next year, serving in the Vicksburg area, in Louisiana, and in operations around Tullahoma. He was killed at Chickamauga. See R. Gerald McMurtry, *Ben Hardin Helm*.

8. James A. Bowers was company surgeon and in November 1861 became regimental surgeon. Born in 1830 in Elkton, he had studied at Jefferson Medical College in Philadelphia, graduating in 1854 and doing postgraduate work at Bellevue Hospital in New York. When Elkton organized a company in 1861, Dr. Bowers became first lieutenant. After the war he returned to Elkton. He died in 1878 (Margaret Butler, *Legacy*, 170–71).

9. Hardee graduated from the U.S. Military Academy in 1838, fought with Maj. Gen. Winfield Scott in the Mexican War, and in 1855 published *Rifle and Light Infantry Tactics*, known popularly as "Hardee's Tactics." See Nathaniel Cheairs Hughes, Jr., *General William J. Hardee: Old Reliable*. For Buell and Crittenden, see Ezra J. Warner, *Generals in Blue: Lives of the Union Commanders*, 51–52, 100–101.

10. Nathaniel Cheairs Hughes, Jr., and Roy P. Stonesifer, Jr., *The Life and Wars of Gideon J. Pillow*. Cheairs to his daughter, Apr. 22, 1862, Cheairs Papers, TSLA.

11. Cook was colonel of the Thirty-second Tennessee, part of the brigade under Colonel Brown.

12. The author continues, solemnly (how fortunate he did not write the rest of the manuscript this way!): "Possibly in future years, when your swords shall be beaten into ploughshares, and when, in the midst of peaceful pursuits, the memory of the bloody scenes of this revolution shall become dim, these pages shall have some small degree of interest to myself and to a few chosen friends, and perhaps, too, their perusal may afford a few moments of pleasure to her, whose devoted love has followed the unfortunate author through camp, field, and prison."

1. FORT DONELSON: FEBRUARY 12–16, 1862

1. For operations at Donelson, far and away the best source is Benjamin Franklin Cooling, *Forts Henry and Donelson: The Key to the Confederate Heartland*.

2. A West Point graduate, and afterward a dental surgeon, Dr. Edward Maynard patented a breech-loading carbine with an excellent rate of fire and impressive accuracy, and before the war it became a favorite with Southern sportsmen and militia members. It remained a favorite during the great conflict; at Donelson Colonel Forrest borrowed a Maynard to kill a Federal sharpshooter. According to one testimony it was "warranted to shoot twelve times a minute, and carry a ball effectually to 1,600 yards. . . . Nothing to do with the Maynard rifle but load her up, turn her North, and pull trigger" (Wayne Austerman, "Maynard," 42–45).

3. Barber here interrupted his narrative with a long description of terrain in and around Fort Donelson together with troop dispositions, which now appears with the chapter map.

4. Appointed brigadier general in the Confederate army, John B. Floyd escaped from Donelson in an ignominious manner that caused his removal from command by President Jefferson Davis (Warner, *Generals in Gray*, 89–90). Sheet-music lyrics in 1862 about "Floyd's Retreat from Fort Donelson" ended with "He who fights and runs away, / May live to run another day."

5. Edward H. Reynolds, private in the Forty-sixth Illinois, kept a remarkable diary of the operation at Fort Donelson, well worth citing to give the Union side of things. Reynolds showed a considerable descriptive power and of course wrote in the heat of the moment. "Early in the morning we arrive and disembark," he noted,

> just out of range of the guns of Fort Donelson, and marched inland west of the forts but had moved but a short distance when we were hurriedly rushed back to the river to guard the transports, and here we witnessed our first little bit of war. The gunboats steamed slowly up the stream and when within easy range, the big guns in the forts opened a lively fire on them which was promptly returned, but at great disadvantage, the river here being narrow and rapid, with no chance to maneuver for position. Heavy shot and shell fell fast among our unprotected vessels and as they became disabled they floated helplessly back among other boats causing a bad situation and much damage. After hours of hard work and the loss of many lives they were towed and floated down out of range of the forts. (Reynolds Diary, Feb. 14, 1862, *Civil War Times Illustrated* Collection, U.S. Army Military History Research Collection, U.S. Army Military History Institute, Carlisle Barracks, Pennsylvania).

6. Private Reynolds arrived on February 14 and was one of the Federal reinforcements.

> At 4:00 P.M. we were marched around west and south of the forts to a position [near] the enemy's works, where all timber had been cleared off and yellow clay was nearly ankle deep. After some investigation and delay we were ordered to remain here for the night, with arms and accouterments ready for instant use. This was indeed a hard problem for us green Yanks to solve. Our first night out, in a strange land, in range of rebel guns where no fire or light is permitted, in pitch darkness we must gnaw our hardtacks and prepare our downy beds of ease. There was no shelter from mud or the threatened storm. We each carried a light single blanket and by two bunking together, spread one in the mud while the other must cover two Yankees with guns, ammunition, haversacks, etc. Rain, sleet, and snow fell almost constantly during the night and it is much easier to imagine than to describe this night and our condition in the morning. (Ibid., Feb. 14, 1862)

7. Before becoming adjutant, Thomas M. Tucker had been second lieutenant of Company E. A youthful student at the Nashville Military School, he was "quite a favorite with the company," according to Barber's history of Company E. He was killed at Chickasaw Bayou.

8. The division order of battle showed two Indiana regiments, two Kentucky, three Illinois, three Ohio, and one Nebraska. *War of the Rebellion: A Compilation of the Official Records of the Union and Confederate Armies*, vol. 7: 169 (hereafter cited as *OR*). See also Robert E. and Katherine M. Morsberger, *Lew Wallace: Militant Romantic.*

The human dimension of war is difficult to capture by reciting troop dispositions and presence of commanders. When Barber wrote of Wallace's division it was of the presence of such individuals as Private Reynolds.

> We were a very sorry looking crowd this morning and possibly some of us wonder why we left home and mother. Crawling out of our muddy nests, and after a few minutes for hardtack and sowbelly, we are again in line and plodding along towards the roar of musketry and cannon. This is our first test under fire, where shells are whizzing over and bursting nearby. No word excepting the loud commands of field officers is heard and no signs of the white feather among our boys.
>
> We were now in heavy timber, moving in four ranks where big shells were shattering trees and felling limbs etc. among us and here we pass over our first fallen comrades. As I stepped over the first, lying directly in our path, I could see that he was still alive and struggling for breath. This seemed wicked, passing him without a word or offer of help and we never forget these first impressions. As we advanced many were passed, both dead and dying.
>
> We are now quickly moved by the left into line of battle and ordered forward to support Dresser's battery which was shelling the rebel works and drawing a heavy fire over us. Nearing the battery we are ordered to halt. In this position a very large tree was directly in our ranks, crowding our company badly, and while in this position a percussion shell from the enemy struck a limb of this tree directly over us, exploding and killing or mortally wounding Jerome Emerson who at the time was crowded tightly against my left side. He could not utter a word, was left where he fell, and never heard from. Poor Jerry was the first killed in our company. He seemed to have a presentiment that something was to happen to him. As we were leaving our muddy camp this morning he remarked that he did not expect to get through this alive. He lived on a farm between Flagg Station and Ashton, Illinois.
>
> We saw General Grant today for the first time, busily riding along the lines, through his first important battle and victory. (Diary, Feb. 15, 1862)

9. Barber of course is setting out the climactic moment at Donelson. Even months later, as he was writing in confinement at Johnson's Island, he could not be sure what happened. He believed Gordon's order broke the Confederate charge and lost the battle. But here he was unfair to Gordon, for no forward movement would have availed against Wallace's lines, which reached out on either side of the Wynn's Ferry road, with a battery squarely on the road. Barber admitted the hail of fire was extraordinary. For excellent description of the scene see Cooling, *Forts Henry and Donelson.* Incarcerated at Fort Warren, Major Cheairs wrote a report of the battle for the Third, and carefully avoided accusing Gordon ("some unfortunate order being given"). Report of Mar. 10, 1862, *OR*, vol. 7:350. Colonel

Brown's report, written earlier at Fort Warren (February 16), names Gordon (ibid., 348).

10. During the Mexican War, Charles F. Smith, with four hundred men, helped storm one of the heights at Monterrey; see Napoleon Jackson Tecumseh Dana, *Monterrey Is Ours! The Mexican War Letters of Lieutenant Dana, 1845–1847,* 131–33. As Barber relates, Smith's rushing of men into the Confederate breastworks, with the general personally leading the assault—hat on the tip of his sword—was a crucial move and caused surrender of the garrison. For this he was promoted to major general (Warner, *Generals in Blue,* 455–56). An infection resulting from an accident caused his death two months later, a tragic loss to the Union side. Maj. Gen. William T. Sherman said that had he lived General Grant would have "disappeared to history" (George W. Cullum, *Biographical Register of the Officers and Graduates of the U.S. Military Academy* 1:357).

11. Pillow unceremoniously escaped across the river in a small flatboat or skiff.

12. Barber was far off in reckoning Federal strength, which at the beginning of the battle was little more than the Confederate strength—twenty-five thousand versus twenty thousand.

13. Barber's description of chaos following the surrender aptly characterized the situation to the south of Donelson in the state capital, Nashville, which now was exposed to Grant's forces. Here nature in the form of flood waters combined with military events. A bewildered Confederate officer, Alexander Winn, wrote Floyd (who of course could do nothing about the problem) of how "Several thousand pounds of bacon are even now floating off and being lost. The river is rapidly rising and bearing off large quantities. Every moment, sides of bacon are floating away on the rising tide. As an officer of the army cognizant of these facts I consider it my duty to represent these facts to you. I will not presume to dictate, to an officer of your standing and experience, but would most respectfully urge that something may be done" (letter of Feb. 19, 1862, Floyd Papers, William R. Perkins Library, Duke University).

2. CAPTIVITY: FEBRUARY 16–SEPTEMBER 16, 1862

1. Again Private Reynolds's diary offers piquant description of the demoralizing scene at the time of the Confederate surrender.

> At daylight we were ordered to advance and on approaching the rebel works discovered white flags floating over their lines and were informed of the surrender that had taken place. We were immediately formed in line of march and entering the strong works with other regiments were kept very busy during the day, receiving the surrender of our fourteen thousand prisoners, a large number of big guns, and all arms, ammunition, mules, wagons, and supplies.
>
> The prisoners are a miscellaneous lot, all sizes, ages, and descriptions, in all sorts of garbs, plug hats, slouch hats, and caps, long and short coats of all colors, just as they left their homes, not having received uniforms from their government.
>
> We are placed on guard at the riverbank, preparing the shipment of all prisoners to Camp Douglas at Chicago and other Northern points. A fleet of steamers is waiting and the prisoners are beginning to move down the

steep bank, perhaps forty feet, like herded sheep. Rain had fallen most of the day and now pouring down and yellow clay daubs everything.

It was interesting and amusing to watch the droves of prisoners, in no order, going down to the landing. The steep bank soon became slippery as ice, and the clumsy ones began to toboggan down on their backs, knocking the feet from others as they glide down, sometimes four or five deep when the bottom is reached. This lasted until late into the night, growing more slippery and difficult to reach the landing right and up, developing many scenes, some jolly clowns, and some piles of grouches going down in bulk. This mussed up their dispositions at times and the guard at the water's edge was kept busy preventing fights among them. We were on guard here on the riverbank most of the day and all throughout the rainy night without shelter. (Feb. 16, 1862)

All prisoners down the hill and away, we return to the camp occupied by us on the fourteenth where we have opportunity to clean up and dry out after our dirty experience the past few days. (Feb. 17)

2. "The next morning after our surrender we were marched to the river where there were several old hulks of steamboats that appeared to be rotten from bottom to top. We were crowded on the lower decks one thousand to the boat. We were in much more danger on the decks of these old boats than we were when we were facing the Yankee bullets" (Memoir of Milton A. Ryan, Ryan Papers, U.S. Army Military History Research Collection). Ryan was in the Fourteenth Mississippi.

3. At the beginning of the war, M. Jeff Thompson was mayor of St. Joseph, Missouri, and organized a battalion and offered it to the governor of his state. When the governor refused, and Maj. Gen. John C. Frémont in August 1861 issued an emancipation proclamation, Thompson issued a counterproclamation and with his "swamp rats" began a series of border raids. He surrendered in May 1865.

4. The dead soldier was Thomas B. King. Ill in quarters during the fight at Donelson, he died on February 18.

5. The men went on to Chicago, arriving February 23. According to Chaplain Deavenport, it was a gloomy day, and muddy—the sun thawed the frozen ground. The men trudged through the streets, guards on each side, for the amusement of the populace. "Ear, mouth, and eyes were all open. To them it was far better than a menagerie." Everything, he wrote, was "hatred, deep and fiendlike." A sole happening caused amusement; namely, the orderly of his company had a favorite chicken named "Jake" that rode on his knapsack, and every few steps Jake would crow. Narrative, Deavenport Papers, TSLA. On the rooster, see W. S. Nye, "Jake Donelson: A 'Cocky' Rebel," 51. Jake belonged to Jerome B. McCanless, Company G. After exchange and return to the South, McCanless had the rooster's portrait painted, which is reproduced in the Nye article. Jake died in 1864 and received a military funeral.

6. For more on Brig. Gen. Lloyd Tilghman, see Warner, *Generals in Gray*, 306. He was killed at Champion's Hill.

7. Designed as an instruction camp for volunteers, Camp Chase became a prison camp in November 1861. William B. Hesseltine, *Civil War Prisons: A Study in War Psychology*, 34–54.

8. Granville Moody, a Methodist minister, consulted church members when asked to be colonel of the Seventy-fourth, and accepted with their permission. At

Stones River he received the nickname of "Fighting Parson" after being wounded four times and having his horse shot out from under him. He resigned in 1863 and returned to the ministry.

9. Joseph H. Parks, *General Leonidas Polk, C.S.A.: The Fighting Bishop.*

10. A native Virginian and distinguished lawyer, Connally F. Trigg moved to Knoxville in 1856 and was an outspoken opponent of secession. When Union troops occupied the city in 1863, he became judge of the U.S. district court for eastern Tennessee. He died in 1880. Herschel Gower and Jack Allen, eds., *Pen and Sword: The Life and Journals of Randal W. McGavock,* 911. McGavock's widow married Trigg in 1868.

11. It was said that Brownlow was intemperate in every public act. Late in life he wrote, "had I my life to live over, I would pursue the same course I have pursued, ONLY MORE SO." Privately he was abstemious to a fault. Ellis Merton Coulter, *William G. Brownlow: Fighting Parson of the Southern Highlands;* James C. Kelly, "William Gannaway Brownlow," 25–43, 155–72.

12. Charlotte M. (Lottie) Clark, wife of James Clark, was a staunch supporter of Ohio politician and Southern sympathizer Clement L. Vallandigham. Three of her brothers served in the Confederate army. Among other acts of helpfulness, she undertook to carry messages through the lines to Richmond and other places. An order went out for her arrest, but she departed on the midnight Northern Express for Niagara Falls and crossed to safety via the suspension bridge. Phillip R. Shriver and Donald J. Breen, *Ohio's Military Prisons in the Civil War,* 54. She returned to Ohio and then went to the South, where she remained until the end of the war. For more information, including a photograph, see William H. Knauss, *The Story of Camp Chase,* 175–78.

13. Lt. Col. William Hoffman, a regular officer of the Eighth U.S. Infantry, commissary general of prisoners, had selected Johnson's Island, obtaining half of the island and receiving control of the rest for an annual rental of five hundred dollars. Half the island's three hundred acres were wooded, solving the problem of fuel. A forty-acre clearing on the waterfront furnished room for barracks for guards and prisoners. The half mile of water separating the island and mainland virtually cut off the possibility of escape; of the twelve thousand prisoners incarcerated on the island during the war, only twelve managed to escape. Edward T. Downer, "Johnson's Island," 98–113. See also Charles R. Shultz, "The Conditions at Johnson's Island Prison during the Civil War."

14. Named after the Union's commissary general of prisoners, the four-hundred-man group was entirely volunteer, recruited by promise of a bounty of one hundred dollars per man. William S. Pierson, a Yale graduate and former mayor of Sandusky, possessed no military experience but had impressed Hoffman with his ability and qualities of a gentleman.

15. Second Lieutenant Elijah Gibson of the Eleventh Arkansas was "a young man very peaceable quiet fellow" (James B. Murphy, ed., "A Confederate Soldier's View of Johnson's Island Prison," 110, quoting the diary of Captain William H. A. Speer).

16. Here Barber began a long narrative of early days in the army, summarized in the introduction.

17. In this entry of August 23, Barber opened with a newspaper summary, remarked the imminence of exchange, and continued his narrative of early days.

18. Joseph H. Parks, *General Edmund Kirby Smith, CSA.* For more on Maj. Gen. William Nelson, see Warner, *Generals in Blue,* 343–44.

19. Barber was passing a string of six Confederate forts along the Mississippi, beginning with Columbus, Kentucky. In the autumn of 1861 the latter locality had been fortified with 140 guns facing north and west across the river. Downriver north of Tiptonville, Tennessee, was a huge, near-circular bend in the river called Island Ten at the junction of the states of Tennessee, Kentucky, and Missouri, where the second fort was located. Northward across the river in New Madrid, Missouri, stood another fort. Fourth was Fort Pillow, near present-day Fulton, Tennessee. Ten miles to the south near Drummonds were batteries on the high bluff at Fort Wright. Downstream, six miles above Memphis, lay the guns of Fort Harris, which protected the city, as did more artillery on the city's bluff. Thomas L. Connelly, *Civil War Tennessee: Battles and Leaders*, 16. All this, Connelly writes, was in order to allow planters and their wives to enjoy the niceties of Memphis, to which they fled from the heat and boredom of the cottonlands. The city meant balls at the magnificent Gayoso House or luxurious meals in the Commercial Hotel dining room featuring calf's-foot jelly, codfish-egg sauce, and roast bear meat. Crisp's Gaiety Theater offered performances by Edwin Booth and Charlotte Cushman.

20. For more on Samuel R. Curtis, see Warner, *Generals in Blue*, 107–8.

3. VICKSBURG: SEPTEMBER 16, 1862–JANUARY 2, 1863

1. The present chapter begins prosaically but turns to the battle of Chickasaw Bayou, an engagement with large Federal losses and a defeat for General Sherman. In this battle Sherman had 30,000 men and used 8,000; the Confederates had under 6,000 and used 3,500. Union casualties were 1,776 (308 killed, 1,005 wounded, 563 missing), Confederate 207. An improvised Confederate defense, resting on the Third Tennessee (Barber's narrative shows this), prevented the Federals from taking Vicksburg without a siege. Years later the Confederate commander, Brig. Gen. Stephen D. Lee, sought to distribute laurels and wrote in "Battle of Chickasaw Bayou" that other regiments deserved credit, but Barber's narrative seems closer to the truth. Too, the battle shows the appalling results of a frontal attack in an era of rifles, not muskets, for which see Earl J. Hess, ed., *A German in the Yankee Fatherland: The Civil War Letters of Henry A. Kircher*, p. 48; Florence M. A. Cox, ed., *Kiss Josey for Me*, 116; Frank L. Byrne and Jean Powers Soman, eds., *Your True Marcus: The Civil War Letters of a Jewish Colonel*, 205–17. For the battle see Herman Hattaway, *General Stephen D. Lee*, 62–77. It was the age-old failure of commanders to appreciate the effect of new weapons on infantry tactics—akin to the appearance of the crossbow or, beginning in 1914, the employment of great numbers of machine guns. On this score, see Grady McWhiney and Perry D. Jamieson, *Attack and Die: Civil War Military Tactics and the Southern Heritage*, 3–24, 143–69.

2. Walker had been commander of Company G.

3. For more on Sterling Price, see Warner, *Generals in Gray*, 246–47.

4. Robert G. Hartje, *Van Dorn: The Life and Times of a Confederate General*. An excellent cavalry commander, also a philanderer, Earl Van Dorn incurred the enmity of the husband of one of his conquests, who in 1863 sought him out (as it happened, in Rippavilla, the house of Major Cheairs) and killed him.

5. For more on John C. Vaughn, Warner, *Generals in Gray*, 316–17.

6. William L. Wessels, *Born to Be a Soldier: The Military Career of William Wing Loring of St. Augustine, Florida.*

7. A native of Alabama, John Gregg had moved to Texas. He became brigadier general after exchange, commanded at the defeat at Raymond, and was killed below Richmond in 1864 (Warner, *Generals in Gray*, 118–19).

8. For more on Claudius C. Wilson, see ibid., 339. Stephen D. Lee graduated from the U.S. Military Academy in 1854 and resigned in 1861 to go with the Confederacy. Thereafter his rise was rapid. Appointed brigadier general, he went to Vicksburg where he commanded in engagements during the winter of 1862–63, including Chickasaw Bayou. A fighter, he saw much action with the Army of Tennessee, becoming a lieutenant general. After the war he was a planter, member of the Mississippi legislature, first president of the Mississippi Agricultural and Mechanical College, and commander in chief of the United Confederate Veterans. He died in 1908 (Hattaway, *General Stephen D. Lee*).

9. Barber may have exaggerated. The most-recent published account of the battle, Hattaway's *Stephen D. Lee*, relates the capture of five hundred rifles (73).

10. Hattaway's stirring *Stephen D. Lee* relates: "Before nightfall Lee had sent litter bearers to bring in the Federal wounded, but they were mistakenly fired upon. After dark some eighty Union wounded were picked up and taken to Confederate hospitals. This kindness probably gave rise to the charge made later that the Southerners plundered the dead and wounded of their clothing and equipment. Of course, the charge was unfounded, and [Union brigadier general George W.] Morgan himself admitted as much in his account of the battle" (74). But see Byrne and Soman, eds., *Your True Marcus*, 215: "Oh such horrid sights: they had stripped all our dead of everything but their Shirt and Drawyers" (Dec. 30).

11. The Federals left their positions as quietly as possible, "at a rapid rate, half the time running, getting tangled among the straggly grapevines and sinking in the mud a foot," and reached their boats at midnight "and had a good night's rest after all" (Frank McGregor to Susie Barton, Jan. 6, 1863, McGregor Papers, U.S. Army Military History Research Collection).

4. PORT HUDSON: JANUARY 2–MAY 3, 1863

1. Vicksburg and Port Hudson together constituted the Confederate bastion on the Mississippi in 1862–63. Indeed, Port Hudson was the stronger place. Because neither Lee, Grant, nor any other Civil War luminary fought at Port Hudson, also because the river shifted and the town now has vanished (without the possibility of a national park and visitors), Port Hudson surely has not had the attention it deserves. See Lawrence L. Hewitt, *Port Hudson: Confederate Bastion on the Mississippi*, xii–xiii.

2. The reason for the attempt to run the batteries at Port Hudson by Rear Adm. David G. Farragut on March 14 was not to blockade the Mississippi from Port Hudson to Vicksburg but to prevent foodstuffs from western Louisiana reaching troops at Port Hudson. In this hope the admiral was proved wrong (Hewitt, *Port Hudson*, 94–95). For more on Franklin Gardner, William N. R. Beall, and Samuel B. Maxey, see Warner, *Generals in Gray*, 21–22, 97, 216.

3. The Federal force on December 31, 1862, comprised 31,253 men, of which a third occupied Baton Rouge (Hewitt, *Port Hudson*, 39). For more on the Union commander, see Fred Harvey Harrington, *Fighting Politician: Major General N. P. Banks.*

4. Rosecrans is in Warner, *Generals in Blue,* 410–11. For his opponent, see Grady McWhiney, *Braxton Bragg and Confederate Defeat.*

5. For Albert Rust, see Warner, *Generals in Gray,* 266–67.

6. For John C. Pemberton, see Michael B. Bullard, *Pemberton: A Biography.*

7. Barber was looking at *Hartford,* Farragut's flagship in the lead, with *Albatross* lashed alongside, followed by *Richmond* with *Genesee,* then *Monongahela* with *Kineo,* and finally *Mississippi.* The admiral had lashed slower vessels to faster ones. A sidewheeler with big paddle boxes, twenty feet out on each side, *Mississippi* had the least chance of getting past the batteries, and Farragut put it last so it could not hinder the squadron if disabled (Hewitt, *Port Hudson,* 74–75).

8. "What did you think of the Port Hudson affair, it was a terrible night, was it not? I thought of you often during that fight. I could not tell you if I wanted to of the fearful cannonading. As one of our men remarked, 'They didn't seem to care whether they hit a fellow or not' " (Lt. Comdr. John E. Hart to wife Hattie, Apr. 16, 1863, Hart Papers, U.S. Army Military History Research Collection). Hart was captain of *Albatross.*

9. Confederate casualties were three men killed and twenty-two wounded (Hewitt, *Port Hudson,* 93).

10. The run past the Confederate batteries was frightening; shells and shot were everywhere. Of Farragut's seven ships, two made the passage, *Hartford* and *Albatross* (Barber mistook the latter for *Monongahela*). Four turned back and *Mississippi* was lost; last in line, the frigate passed the lower batteries but grounded on the shoal jutting from the west bank at the bend, was abandoned, slid off early the next morning, floated past the remaining ships, and at 5:05 A.M. blew up (Hewitt, *Port Hudson,* 72–95).

11. Union troops captured Deavenport near Florence, Alabama, in November 1864, and he escaped a week or so later, leaving among his belongings a book containing a short narrative and diary, the former a reminiscence of wartime service, the latter entries from March 31 through September 23, 1864. His captor, Capt. James K. McLean of the Third Illinois Cavalry, kept the book. Years later, in 1895, McLean's son placed advertisements in Southern newspapers, received a letter from Deavenport's widow, and returned the book. In 1965 the chaplain's daughter, Liza Deavenport Jamison, presented it to the Tennessee State Library and Archives. In an accompanying explanation, Mrs. Jamison related that Federal troops captured her father six times and that he escaped every time. Once when near Pulaski, Tennessee, he went to his former church to hold a prayer meeting and was in the midst of it, and a friend rushed in and announced, "The Yankees are coming! Run!" Deavenport called upon the superintendent of the Sunday school to take over, opened his hymnal without looking at the hymn, handed the book to the superintendent, and climbed the steps to the slaves' gallery and thence through the trap door to the belfry. All the while the congregation was singing "Could I but Climb Where Moses Stood and View the Landscape O'er." He remained in the belfry five days, supplied with food and water by two cousins. Deavenport Papers, TSLA.

12. "I have a large amount of cotton bales upon my decks and hung over the vessel's sides, so as to resist shot, shells and all that sort of thing. I have also slung to my sides great logs of timber, so as to keep off 'rams.' My little gunboat is a sight to see" (Lt. Comdr. John E. Hart to Hattie, Apr. 16, 1863, Hart Papers).

13. Jerry Thompson, *Henry Hopkins Sibley: Confederate General of the West.* For Christopher C. Augur, see Warner, *Generals in Blue,* 12.

14. For James R. Chalmers, see Warner, *Generals in Gray,* 46.

15. Between April 17 and May 2, 1863, Col. Benjamin H. Grierson led a brigade of 1,700 cavalrymen from La Grange, Tennessee, to Baton Rouge to disrupt Confederate communications and transport and distract attention from Grant's main move against Vicksburg. See Dee Alexander Brown, *Grierson's Raid*.

16. For John S. Bowen, see Warner, *Generals in Gray*, 29–30.

17. The last two sentences of this entry open the next chapter.

5. MARCHING THROUGH MISSISSIPPI: MAY 3–AUGUST 24, 1863

1. For the beginning of this entry see last line of preceding chapter.

2. Surgeon Erastus Yule was left behind with Lt. Col. William Blackburn, who later died. Brown, *Grierson's Raid*, 197–203, 241.

3. Grant had launched his great maneuver around Vicksburg, besieging the town and at the same time preventing Confederate forces in the vicinity from linking up with the defenders; Barber seems not to have known about it. For what was happening with the Third Tennessee, Edwin C. Bearss, *The Campaign for Vicksburg: Grant Strikes a Fatal Blow*, describes the scene (483–517): "As the Confederates debouched from the timber, a close-range volley crashed into their left flank, shattering it and hurling it back into the shelter of the woods. . . . It had been fired by Colonel McCook's 31st Illinois. It had lost its way earlier in the day, but it now waited at the edge of the woods. When the Rebel line came out of the timber, the Illinoisans did an about-face and fired at point-blank range into the flank of the enemy battle line" (499). The basic problem was not anything the Third Tennessee had done, nor was it the fortune of the Illinois regiment; rather, it was a miscalculation by General Gregg, who with three thousand men believed he faced a Federal brigade when in fact he faced Maj. Gen. James B. McPherson's corps. The division of Maj. Gen. John A. Logan, sixty-five hundred strong, bore the brunt of the fighting. Toward the end Logan received reinforcement from two brigades of another division, four thousand more men.

4. Barber sent these losses to Gregg; the Third's report is in Barber's hand (roll 2, RG 45, National Archives). The other Confederate regiment that lost badly at Raymond was the Seventh Texas. "The Seventh Texas, which boasts that it never before gave way, was lying in ambush when the Twentieth Ohio first marched into the woods. With all its advantage of position, this regiment was slaughtered and driven. Twenty-three dead were found in half an acre in front of the line of the Twentieth: 7 dead were found behind a log, which was pierced by seventy-two balls. One tree in front of my line was stripped and hacked near the root by balls, though not a mark was found more than 2 feet above the ground" (Report of Col. Manning F. Force, Twentieth Ohio, 1863 [no date], *OR*, vol. 24, pt.1:715. Total Confederate losses were 514: 73 killed, 251 wounded, 190 captured or missing. Gregg's May 20, 1863, report is in ibid., 736–39. Logan reported a total of 437: 62 killed, 338 wounded, 37 captured or missing (ibid., 705–6).

5. For William H. T. Walker, see Warner, *Generals in Gray*, 323–24.

6. The general hoped to join Pemberton at Vicksburg. He sought to make a stand at Jackson but withdrew because his rear was vulnerable. The Federals would move back to Vicksburg.

7. For John Adams, see Warner, *Generals in Gray*, 2; and for States Rights Gist, see ibid., 106–7.

8. Pitt enlisted as a private in Company B, Thirtieth Tennessee, in 1861. According to another of his auditors, William T. McGlothlin of the Thirtieth, he "preached for us today a good and appropriate sermon. He gave the boys some good advice" (Diary, May 24, 1863, McGlothlin Papers, U.S. Army Military History Research Collection).

9. For John S. Marmaduke, see Warner, *Generals in Gray*, 211–12.

10. For Ambrose E. Burnside, see William Marvel, *Burnside*.

11. For John C. Breckinridge, see William C. Davis, *Breckinridge: Statesman, Soldier, Symbol*.

12. For John A. McClernand, see Warner, *Generals in Blue*, 293–94.

13. Arthur W. Bergeron, Jr., "General Richard Taylor as a Military Commander," 35–47. The author considers him near Forrest among civilian generals. But for Taylor's fondness for the offensive, see McWhiney and Jamieson, *Attack and Die*, 144–46.

14. For Samuel G. French, see Warner, *Generals in Gray*, 93–94.

15. Richard S. Ewell is also in ibid., 84–85.

16. "The Sabbath. A rumor is current in the evening that Vicksburg is surrendered. A *death knell* runs through the whole army and but few can be reconciled to believe it" (Diary, July 5, 1863, McGlothlin Papers).

17. "A still darker gloom seems to settle down upon the army. Is *Vicksburg* gone? Our last stronghold on the river. Horrible! Horrible! Mississippi is gone. . . . This evening we still get news that the Gibraltar of the west is no longer in Confederate hands" (ibid., July 6, 1863).

18. For Abraham Buford, see Warner, *Generals in Gray*, 39.

19. The simple detailing of a casualty, of a man wounded, gives little indication of what happened. A surgeon wrote to General Gregg,

> Col. Moody is apparently doing as well as we could expect or even far better than was at first expected. Up to this time he has never had much fever and little or none for four or five days past. This wound has caused but little pain—during the last four or five days he has rolled and turned himself about in the bed and occasionally in moving. When the tendons down or at the lower extremity of the spine became taut, he feels slight throbbing sensations about the wound. He has felt these throbbing sensations at no other time and then not painful. The swelling has nearly subsided. It seems to be more stubborn on the left of the wound—about [illegible] 1 1/2 inches to the left of the wound. There appears to be a hard flat substance from 1 to 2 inches in diameter at right angles from the spine and between two and three inches in length starting nearly opposite the wound and extending downwards. As the swelling began to assuage and we first discovered it, we thought it was the ball, but since the swelling has subsided sufficiently we have arrived at a definite conclusion, or rather that it was not the ball, though we do not know how to account for it. At the upper extremity of this surface it is more sensitive to the touch than anywhere else. For five or six days the wound has been discharging a cream-colored matter and has been healing up very fast. The granulations are healthy and the orifice is nearly closed. We fear it is healing too fast, that the wound will close externally before it has healed internally and that an abscess will be the consequence. We wish to avoid the abscess if possible, but if further examination should show the ball to be near the wound, would it not be better to cut it out now

before the orifice entirely closes? We wish you to show this to the surgeon and get him (or you) to write to us by return mail. Also write how to keep the orifice open, whether injections of castile soap and water or exercise would be improper. ([First name illegible] Walker to Gregg, July 27, 1863, Gregg Papers, U.S. Army Military History Research Collection)

20. "I have just assisted in laying Adjutant Dulin of the First Battalion of Sharpshooters in his coffin. He was shot through the heart yesterday evening while out with his battalion skirmishing. I am now sitting by the side of another corpse killed at the same time. He is a private far from home and with not a single relative. Now good night" (Hubbard T. Minor Diary, July 13, 1863, Minor Papers, U.S. Army Military History Research Collection).

21. "One man was shot this evening by military order, in Wilson's brigade. It seemed to create a high sensation among the men. We are having a quantity of desertions since the fall of Vicksburg" (Diary, July 21, 1863, McGlothlin Papers).

22. Reference to Battery Wagner is to the assault led by Robert Gould Shaw and the 54th Massachusetts.

23. For Nathan G. Evans, see Warner, *Generals in Gray*, 83–84.

6. GEORGIA: DECEMBER 3, 1863–MARCH 28, 1864

1. As mentioned in the editorial comments, this passage is clear enough; it is about starting a diary volume at Enterprise. No such volume has survived for the period between August 25 and December 2. All one knows is what Barber wrote about himself in the second set of regimental rolls early in 1864, namely that he obtained a furlough and was absent from the field at Chickamauga but present at Missionary Ridge.

2. The sentiments were admirable, the dejection plain. Well it should have been, considering the prospect. Although he hardly could sense what was to happen, from the beginning of service Barber had been in the midst of great events. The decision in the war was not to be taken in the East but the West. In the East the two armies, of the Potomac and of Northern Virginia, fought evenly until near the end in April 1865. In the West the Union strategy, attributed to General Scott, general in chief at the outset, was that of an anaconda, in which Union troops squeezed out Confederate resistance. The first Union move was to take Forts Henry and Donelson, then Vicksburg and Port Hudson. Next was the defeat of the Army of Tennessee before Atlanta. In the spring of 1864, Barber participated in Atlanta's defense and with his fellow Tennesseans came up against the juggernaut of Sherman, for which "Old Joe" Johnston and his successor, Lt. Gen. John B. Hood, were utterly no match. The capture of Atlanta ensured Lincoln's reelection. The Union general then rolled up the Deep South and made Lee's situation impossible. See these two splendid books on the Army of Tennessee: Craig L. Symonds, *Joseph E. Johnston: A Civil War Biography*, and Albert Castel, *Decision in the West: The Atlanta Campaign of 1864*.

3. See Stanley P. Hirshson, *Grenville M. Dodge: Soldier, Politician, Railroad Pioneer*.

4. Anderson Searcy was colonel of the Forty-fifth Tennessee.

5. William R. Butler was lieutenant colonel of the Eighteenth Tennessee.

6. For Alexander W. Reynolds, see Warner, *Generals in Gray*, 254–55.

7. For Otho F. Strahl, see ibid., 295–96.

8. Edwin C. Bearss, "Pat Cleburne: The Stonewall Jackson of the West"; Howell and Elizabeth Purdue, *Pat Cleburne, Confederate General: A Definitive Biography.*

9. For Zachariah C. Deas, see Warner, *Generals in Gray*, 70–71.

10. For Philip Dale Roddey see ibid., 262.

11. For Carter L. Stevenson, see ibid., 292–93.

12. Christopher Losson, *Tennessee's Forgotten Warriors: Frank Cheatham and His Confederate Division.*

13. For the general, see Richard M. McMurry, *John Bell Hood and the War for Southern Independence.*

14. Brown advocated states' rights in an insistent and, for President Davis in Richmond, embarrassing way. See Joseph H. Parks, *Joseph E. Brown of Georgia.*

15. For James B. McPherson the best source is Albert Castel, *Decision in the West*, passim, esp. 79–81, 411.

16.   On the twenty-eighth of last month I began a meeting of this brigade, which has been in progress since that time. Brother Chapman, chaplain of the Thirty-Second Tennessee, having met with an accident, I have been alone most of the time. It has been a precious season. Nineteen have professed faith in Christ, many more are inquiring. It is magnificent to preach to these boys and see them enlisting under the banner of heaven. May God continue the good work. I have labored much but am not wearied. We have a shelter about sixty feet long and here crowds meet every night. It is delightful to hear the rich volume of song ascending. (Diary, Deavenport Papers, Mar. 31, 1864)

Had a good meeting last night, one conversion, an old schoolmate, Pat Good. The altar was crowded with mourners, more than at any previous time. Attended prayer meeting this morning, a good congregation, profitable time. There are rumors of leaving here, hope we may stay. Some skirmishing in front yesterday. (Apr. 1)

There was still an increase of mourners and interest, three conversions. The night was cold and wet but the crowd large and attentive. The prayer meeting this morning was sweet. (Apr. 2)

The meeting still continues with increasing interest. Last night the spirit descended in power and God's was mightily revived. Since my last note twelve or fifteen have embraced religion and the number of penitents have been more than doubled. Yesterday an old Negro said to his master, "Mas John, if the Yankee let us stay here three months dey can't whip us, if dey could whip us when we were wicked, I know they can't when we got religion." (Apr. 5)

Yesterday was the day set about by the Congress of the Confederacy for fasting, humiliation and prayer. It was generally assumed in this brigade. We had prayer meeting at 7:00 a.m., preaching at 11:00, prayer meeting at 2:30 p.m., and preaching at 6:30. All these were well attended notwithstanding it was a gloomy day. Last night we had a precious season and several were converted. Praise be to God. (Apr. 9)

On April 26 the chaplain calculated that 101 men had been converted, seventy-three joining the church. See also G. Clinton Prim, Jr., "Born Again in the Trenches," 250–72.

17. For Edmund W. Pettus and Arthur M. Manigault, see Warner, *Generals in Gray*, 210–11, 232–39. Also R. Lockwood Tower, Warren Ripley, and Arthur M. Wilcox, eds., *A Carolinian Goes to War: The Civil War Narrative of Arthur Middleton Manigault, Brigadier General, C.S.A.* For perhaps the greatest snowballing in history, see William G. Bentley, "The Great Snowball Battle," 22–23, and Steve Davis, "The Great Snow Battle of 1864," 32–35. It involved five thousand men and was principally between Tennessee and Georgia troops. Tennessee won.

7. THE LAST ATTACK: MARCH 29–MAY 15, 1864

1. For William B. Bate, see Warner, *Generals in Gray*, 19–20.
2. Lovell B. Rousseau is in idem, *Generals in Blue*, 412–13.
3. Four daily newspapers were normally published in Atlanta: the *Daily Intelligencer*, the *Southern Confederacy*, the *Reveille*, and the *Commonwealth*. Three papers fled toward Atlanta: the *Knoxville Register*, *Memphis Daily Appeal* (known as the "Moving Appeal" as it wandered across the South), and the *Chattanooga Rebel*. The latter's editor was the redoubtable Henry Watterson, who resigned after the paper moved to Marietta. Watterson came to admire President Lincoln as the greatest man of all time, but during the war he described him as a "raw-boned, shamble-gaited, knock-kneed, pigeon-toed, swob-sided, shapeless skeleton in a very tough, very dirty, unwholesome skin" (Henry T. Malone, "Atlanta Journalism during the Confederacy," 210–19). For the *Rebel* see Roy Morris, "That Improbable, Praiseworthy Paper," 16–18, 20–24.
4. For Alfred Cumming, see Warner, *Generals in Gray*, 66.
5. Burwell Abernathy II was the half brother of Barber's wife, Mary Paine Abernathy.
6. Exact figures for the Army of Tennessee at this time are difficult to come by because of different categories used in assessing manpower. Richard M. McMurry has calculated 55,000 and by mid-May, with the addition of Leonidas Polk's troops, 70,000. In opposition, Sherman, on April 30, had 110,000. See "A New Look," 12–13.

7.   Today I witnessed a sight sad indeed, I saw fourteen men shot for desertion. I visited them twice yesterday and attended them to the place of execution. Most of them met death manfully. Some, poor fellows, I fear were unprepared. I saw them wash and dress themselves for the grave. It was a solemn scene, they were tied to the stake, there was the coffin, there the open grave ready to receive them. I have seen a man die at home surrounded by loved ones, I have seen him die on the battlefield among the noble and brave, I have seen him die in prison in an enemy land, but the saddest of all was the death of the deserter, but even there Christ was sufficient. "Tell my wife," said one but a few minutes before the leaden messengers pierced his breast, "not to grieve for me, I have no doubt of reaching a better world." Let me then continue to hold up that savior and point sinners to him. I think they were objects of pity, many were ignorant, poor, and had families dependent upon them. It is a cruel thing, it heeds not the widow's tears, the orphan's pain, or the lover's anguish. (Diary, May 4, 1864, Deavenport Papers)

8. Unknown to Barber, Sherman that day commenced a complicated operation to turn the Confederates out of their position along Rocky Face Ridge. Johnston was expecting an attack on the Confederate right, but Sherman moved against his left—toward Resaca, south of Dalton. Meanwhile the Union general pressed the Confederates on Rocky Face and at Mill Creek and Dug gaps, so they could not guess where the real push would come. This was to be McPherson's army of twenty thousand. Screened by Taylor's Ridge it moved down toward undefended Snake Creek Gap in front of Resaca, passed through, and almost got into the town, which McPherson could have taken if he had thrown his full force at it. To Sherman's dismay, he moved back into the gap and dug trenches. All this occurred between May 4 and May 9.

9. Michael B. Dougan, "Thomas C. Hindman: Arkansas Politician and General," 21–38.

10. Benjamin J. Hill was colonel of the Thirty-fifth Tennessee.

11. John P. McGuire was major of the Thirty-second Tennessee.

12. For George E. Maney, see Warner, *Generals in Gray*, 210.

EPILOGUE

1. Southern Historical Collection, Wilson Library, University of North Carolina, Chapel Hill.

2. John Thomas Smith, *A History of the Thirty-First Regiment of Indiana Volunteer Infantry in the War of the Rebellion*, 100; George W. Morris, *History of the Eighty-First Regiment of Indiana Volunteer Infantry*, 88–90; Lewis W. Day, *Story of the One Hundred and First Ohio Infantry*, 204–8; David S. Stanley, *Personal Memoirs*, 164–65; 4th Corps Diary, May 14, 1864, West-Stanley-Wright Papers, U.S. Army Military History Research Collection; Milo M. Quaife, ed., *From The Cannon's Mouth: The Civil War Letters of General Alphaeus S. Williams*, 308; Jeffrey C. Charmley, " 'Neglected Honor' : The Life of General A. S. Williams of Michigan (1810–1878)"; also Castel, *Decision in the West*, 163–66.

3. Diary, May 16, 1864, Deavenport Papers.

4. Tennessee Civil War Centennial Commission, *Tennesseans in the Civil War* 1:181–82.

5. According to the Giles County Court Record Book 1, April 1865–June 1871, the administrator of Barber's estate, A. M. Wilson, in 1866 "suggested the insolvency of said estate" (98). Burwell Abernathy II to Thomas James Paine, in Margaret Butler, *Legacy*, 29–30.

Bibliography

MANUSCRIPT RECORDS

Company Rolls, Third Tennessee Infantry, William R. Perkins Library, Duke University, Durham, North Carolina

Compiled Records of Confederate Units, Roll 51, M861, Record Group 109, National Archives, Washington, D.C.

Confederate States Army Casualties: Lists and Narrative Reports, 1861–65, Roll 2 (Battle of Raymond), M836, Record Group 45, National Archives.

Court Record Book 1, April 1866–June 1871, Giles County Courthouse, Pulaski, Tennessee

UNPUBLISHED PAPERS AND DIARIES

Barber, Flavel C. Papers. Lilly Library, Indiana University, Bloomington.

Beatty, Taylor. Diary. Southern Historical Collection, Wilson Library, University of North Carolina, Chapel Hill.

Brown, John C. Papers. Civil War Collection, Tennessee State Library and Archives, Nashville.

Cheairs, Nathaniel F. Papers. Civil War Collection (also Sherrell Figuers Papers), Tennessee State Library and Archives.

Deavenport, Thomas H. Papers. Civil War Collection, Tennessee State Library and Archives.

Floyd, John B. Papers. William R. Perkins Library, Duke University.

Gregg, John. Papers. U.S. Army Military History Research Collection, Military History Institute, Carlisle Barracks, Carlisle, Pennsylvania.

Hancock, Enoch. Papers. Civil War Collection, Tennessee State Library and Archives.

Hart, John E. Papers. U.S. Army Military History Research Collection.

McGlothlin, William T. Papers. U.S. Army Military History Research Collection.

McGregor, Frank. Papers. U.S. Army Military History Research Collection.

Minor, Hubbard T. Papers. U.S. Army Military History Research Collection.

Reynolds, Edward H. Diary. *Civil War Times Illustrated* Collection, U.S. Army Military History Research Collection.

Ryan, Milton A. Papers. U.S. Army Military History Research Collection.

West-Stanley-Wright Papers. U.S. Army Military History Research Collection.

BOOKS

Ankeny, Henry G. *Kiss Josey for Me.* Ed. Florence M. A. Cox. Santa Ana, Calif.: Fries-Pioneer, 1974.

Ballard, Michael B. *Pemberton: A Biography.* Jackson: Univ. of Mississippi Press, 1991.

Barber, Edwin A. *Genealogy of the Barber Family: The Descendants of Robert Barber of Lancaster, Pennsylvania.* Philadelphia: William F. Fell, 1890.

Barbiere, Joe. *Scraps from the Prison Table, at Camp Chase and Johnson's Island.* Doylestown, Pa.: W. W. H. Davis, 1868.

Barnard, George N. *Photographic Views of Sherman's Campaign.* 1866. New York: Dover, 1977.

Bearss, Edwin C. *The Campaign for Vicksburg.* 3 vols. Dayton, Ohio: Morningside Bookshop, 1985–88.

———. *Decision in Mississippi: Mississippi's Important Role in the War Between the States.* Jackson: Mississippi Commission on the War Between the States, 1962.

Beringer, Richard E., Herman Hattaway, Archer Jones, William N. Still, Jr. *Why the South Lost the Civil War.* Athens: Univ. of Georgia Press, 1986.

Boatner, Mark M., III. *The Civil War Dictionary.* New York: David McKay, 1959.

Brown, Dee Alexander. *Grierson's Raid.* Urbana: Univ. of Illinois Press, 1954.

Buck, Irving A. *Cleburne and His Command.* 2d ed. Ed. Thomas Robson Hay. Jackson, Tenn.: McCowat-Mercer, 1959.

Butler, Margaret. *Legacy: Early Families of Giles County.* Pulaski, Tenn.: Privately published, 1991.

Castel, Albert. *Decision in the West: The Atlanta Campaign of 1864.* Lawrence: Univ. Press of Kansas, 1992.

Civil War Collection, Confederate and Federal. Ed. Harriet C. Owsley. Nashville: Tennessee State Library and Archives, 1966.

Civil War Eyewitnesses: An Annotated Bibliography of Books and Articles, 1955–1986. Ed. Garold L. Cole. Columbia: Univ. of South Carolina Press, 1988.

Connelly, Thomas L. *Army of the Heartland: The Army of Tennessee, 1861–1862.* Baton Rouge: Louisiana State Univ. Press, 1967.

———. *Autumn of Glory: The Army of Tennessee, 1862–1865.* Baton Rouge: Louisiana State Univ. Press, 1971.

———. *Civil War Tennessee: Battles and Leaders.* Knoxville: Tennessee Historical Commission with the Univ. of Tennessee Press, 1979.

Cooling, Benjamin Franklin. *Forts Henry and Donelson: The Key to the Confederate Heartland.* Knoxville: Univ. of Tennessee Press, 1987.

Corlew, Robert E. *Tennessee: A Short History.* 2d ed. Knoxville: Univ. of Tennessee Press, 1981.

Coulter, Ellis Merton. *William G. Brownlow: Fighting Parson of the Southern Highlands.* Chapel Hill: Univ. of North Carolina Press, 1937.

Cullum, George W. *Biographical Register of the Officers and Graduates of the U.S. Military Academy . . .* 3d ed. 8 vols. Boston: Houghton Mifflin, 1891–1930.

Cunningham, Edward. *The Port Hudson Campaign: 1862–1863.* Baton Rouge: Louisiana State Univ. Press, 1963.

Current, Richard N. *Lincoln's Loyalists: Union Soldiers from the Confederacy.* Boston: Northeastern Univ. Press, 1992.

Dana, Napoleon Jackson Tecumseh. *Monterrey Is Ours! The Mexican War Letters of Lieutenant Dana, 1845–1847.* Ed. Robert H. Ferrell. Lexington: Univ. Press of Kentucky, 1990.

Day, Lewis W. *Story of the One Hundred and First Ohio Infantry.* Cleveland: W. M. Bayne, 1894.

Dougan, Michael B. "Thomas C. Hindman: Arkansas Politician and General." *Rank and File: Civil War Essays in Honor of Bell Irvin Wiley.* Eds. James I. Robertson, Jr., and Richard M. McMurry. San Rafael, Calif.: Presidio, 1976.

Durham, Walter T. *Rebellion Revisited: A History of Sumner County, Tennessee, from 1861 to 1870.* Gallatin, Tenn.: Sumner County Museum Association, 1982.

Dyer, Frederick H. *A Compendium of the War of the Rebellion.* Dayton, Ohio: National Historical Society with Morningside Bookshop, 1979.

Edmonds, David C. *The Guns of Port Hudson.* 2 vols. Lafayette, La.: Acadiana, 1983–84.

Frohman, Charles E. *Rebels on Lake Erie.* Columbus: Ohio Historical Society, 1965.

Govan, Gilbert E., and James W. Livingood. *A Different Valor: The Story of General Joseph E. Johnston, C.S.A.* Indianapolis: Bobbs-Merrill, 1956.

Hallock, Judith Lee. *Braxton Bragg and Confederate Defeat.* Vol. 2. Tuscaloosa: Univ. of Alabama Press, 1991.

Hamilton, James J. *The Battle of Fort Donelson.* South Brunswick, N.J.: T. Yoseloff, 1968.

Harrington, Fred Harvey. *Fighting Politician: Major General N. P. Banks.* Philadelphia: Univ. of Pennsylvania Press, 1948.

Hattaway, Herman. *General Stephen D. Lee.* Jackson: Univ. Press of Mississippi, 1976.

Hattaway, Herman, and Archer Jones. *How the North Won: A Military History of the Civil War.* Urbana: Univ. of Illinois Press, 1983.

Hesseltine, William B., ed. *Civil War Prisons.* Kent, Ohio: Kent State Univ. Press, 1972.

Hewitt, Lawrence L. *Port Hudson: Confederate Bastion on the Mississippi.* Baton Rouge: Louisiana State Univ. Press, 1987.

Hirshson, Stanley P. *Grenville M. Dodge: Soldier, Politician, Railroad Pioneer.* Bloomington: Indiana Univ. Press, 1967.

Hopkins, Owen Johnston. *Under the Flag of the Nation: Diaries and Letters of a Yankee Volunteer in the Civil War.* Ed. Otto F. Bond. Columbus: Ohio Historical Society with Ohio State Univ. Press, 1961.

Hughes, Nathaniel Cheairs, Jr. *The Battle of Belmont: Grant Strikes South.* Chapel Hill: Univ. of North Carolina Press, 1991.

———. *General William J. Hardee: Old Reliable.* Baton Rouge: Louisiana State Univ. Press, 1965.

Hughes, Nathaniel Cheairs, Jr., and Roy P. Stonesifer, Jr. *The Life and Wars of Gideon J. Pillow.* Chapel Hill: Univ. of North Carolina Press, 1993.

Kircher, Henry A. *A German in the Yankee Fatherland: The Civil War Letters of Henry A. Kircher.* Ed. Earl J. Hess. Kent, Ohio: Kent State Univ. Press, 1983.

Knauss, William H. *The Story of Camp Chase.* Nashville, Tenn.: Methodist Episcopal Church, South, 1906.

Leckie, William H., and Shirley A. *Unlikely Warriors: General Benjamin H. Grierson and His Family.* Norman: Univ. of Oklahoma Press, 1984.

Losson, Christopher. *Tennessee's Forgotten Warriors: Frank Cheatham and His Confederate Division.* Knoxville: Univ. of Tennessee Press, 1989.

McCallum, James. *A Brief Sketch of the Settlement and Early History of Giles County, Tennessee.* Pulaski, Tenn.: Pulaski Citizen, 1928.

McGavock, Randal W. *Pen and Sword: The Life and Journals of Randal W. McGavock.* Eds. Herschel Gower and Jack Allen. Nashville: Tennessee Historical Commission, 1959.

McKee, Irving. *"Ben-Hur" Wallace: The Life of General Lew Wallace.* Berkeley: Univ. of California Press, 1947.

McMurry, Richard M. *John Bell Hood and the War for Southern Independence.* Lexington: Univ. Press of Kentucky, 1982.

———. *Two Great Rebel Armies: An Essay in Confederate Military History.* Chapel Hill: Univ. of North Carolina Press, 1989.

McWhiney, Grady. *Braxton Bragg and Confederate Defeat.* New York: Columbia Univ. Press, 1969.

McWhiney, Grady, and Perry D. Jamieson. *Attack and Die: Civil War Military Tactics and the Southern Heritage.* University: Univ. of Alabama Press, 1982.

Manigault, Arthur Middleton. *A Carolinian Goes to War: The Civil War Narrative of Arthur Middleton Manigault, Brigadier General, C.S.A.* Ed. R. Lockwood Tower, Warren Ripley, and Arthur M. Wilcox. Columbia: Charleston Library Society with Univ. of South Carolina Press, 1983.

Marszalek, John F. *Sherman: A Soldier's Passion for Order.* New York: Free Press, 1993.

Marvel, William. *Burnside.* Chapel Hill: Univ. of North Carolina Press, 1991.

Morris, George W. *History of the Eighty-First Regiment of Indiana Volunteer Infantry . . .* Louisville, Ky.: Franklin, 1901.

Morsberger, Robert E., and Katherine M. *Lew Wallace: Military Romantic.* New York: McGraw-Hill, 1980.

Parks, Joseph H. *General Edmund Kirby Smith, C.S.A.* Baton Rouge: Louisiana State Univ. Press, 1954.

———. *General Leonidas Polk, C.S.A.: The Fighting Bishop.* Baton Rouge: Louisiana State Univ. Press, 1962.

———. *Joseph E. Brown of Georgia.* Baton Rouge: Louisiana State Univ. Press, 1976.

Purdue, Howell, and Elizabeth Purdue. *Pat Cleburne, Confederate General: A Definitive Biography.* Hillsboro, Texas: Hill Junior College Press, 1973.

Shriver, Phillip R., and Donald J. Breen. *Ohio's Military Prisons in the Civil War.* Columbus: Ohio State Univ. Press, 1964.

Silver, James W. *Confederate Morale and Church Propaganda.* Tuscaloosa, Ala.: Confederate Publishing Company, 1957.

Smith, John Thomas. *A History of the Thirty-First Regiment of Indiana Volunteer Infantry in the War of the Rebellion.* Cincinnati: Western Methodist, 1900.

Spiegel, Marcus M. *Your True Marcus: The Civil War Letters of a Jewish Colonel.* Ed. Frank L. Byrne and Jean Powers Soman. Kent, Ohio: Kent State Univ. Press, 1985.

Stanley, David S. *Personal Memoirs.* Cambridge: Harvard Univ. Press, 1917.

Stickles, Arndt M. *Simon Bolivar Buckner: Borderland Knight.* Chapel Hill: Univ. of North Carolina Press, 1940.

Symonds, Craig L. *Joseph E. Johnston: A Civil War Biography.* New York: W. W. Norton, 1992.

Tennesseans in the Civil War: A Military History of Confederate and Union Units with Available Rosters of Personnel. 2 vols. Nashville: Tennessee Civil War Centennial Commission, 1964–65.

Thompson, Jerry D. *Henry Hopkins Sibley: Confederate General of the West.* Natchitoches, La.: Northwestern State Univ. Press, 1987.

U.S. War Department. *The War of the Rebellion: A Compilation of the Official Records of the Union and Confederate Armies.* 128 vols. Washington, D.C.: Government Printing Office, 1880–1901.

Warner, Ezra J. *Generals in Blue: Lives of the Union Commanders.* Baton Rouge: Louisiana State Univ. Press, 1964.

———. *Generals in Gray: Lives of the Confederate Commanders.* Baton Rouge: Louisiana State Univ. Press, 1959.

Wessels, William L. *Born to be a Soldier: The Military Career of William Wing Loring of St. Augustine, Florida.* Fort Worth: Texas Christian Univ. Press, 1971.

Whaley, Elizabeth J. *Forgotten Hero: General James B. McPherson.* New York: Exposition, 1955.

Williams, Alpheus S. *From the Cannon's Mouth: The Civil War Letters of General Alphaeus S. Williams.* Ed. Milo M. Quaife. Detroit: Wayne State Univ. Press, 1959.

ARTICLES

Austerman, Wayne. "Maynard." *Civil War Times Illustrated* 25 (April 1986): 42–45.

Bearss, Edwin C. "Unconditional Surrender: The Fall of Fort Donelson." *Tennessee Historical Quarterly* 21 (1962): 47–65, 140–61.

Bentley, William G. "The Great Snowball Battle." *Civil War Times Illustrated* 5 (January 1967): 22–23.

Bergeron, Arthur W., Jr. "General Richard Taylor as a Military Commander." *Louisiana History* 23 (1982): 35–47.

Brown, Dee Alexander. "Battle at Chickasaw Bluffs." *Civil War Times Illustrated* 9 (July 1970): 4–9, 44–48.

Davis, Steve. "The Great Snow Battle of 1864." *Civil War Times Illustrated* 15 (June 1976): 32–35.

Downer, Edward T. "Johnson's Island." *Civil War History* 8 (1962): 202–17.

Hattaway, Herman. "Confederate Myth Making: Top Command and the Chickasaw Bayou Campaign." *Journal of Mississippi History* 32 (1970): 311–26.

Ikard, Robert W. "Lieutenant Thompson Reports on Chickamauga: A Companion of Immediate and Historical Perspectives of the Battle." *Tennessee Historical Quarterly* 44 (1985): 417–38.

Kelley, James C. "William Gannaway Brownlow, Part I." *Tennessee Historical Quarterly* 43 (1984): 25–43.

Kime, Marlin G. "Sherman's Gordian Knot: Logistical Problems in the Atlanta Campaign." *Georgia Historical Quarterly* 70 (1986): 102–10.

Lee, Stephen D. "Battle of Chickasaw Bayou." *Confederate Veteran* 6 (1898): 519.

Lowry, J. T. "A Fort Donelson Prisoner of War." *Confederate Veteran* 3 (1895): 110.

McBride, Robert M. "The 'Confederate Sins' of Major Cheairs." *Tennessee Historical Quarterly* 23 (1964): 121–35.

McMurry, Richard M. "The Atlanta Campaign of 1864: A New Look." *Civil War History* 22 (1976): 5–15.

———. "Resaca: 'A Heap of Hard Fiten.' " *Civil War Times Illustrated* 9 (November 1970): 4–12, 44–48.

Malone, Henry T. "Atlanta Journalism during the Confederacy." *Georgia Historical Quarterly* 37 (1953): 210–19.

Moore, Josephus C. "Diary of a Confederate Soldier." Ed. Larry G. Bowman and Jack B. Scroggs. *Military Review* 62 (February 1982): 20–34.

Morris, Roy. "That Improbable, Praiseworthy Paper." *Civil War Times Illustrated* 23 (November 1984): 16–18, 20–24.

Norton, Herman. "Revivalism in the Confederate Armies." *Civil War History* 6 (1960): 410–24.

Nye, W. S. "Jake Donelson: A 'Cocky' Rebel." *Civil War Times Illustrated* 1 (April 1962): 51.

Peeke, Hewson L. "Johnson's Island." *Ohio Archeological and Historical Publications* 26 (1917): 470–76.

Prim, G. Clinton, Jr. "Born Again in the Trenches." *Tennessee Historical Quarterly* 43 (1984): 250–72.

Romero, Sidney J. "The Confederate Chaplain." *Civil War History* 1 (1955): 127–40.

Sanders, Lorenzo J. "The Diary of an 'Average' Confederate Soldier." Ed. Lowell H. Harrison. *Tennessee Historical Quarterly* 29 (1970–71): 256–71.

Sherman, William T. "Vicksburg by New Years." *Civil War Times Illustrated* 16 (January 1978): 44–48.

Speer, William H. A. "A Confederate Soldier's View of Johnson's Island Prison." Ed. James B. Murphy. *Ohio Historical Quarterly* 79 (1970): 101–11.

Stonesifer, Roy D., Jr. "Gideon J. Pillow: A Study in Egotism." *Tennessee Historical Quarterly* 25 (1966): 340–50.

Walker, Peter Franklin. "Command Failure: The Fall of Forts Henry and Donelson." *Tennessee Historical Quarterly* 16 (1957): 335–60.

UNPUBLISHED THESES, DISSERTATIONS, AND REPORTS

Bearss, Edwin C. "The Battle of Raymond." Typescript report for the National Park Service, 1960. Copy in Tennessee State Library and Archives.

———. "Pat Cleburne: The Stonewall Jackson of the West." Master's thesis, Indiana University, 1954.

Butler, Margaret. "The Life of John C. Brown." Master's thesis, University of Tennessee, 1936.

Charmley, Jeffrey G. " 'Neglected Honor': The Life of General A. S. Williams of Michigan (1810–1870)." Dissertation, Michigan State University, 1983.

Newman, M. T. "Bethany Presbyterian Church: Historic Sketch of Famous Old Institution." Typescript, Margaret Butler, Pulaski, Tennessee.

Shultz, Charles R. "The Conditions at Johnson's Island Prison During the Civil War." Master's thesis, Bowling Green State University, 1960.

Index

HOLDING THE LINE

was composed in 9¹/₂-point Trump Mediæval leaded 3 points
on a Macintosh using Quark XPress with Agfa Accuset output
by BookMasters, Inc.;
printed by sheet-fed offset
on Glatfelter 50-pound Supple Opaque Natural stock
(an acid-free recycled stock),
notch bound over 88-point binder's boards
in ICG Kennett cloth,
and wrapped with dust jackets printed in two colors
on 100-pound enamel stock finished with polyester film lamination
by Thomson-Shore, Inc.;
designed by Will Underwood;
and published by
The Kent State University Press
KENT, OHIO 44242